CW00421033

Microsoft Defender for Cloud

Yuri Diogenes and Tom Janetscheck

Microsoft Defender for Cloud

Published with the authorization of Microsoft Corporation by:
Pearson Education, Inc.

ISBN-13: 978-0-13-787845-1
ISBN-10: 0-13-787845-1

Library of Congress Control Number: 2022944665

1 2022

TRADEMARKS

PERMISSIONS

Chapter 2, Icons of AWS: Amazon Web Services, Inc, Chapter 6, Figure 06-30: United States Department of Commerce

WARNING AND DISCLAIMER

SPECIAL SALES

For information about buying this title in bulk quantities, or for special sales opportunities (which may include electronic versions; custom cover designs; and content particular to your business, training goals, marketing focus, or branding interests), please contact our corporate sales department at corpsales@pearsoned.com or (800) 382-3419.

For government sales inquiries, please contact governmentsales@pearsoned.com.

For questions about sales outside the U.S., please contact intlcs@pearson.com.

CREDITS

EDITOR-IN-CHIEF
Brett Bartow

EXECUTIVE EDITOR
Loretta Yates

SPONSORING EDITOR
Charvi Arora

DEVELOPMENT EDITOR
Rick Kughen

MANAGING EDITOR
Sandra Schroeder

PROJECT EDITOR
Tracey Croom

COPY EDITOR
Rick Kughen

INDEXER
Tim Wright

PROOFREADER
Jen Hinchliffe

TECHNICAL EDITOR
Liana Tomescu

EDITORIAL ASSISTANT
Cindy Teeters

COVER DESIGNER
Twist Creative, Seattle

COMPOSITOR
codeMantra

GRAPHICS
codeMantra

Pearson's Commitment to Diversity, Equity, and Inclusion

Pearson is dedicated to creating bias-free content that reflects the diversity of all learners. We embrace the many dimensions of diversity, including but not limited to race, ethnicity, gender, socioeconomic status, ability, age, sexual orientation, and religious or political beliefs.

Education is a powerful force for equity and change in our world. It has the potential to deliver opportunities that improve lives and enable economic mobility. As we work with authors to create content for every product and service, we acknowledge our responsibility to demonstrate inclusivity and incorporate diverse scholarship so that everyone can achieve their potential through learning. As the world's leading learning company, we have a duty to help drive change and live up to our purpose to help more people create a better life for themselves and to create a better world.

Our ambition is to purposefully contribute to a world where:

- Everyone has an equitable and lifelong opportunity to succeed through learning.
- Our educational products and services are inclusive and represent the rich diversity of learners.
- Our educational content accurately reflects the histories and experiences of the learners we serve.
- Our educational content prompts deeper discussions with learners and motivates them to expand their own learning (and worldview).

While we work hard to present unbiased content, we want to hear from you about any concerns or needs with this Pearson product so that we can investigate and address them.

- Please contact us with concerns about any potential bias at https://www.pearson.com/report-bias.html.

Contents at a Glance

Acknowledgments   xiii

About the authors   xv

Foreword   xvii

Introduction   xix

CHAPTER 1   The threat landscape   1

CHAPTER 2   Planning Microsoft Defender for Cloud adoption   27

CHAPTER 3   Onboarding Microsoft Defender for Cloud   45

CHAPTER 4   Policy management   67

CHAPTER 5   Strengthening your security posture   105

CHAPTER 6   Threat detection   155

CHAPTER 7   Better together   189

CHAPTER 8   Enhanced security capabilities   201

CHAPTER 9   Accessing Defender for Cloud from APIs   223

CHAPTER 10   Deploying Microsoft Defender for
               Cloud at scale   235

APPENDIX   Microsoft Defender for DevOps   245

               Index   259

Contents

Acknowledgments   *xiii*

About the authors   *xv*

Foreword   *xvii*

Introduction   *xix*

Chapter 1   The threat landscape   1

The state of cybercrime..1

Understanding the cyberkill chain.................................... 3

    Using the MITRE ATT&CK Framework to protect and detect   5

    Common threats   6

    Improving security posture   6

    Adopting an assume-breach mentality   8

Cloud threats and security 9

    Compliance   11

    Risk management   11

    Identity and access management   12

    Operational security   12

    Endpoint protection   12

    Data protection   13

    Azure security   13

    VM protection   14

    Network protection   15

    Storage protection   19

    Identity   21

    Logging   21

    Container security   22

Chapter 2   Planning Microsoft Defender for Cloud adoption   27

Deployment scenarios...27

Understanding Defender for Cloud...............................28

Defender for Cloud architecture   **29**

Defender for Cloud dashboard   **33**

Planning adoption **34**

Considerations for CSPM   **35**

Considerations for CWPP   **38**

Considerations for multi-cloud   **39**

Considerations for vulnerability assessment   **40**

Considerations for EDR   **42**

Considerations for multi-tenant   **42**

Chapter 3   **Onboarding Microsoft Defender for Cloud**   **45**

Planning your Azure environment for Defender for Cloud **45**

Designing your environment   **46**

Onboarding VMs from an Azure subscription **49**

Understanding auto-provisioning **51**

Auto provision the Log Analytics agent for Azure VMs   **52**

Deploy the Log Analytics agent to Azure Arc machines   **55**

Auto-provisioning of vulnerability assessment solutions   **56**

Auto-deployment of guest configuration agent   **57**

Deploy Microsoft Defender for Containers components   **58**

Connecting to Amazon Web Services (AWS) **59**

Onboard AWS VMs. **62**

How to onboard subscriptions at scale. **63**

Registering the Microsoft.Security resource provider   **63**

Assign the Azure security Benchmark   **65**

Configure auto-provisioning at scale   **66**

Chapter 4   **Policy management**   **67**

Introduction to Azure Policy **67**

Policy exemptions   **70**

Understanding Azure Security Benchmark. **73**

Fine-tuning policies in Defender for Cloud. **75**

Creating custom policies in Microsoft Defender for Cloud **78**

Policy enforcement and governance 81

How to overcome reactive security management   83

Prevent security misconfigurations with Defender
for Cloud   83

Large-scale provisioning with Azure Blueprints   85

Policy deployment and best practices 88

Regulatory standards and compliance. 90

Regulatory compliance in Microsoft Defender for Cloud   92

Customize your regulatory compliance experience   94

Build your own compliance initiative   96

Creating custom assessments for AWS and GCP. 99

Chapter 5   Strengthening your security posture   105

Driving security posture improvement using Secure Score. 105

Fine-tuning your Secure Score   109

Using APIs and Continuous Export to create reports. 111

Get Secure Score data   112

Secure Score over time report   114

Notify on Secure Score downgrade   115

Remediating recommendations. 115

Enable multi-factor authentication (MFA)   118

Recommendations and controls focused on compute   121

Networking   131

Data and storage   135

Using workflow automation to remediate
security recommendations. 138

Resource exemptions and automation   141

Security governance and contextual security 143

Using security governance to create responsibility   144

Using Attack Paths to focus on the right resources   149

Build your own views with Cloud Security Map   152

Chapter 6	**Threat detection**	**155**

Methods of threat protection **155**

Understanding alerts **156**

    Accessing security alerts   **157**

    Alert suppression   **161**

    Alerts in Azure Resource Graph (ARG)   **163**

Defender for Servers **164**

    Windows   **165**

    Linux   **166**

    Defender for Containers   **166**

    Vulnerability Assessment   **167**

    Threat detection   **168**

Defender for App Service **169**

Defender for Storage **171**

    Considerations before enabling Defender for Storage   **172**

Defender for SQL **173**

    Vulnerability Assessment for SQL   **174**

Defender for Cosmos DB **177**

Defender for Open-Source Relational Databases **178**

Defender for Key Vault **179**

Defender for Resource Manager **180**

Defender for DNS **181**

The cyberkill chain and fusion alerts **182**

Threat intelligence in Defender for Cloud **185**

Responding to alerts **187**

    Contact   **187**

    Mitigation   **187**

    Impact   **188**

    Take action   **188**

Chapter 7	**Better together**	**189**
	Defender for Cloud and Microsoft Sentinel **189**
	Integration with Microsoft Sentinel	**190**
	Accessing alerts in Microsoft Sentinel	**192**
	Defender for Cloud and Microsoft Purview **194**
	Defender for Cloud and Microsoft Defender for Endpoint **196**

Chapter 8	**Enhanced security capabilities**	**201**
	Just-in-time virtual machine access. **201**
	Recommendation to enable JIT	**203**
	JIT dashboard	**206**
	Requesting access	**207**
	File integrity monitoring. **209**
	Customizing your settings	**210**
	Visualizing changes	**213**
	Adaptive Application Control **215**
	Configuring Adaptive Application Control	**217**

Chapter 9	**Accessing Defender for Cloud from APIs**	**223**
	Understanding REST API. **223**
	Accessing alerts using the Defender for Cloud REST API **224**
	Accessing alerts using the Graph Security API. **230**
	Using the Graph Security API	**232**

Chapter 10	**Deploying Microsoft Defender for Cloud at scale**	**235**
	The three cornerstones of deployment at scale **235**
	Defender for Cloud, Azure Policy, and Management Groups—better together	**238**
	Best practices for managing Defender for Cloud at scale **239**
	How to get started with ARM templates **240**
	Export templates from the Azure portal	**240**
	Use Visual Studio Code to create ARM templates	**241**

Appendix **Microsoft Defender for DevOps** **245**

Shift left 245

Understanding Defender for DevOps. **247**

Connect your source code management system to
    Defender for Cloud. **249**

    Configure pull request annotations **252**

    Discover security issues when developers commit code **253**

    Discover security issues in Infrastructure as Code (IaC) **255**

    Discover security issues during development **256**

Index *259*

Acknowledgments

The authors would like to thank Loretta Yates and the entire Microsoft Press/Pearson team for their support in this project, Gilad Elyashar for writing the foreword, and also our friends from Defender for Cloud Engineering in Israel: Or Serok Jeppa, Meital Taran-Gutman, Ron Matchoro, Tamer Salman, Ram Pliskin, Lior Arviv, Melvyn Mildiner, Amit Biton, Omer Chechik, Arik Noyman, Liron Kachko, Denis Mizetski, Ofir Monza, Shahar Razon, Yael Genut, Inbal Argov, Eitan Shteinberg, Ido Keshet, Maya Herskovic, Tomer Spivak, Miri Kreitenberger, Aviv Mor, Tal Rosler, Netta Norman, Nir Sela, Elazar Krieger, Ben Mansheim, and Erel Hansav.

We also would like to thank all our teammates from the CxE MDC Team (Safeena, Stan, Fernanda, Dick, Giulio, Future, Shay, Vasavi, and Bojan), our manager Rebecca Halla for encouraging us to embrace new challenges, a special thanks to Liana Tomescu for reviewing this book and thanks to George Wilburn for writing the Defender for DevOps appendix.

Yuri would also like to thank: my wife and daughters for their endless support; my great God for giving me strength and guiding my path each step of the way; my great friend and co-author, Tom Janetscheck for this awesome partnership. Thanks to my parents for working hard to give me an education, which is the foundation I use every day to keep moving forward in my career. Last but not least, thanks to all followers of the *Defender for Cloud in the Field* show, and the entire Defender for Cloud community members for inspiring us to do more.

Tom would also like to thank: my wife and sons for always supporting me in whatever I do and for being my bastion of calm; my great friend and my manager and co-author, Yuri Diogenes for the awesome partnership on this project. Special thanks to Ben Kliger, who encouraged me to move out of my comfort zone and take the step into Defender for Cloud engineering. Last but not least, thanks to my friends Sarah and Dominik for all the inspiration and for letting me support you in pursuing your goals.

About the authors

Yuri Diogenes, MsC

Yuri holds a Master of Science in cybersecurity intelligence and forensics investigation from UTICA College and is currently working on his Ph.D. in Cybersecurity Leadership from Capitol Technology University. Yuri has been working at Microsoft since 2006, and currently, he is a Principal PM Manager for the CxE Microsoft Defender for Cloud Team. Yuri has published a total of 26 books, mostly about information security and Microsoft technologies. Yuri is also a professor at EC-Council University, where he teaches in the Bachelor in Cybersecurity Program. Yuri holds an MBA and many IT/Security industry certifications, such as CISSP, MITRE ATT&CK Cyber Threat Intelligence Certified, E|CND, E|CEH, E|CSA, E|CHFI, CompTIA Security+, CySA+, Network+, CASP, and CyberSec First Responder. You can follow Yuri on Twitter at @yuridiogenes.

Tom Janetscheck

Tom is a Senior Program Manager in the CxE Microsoft Defender for Cloud team, where he works with his friend Yuri, helping customers onboard and deploy Microsoft Defender for Cloud. As a former Microsoft MVP, Tom joined the team during COVID-19 in Spring 2020, and he deeply missed in-person conferences, as he loves to speak to audiences all over the world. With almost 20 years of experience in various IT admin and consulting roles, Tom has a deep background in IT infrastructure and security, and he holds various certifications, including MCSE and MCTS. When Tom is not writing a book, preparing a conference or user group session, or helping his customers onboard Defender for Cloud, he is an enthusiastic motorcyclist, scuba diver, and musician. He plays the guitar, bass, and drums. He also volunteers as a firefighter at his local fire department and can usually be met attending rock concerts all over the place. You can follow Tom on Twitter at @azureandbeyond.

Foreword

As customers' path toward the cloud and digital transformation continues, we see increased complexity in our cloud environments, moving from traditional VM workloads to cloud-native applications and leveraging an increasing selection of PaaS services. This introduces new challenges to cloud providers, security vendors, and security teams who have to familiarize themselves with dozens—or even hundreds—of PaaS services and ensure each is secured properly, given the correct context.

Securing these cloud workloads starts with reducing the attack surface by maintaining the security posture and defense-in-depth. This can be quite a challenge given the variety and the sheer number of posture misconfigurations and vulnerabilities found on an average cloud workload. This book goes into detail on how Defender for Cloud can be used to fully visualize the customer's cloud estate. It also helps identify the attack surface across all workload types (prioritizing risks using Secure Score, guiding customers to which threat to address first, and providing the customers with at-scale tooling to build cloud-native applications that are secure from day-1). Lastly, this book helps you enforce the correct set of policies to avoid drift.

While posture management is a must, it must be complemented with threat detection capabilities that can detect sophisticated attackers in a timely manner and assist SOC teams' response by blocking or mitigating these threats. In this book, Yuri and Tom share their knowledge of how Defender for Cloud identifies cyberattacks by leveraging signals from across the cloud workload, including VMs, containers, PaaS access logs, admin activity, networking, and more. And they tell you how this knowledge can be applied in a modern SOC to respond to such attacks.

If you are an IT or Security leader, I highly recommend you share this book with your teams. It is relevant to any organization that needs to protect and defend IT workloads across clouds and hybrid environments.

Gilad Elyashar,
Partner Director on Product Management
Microsoft Cloud Security

Introduction

Welcome to *Microsoft Defender for Cloud,* a book that was developed together with the Microsoft Defender for Cloud product group to provide in-depth information about Microsoft Defender for Cloud and to demonstrate best practices based on real-life experience with the product in different environments.

The purpose of this book is to introduce the wide array of security features and capabilities available in Microsoft Defender for Cloud. After being introduced to all of these security options, you will dig in to see how they can be used in a number of operational security scenarios so that you can get the most out of the protect, detect, and respond skills provided only by Microsoft Defender for Cloud.

Who is this book for?

Microsoft Defender for Cloud is for anyone interested in Azure security or multicloud security: security administrators, support professionals, developers, and engineers.

Microsoft Defender for Cloud is designed to be useful for the entire spectrum of Azure users. You will find this book to be a valuable resource, regardless of whether you have no security experience, some experience, or you are a security expert. This book provides introductory, intermediate, and advanced coverage on a large swath of security issues that are addressed by Microsoft Defender for Cloud.

The approach is a unique mix of didactic, narrative, and experiential instruction. Didactic covers the core introductions to the services. The narrative leverages what you already understand, and we bridge your current understanding with new concepts introduced in the book.

Finally, we share our experiences with Microsoft Defender for Cloud, how to get the most out of it by showing, in a stepwise, guided fashion, how to configure it to gain all the benefits it has to offer.

In this book, you will learn:

- How to secure your Azure assets no matter what your level of security experience
- How to protect resources in AWS and GCP

- How to save hours, days, and weeks of time by removing the need for trial and error

- How to protect, detect, and respond to security threats better than ever by knowing how to get the most out of the different Microsoft Defender for Cloud plans

System requirements

- Anyone with access to a Microsoft Azure subscription can use the information in this book. If you are integrating with AWS and GCP, you will also need an account on each cloud provider.

Errata, updates & book support

We've made every effort to ensure the accuracy of this book and its companion content. You can access updates to this book—in the form of a list of submitted errata and their related corrections—at:

MicrosoftPressStore.com/DefenderforCloud/errata

If you discover an error that is not already listed, please submit it to us at the same page.

For additional book support and information, please visit *http://www.MicrosoftPressStore.com/Support.*

Please note that product support for Microsoft software and hardware is not offered through the previous addresses. For help with Microsoft software or hardware, go to *http://support.microsoft.com.*

Stay in touch

Let's keep the conversation going! We're on Twitter: *http://twitter.com/MicrosoftPress.*

Chapter 1

The threat landscape

According to the Cybersecurity & Infrastructure Security Agency (CISA) Alert Report (AA22-040A) issued in February 2022, ransomware attacks tactics, and techniques evolved in 2021, and it was possible to see that cybercriminals were still using old methods of attack with a high rate of success, such as accessing network infrastructure via phishing emails, stolen credentials via Remote Desktop Protocol (RDP) brute-force attack, and exploitation of known unpatched vulnerabilities.

The same report emphasizes the level of professionalism that was introduced in 2021 regarding Ransomware as a Service (RaaS). Cybercriminals now hire online services that can help them perform their attack campaigns and negotiate payments. The sophistication of these cyberattacks is growing and pushing organizations to continue elevating their security postures to tackle proactive actions to reduce exposure and employ intelligent analytics that can quickly identify attempts to compromise their systems. This chapter explores some of these threats to prepare you to use Microsoft Defender for Cloud to protect against them. This chapter also discusses cybercrime, the MITRE ATT&CK framework, establishing your security posture, and the assume-breach approach.

The state of cybercrime

Amateur threat actors with low technical level skills are investing in RaaS kits for their campaigns because the ransomware kits provided by these professional cybercriminals are very sophisticated and easy to use. According to the Microsoft Digital Defense Report 2021, payment for these ransomware kits can be based on a percentage over the profit, such as 30 percent of the ransom. This model encourages amateur threat actors to take the risk because there will be zero upfront investment.

In 2021, ransomware gained a lot of visibility, mainly after the Colonial Pipeline incident. The Colonial Pipeline is one of the largest oil pipelines in the United States, and while the news emphasized the ransomware attack, it is important to understand that the threat actor first had to establish a foothold in the network—which was done by exploiting a legacy VPN. Also in 2021, threat actors were targeting VPN infrastructure, such as exploiting known vulnerabilities in the Pulse Secure VPN appliances.

However, it is not only about RaaS; professional cybercriminals also have different online offerings. For example, they might offer counter-antivirus (CAV) services, which scan antivirus engines to ensure new malware can be successfully deployed without being detected. Another offering is bulletproof hosting services for online criminal activity. (They're called "bulletproof" because the owners of these servers do not cooperate with local law enforcement.) There are even escrow services that act as a third party in online transactions between technical criminals and their criminal clients.

> **NOTE** To download the Microsoft Digital Defense Report 2021, see *www.microsoft.com/ digitaldefensereport.*

In 2021, we also saw Acer get hit by REvil ransomware (a Russian-based RaaS), where the threat actors demanded the largest known ransom to date—$50 million. You can see a list of all known techniques used by REvil at *https://attack.mitre.org/software/S0496*. JBS Foods was also attacked by REvil, and as a result, JBS had to temporarily close operations in Canada, Australia, and the United States. JBS ended up paying $11 million in ransom (see *https://www.cbsnews. com/news/jbs-ransom-11-million*), which is one of the biggest ransomware payments of all time.

Also, cybercriminals might use advanced code injection methods, such as a file-less attack, which usually leverages tools already in the target system, such as PowerShell. By leveraging a tool that is already on the computer, they don't need to write to the hard drive; instead, they only need to take over the target process, run a piece of code in its memory space, and then use that code to call the tool that will be used to perform the attack. The question here is this: Do you have detections for that? Microsoft Defender for Cloud does!

Email phishing continues to grow as an attack vector, and cybercriminals continue to use this method according to the main theme (the topic to be used to drive attention) of the moment. In 2020, the main theme was COVID-19, which meant the core structure of the attack didn't really change from past attacks. Figure 1-1 shows an example of a credential phishing attack (a spearphishing attack).

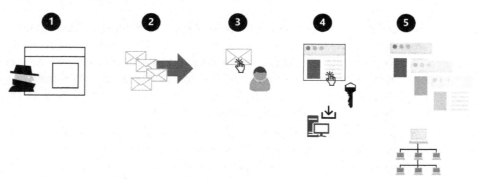

FIGURE 1-1 Typical credential phishing flow

Figure 1-1 shows a summary of the five main phases of a spearphishing attack targeting the user's credentials. The five phases shown in this figure are explained in more detail below:

1. The threat actor prepares a cybercriminal infrastructure by configuring fake or compromised domains. During this process, the threat actor will also gather information about the potential target.

2. Next, the malicious email is sent to the target.

3. The email is well-crafted and leverages social engineering techniques that will entice the user to click a hyperlink embedded in the email.

4. At this point, there are usually two scenarios for credential theft:

   - The victim will be redirected to a fake or compromised domain, and there, they will have to type their credentials.

   - Upon clicking the hyperlink, malware is downloaded to the victim's device, which will harvest the user's credentials.

5. Now that the threat actor has the user's credentials, they will use those credentials on other legitimate sites or to establish network access to the company's network.

Although the example above refers to a spearphishing attack, which is an old technique, cybercriminals may also use advanced methods of code injection, such as file-less techniques.

In November 2021, the world was surprised by the CVE-2021-44228, which was related to Log4Shell. This vulnerability affected Log4j, which is an open-source logging framework in Java that is widely used by cloud and enterprise application developers. At that point, threat actors began to exploit this vulnerability. The exploitation could be done by creating a specially crafted Java Naming and Directory Interface (JNDI) command, sending it to a vulnerable server (hosting a vulnerable version of Log4J) that uses a protocol such as LDAP, RMI, NDS, or DNS, and then running the code remotely. Organizations that were using Microsoft Defender for Cloud could quickly identify which machines were vulnerable to this CVE by using the Inventory feature.

> **NOTE**   You can read more about this scenario at *http://aka.ms/MDFCLog4J*.

Understanding the cyberkill chain

One of the most challenging aspects of defending your systems against cybercriminals is recognizing when those systems are being used for some sort of criminal activity in the first place—especially when they are part of a botnet. A *botnet* is a network of compromised devices that are controlled by an attacker without the knowledge of their owners. Botnets are not new. As a matter of fact, a 2012 Microsoft study found that cybercriminals infiltrated unsecure supply chains using the Nitol botnet, which introduced counterfeit software embedded with malware to secretly infect computers even before they were purchased.

In 2020, we saw one of the most famous supply chain attacks utilizing malicious SolarWinds files and potentially giving nation-state actors access to some victims' networks. This supply chain attack took place when attackers inserted malicious code into a DLL component of the legitimate software (`SolarWinds.Orion.Core.BusinessLayer.dll`). The compromised DLL was distributed to organizations that were using this software.

The execution phase just needed the user or system to start the software and load the compromised DLL. Once this was done, the inserted malicious code performed a call to maintain long-term access through the backdoor capability to establish persistence. The entire process was very well thought out; the backdoor avoided detection by running an extensive list of checks to ensure that it was actually running on a compromised network. The backdoor performed the initial reconnaissance to gather the necessary information and connected to a C2 (command-and-control) server. As part of the exfiltration, the backdoor sent gathered information to the attacker. Also, the attacker received a wide range of other backdoor capabilities to perform additional activities, such as credential theft, privilege escalation, and lateral movement.

The best way to prevent this type of attack, or any other, is to improve your overall security posture by hardening your resources and improving your detection capabilities. The detection capabilities are needed to understand the attack vectors—that is, how an attacker will attack your environment. To help you understand this, we will use the Lockheed Martin cyberkill chain. Each step in this chain represents a particular attack phase (see Figure 1-2).

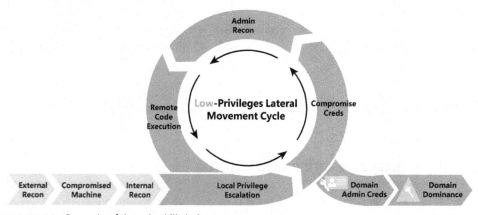

FIGURE 1-2   Example of the cyberkill chain steps

Below are the main steps in this chain, as shown in Figure 1-2:

1. **External recon**   During this step, attackers typically search publicly available data to identify as much information as possible about their target. The aim is to obtain intelligence, or *intel*, to better perform the attack and increase the likelihood of success.

2. **Compromised machine** During this step, attackers leverage different techniques, such as social engineering, to entice users to do something. For example, the attacker might send a phishing email to lure the user into clicking a link that will compromise the machine. The goal is to establish a foothold in the victim's network.

3. **Internal recon and lateral movement** During this step, the attacker performs host discovery and identifies and maps internal networks and systems. The attacker might also start moving laterally between hosts, looking for a privileged user's account to compromise.

4. **The low-privileges lateral movement cycle** During this cycle, the attacker continues to search for accounts with administrative privileges so that they can perform a *local privilege escalation* attack. Typically, this cycle continues until the attacker finds a domain administrative user account that can be compromised.

5. **Domain admin creds** At this point, the attacker needs complete *domain dominance*. To achieve this, the attacker will pivot through the network, either looking for valuable data or installing ransomware or any other malware that can be used for future extortion attempts.

It is important to understand these steps because, throughout this book, you will learn how Defender for Cloud can be used to disrupt the cyberkill chain by detecting attacks in different phases.

Using the MITRE ATT&CK Framework to protect and detect

MITRE ATT&CK (*https://attack.mitre.org/*) is a knowledge base of adversary tactics and techniques based on real-world experiences. For three years in a row (2019-2021), Microsoft successfully demonstrated industry-leading defense capabilities in the independent MITRE Engenuity ATT&CK Evaluation (adversarial tactics, techniques, and common knowledge).

In 2021, Microsoft also released the MITRE ATT&CK mappings for built-in Azure security controls. Also in 2021, Microsoft Defender for Cloud started mapping all security recommendations to MITRE ATT&CK, which helps defenders understand which preventative actions can be done to reduce the likelihood that a threat actor will exploit a vulnerability based on the different MITRE ATT&CK tactics and techniques. The security alerts triggered by the different Microsoft Defender for Cloud plans also map to MITRE ATT&CK tactics and techniques, ensuring that the Security Operation Center (SOC) analyst has a better understanding of the stage of the attack and how it potentially happened. In Chapter 5, "Strengthening your security posture," you will learn more about using MITRE ATT&CK tactics and techniques to prioritize the remediation of security recommendations.

> **TIP** To learn more about MITRE ATT&CK, you can download this free ebook at *https://www.mitre.org/sites/default/files/publications/mitre-getting-started-with-attack-october-2019.pdf.*

Common threats

Ransomware is a threat that grew exponentially at the peak of the COVID-19 pandemic. According to the Microsoft Digital Defense Report of September 2020, 70 percent of human-operated ransomware attacks were brute-force Remote Desktop Protocol (RDP) attacks. This is an alarming number for a problem that can be easily fixed by using technologies such as just-in-time VM access, available in Defender for Server, which is part of Defender for Cloud.

Threat actors are also using existing attack methods against new workloads, such as Kubernetes. The Defender for Cloud research team started mapping the Kubernetes security landscape and noticed that although the attack techniques are different than those targeting single hosts running Linux or Windows, the tactics are similar. When the Kubernetes cluster is deployed in a public cloud, threat actors who can compromise cloud credentials can take over a cluster. Again, the impact of the attack is different to single hosts because this leads to the whole cluster being compromised, though the tactic used is similar to the one used to compromise a single host.

According to the Verizon Data Breach Report of 2021, phishing attacks are still the predominant method of delivering malware. This makes sense because the end-user is almost always the target because they are the weakest link. With the proliferation of mobile devices, bring-your-own-device (BYOD) models, and cloud-based apps, users are installing more and more apps. All too often, these apps are merely malware masquerading as valid apps. It is important to have solid endpoint protection and a detection system that can look across different sources to intelligently identify unknown threats by leveraging cutting-edge technologies such as analytics and machine learning.

The likelihood that a threat actor can exploit a system based on the attacks mentioned above is higher today because of the lack of security hygiene. According to the Verizon Data Breach Report from 2020, misconfiguration accounted for 40 percent of the root cause of compromised systems. Because the user often provides a storage account and leaves it open for an Internet connection is enough to increase the attack vector. That's why it is so important to have a tool such as Microsoft Defender for Cloud that will bring visibility and control over different cloud workloads.

Improving security posture

It used to be the case that cybersecurity experts recommended that organizations simply invest more in protecting their assets. Nowadays, however, simply investing in protecting your assets is not enough. The lack of security hygiene across the industry was mentioned in the Cybersecurity and Infrastructure Security Agency (CISA) Analysis Report (AR21-013A), released in January 2021. The report, "Strengthening Security Configurations to Defend Against Attackers Targeting Cloud Services," stated that most threat actors successfully exploited resources because of "poor cyber hygiene practices."

To strengthen the security posture of your organization, you should invest equally in protection, detection, and response, as shown in Figure 1-3.

Protect
Across all Endpoints, from
Sensors to the Datacenter

Detect
Using Targeted Signals, Behavioral
Monitoring, and Machine Learning

Your
Security Posture

Respond
Closing the Gap Between
Discovery and Action

FIGURE 1-3   The three pillars of your security posture

It is important to expand the rationale of the triad (protection, detection, and response) shown in Figure 1-3. When it comes to protection, you need to think of proactive actions that must be taken to decrease the likelihood that resources will be compromised. This must be done as part of your security hygiene. Once all practice actions are done, vulnerabilities are remediated, and the system is hardened, you must actively monitor the system and identify potential threat actors who are trying to break in. You need a strong detection mechanism across different workloads to increase the likelihood that you will detect these attacks, and you need to have a different set of analytics for different workloads and analytics that are relevant for that use case. For example, you can't expect to have good analytics for your storage accounts if you only have detection for your Key Vault. This is a typical example of two different workloads that have different threat landscapes. Therefore, it is imperative to have good detection created specifically for the workload that you want to monitor. Once you detect an attack, you need to respond, which means you need to have a good incident response in place to reduce the time between detection and response. This will determine how fast you can mitigate the attack and avoid the proliferation of the threat. Also, it's important that you use the lessons learned from each incident response to feed your security hygiene. In other words, learn from it and improve your protection. This is a constant loop, and you must continuously improve.

By having a solid security posture, you also prevent threat actors from staying in your network for a long time. According to the InfoSec Institute, attackers lurk on networks for an average of 200 days without being detected. (See *http://resources.infosecinstitute.com/the-seven-steps-of-a-successful-cyber-attack* for more information.) No doubt, this is a tremendous amount of time to have an attacker inside your network. But the key word here is actually *detected*. Without a good detection mechanism, you have no way of disrupting an attack, so it is imperative that you invest in a holistic solution to monitor cloud-based resources and on-premises assets. You must be able to quickly detect an attack and use actionable data to improve your response.

All that being said, collecting data without analyzing it only delays the response process. That's why it is so important to use tools that leverage technologies, such as behavior analytics, threat intelligence, and machine learning for data correlation. Defender for Cloud will do all that for you, reducing false positives and showing what's relevant for proceeding with your investigation.

Adopting an assume-breach mentality

Microsoft recognizes the fact that preventing a breach is not enough. Microsoft hasn't "given up" or "thrown up the white flag" and continues to use all the traditional prevent-breach processes and technologies. However, in addition to those processes and technologies, Microsoft has encompassed an *assume-breach* philosophy, meaning it's okay to hope you'll never be breached, so long as you know that hope is a poor strategy. Therefore, Microsoft assumes its public cloud network is about to be breached—or has already been breached, so Microsoft identifies the people, processes, and technologies that will help us learn as early as possible when the breach occurred, identify the type of breach, and then eject the attacker. The goal is to limit the expansion of the breach as much as possible.

Microsoft uses the assume-breach approach to help it understand how attackers gain access to the system, and then Microsoft develops methods that enable it to catch the attacker as soon after the breach as possible. Because attackers typically enter a system via a low-value target (for example, a compromised user credential), if a compromised target is detected quickly, it can block the attacker from expanding outward from the low-value asset to higher-value assets (such as an administrative type of credential). Ultimately, it's these high-value assets that are the attacker's ultimate target.

Microsoft uses a very effective method called *red-teaming*, or *red/blue team simulations*. In these exercises, the red team takes on the role of the attacker, and the blue team takes on the defender role. After the exercise parameters and agreed-upon duration of the exercise are determined, the red team tries to attack the Azure infrastructure. Then the blue team tries to discover what the red team has done and then attempts to block the red team from compromising additional systems (if indeed the red team was able to compromise any systems).

At the end of the exercise, the red and blue teams discuss what happened, how the red team might have got in, and how the blue team discovered and ejected the red team, and then suggestions are made for new technologies and operational procedures that will make it easier and faster to discover a compromise.

Cloud threats and security

Visibility and control of different workloads is an area that is becoming critical when it comes to security hygiene. Typical targets of threat actors are exposed storage containers; these actors use custom scanners they've built to identify public containers.

Threat actors actively scan public storage to find "sensitive" content, and they usually leverage the Azure Storage API to list content available within a public storage container. Usually, this process takes place in the following phases:

- **Finding storage accounts** During this phase, threat actors will try to find Azure Storage accounts using the blob storage URL pattern, which is `<storage-account>.blob.core.windows.net`.

- **Finding containers** After finding the storage accounts, the next step is to find any publicly accessible containers in those storage accounts by guessing the container's name. This can be done using an API call to list blobs or any other read operation.

- **Finding sensitive data** In this phase, threat actors can leverage online tools that search through large volumes of data looking for keywords and secrets to find sensitive information.

When you enable Defender for Storage, you have a series of analytics created for different scenarios, one of which is the anonymous scan of public storage containers.

The Microsoft Security Intelligent Report Volume 22 shows the global outreach of cloud weaponization, which is the act of using cloud computing capabilities for malicious purposes. According to this report, more than two-thirds of incoming attacks on Azure services in the first quarter of 2017 came from IP addresses in China (35.1 percent), the United States (32.5 percent), and Korea (3.1 percent); the remaining attacks were distributed across 116 other countries and regions. Sometimes, threat actors will weaponize the cloud to send an attack to a target system (see Figure 1-4). Other times, threat actors simply hijack the resources of the target system. For example, let's say a cloud admin misconfigured a Kubernetes or Docker registry, and this misconfiguration exposed the system to allow free public access to it. Attackers could deploy containers that will mine crypto. The diagram shown in Figure 1-4 represents an attacker gaining access to VMs located in the cloud and leveraging compute resources from these VMs to attack on-premises assets. You can also see some users connect remotely to those VMs and, ultimately, they will also be affected. This is a typical cloud weaponization scenario.

Another potential threat in the cloud happens because of flaws in configuration—again, because of the lack of security hygiene. One common scenario is a public key secret being shared publicly. You might think this doesn't happen, but it does! During a study conducted by North Carolina State University (NCSU) in 2019, billions of files from 13 percent of all GitHub public repositories were scanned for six months. The result showed that 100,000 GitHub repositories had leaked API or cryptographic keys.

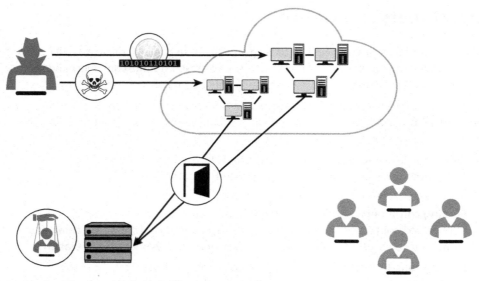

FIGURE 1-4 Cloud weaponization targeting on-premises resources

Figure 1-5 illustrates a scenario in which bots were scanning GitHub to steal keys.

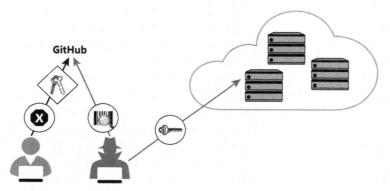

FIGURE 1-5 Public secret attack scenario

Attackers are also shifting efforts to evade detections provided by cloud workload protection platforms (CWPP). In January 2019, a report from Palo Alto Networks showed how malware used by the Rocke group was able to uninstall the CWPP agent before showing signs of malicious behavior. Cloud providers must act quickly to remediate scenarios like this, and when selecting your CWPP agent, you need to be aware of how quickly they can respond to new threat vectors like this.

For this reason, it is imperative that before adopting cloud computing, organizations must first understand the security considerations that are inherited by the cloud computing model. These considerations must be revised before adoption—ideally, during the planning process.

Without a full understanding of cloud security considerations, the overall successful adoption of cloud computing may be compromised.

Consider the following areas for cloud security:

- Compliance
- Risk management
- Identity and access management
- Operational security
- Endpoint protection
- Data protection

Each of these areas must be considered. Depending on the type of business you are dealing with, some areas can be explored in more depth than others. The following sections describe each of these cloud security areas in more detail.

Compliance

During migration to the cloud, organizations need to retain their own compliance obligations. These obligations could be dictated by internal or external regulations, such as compliance with industry standards to support their business models. Cloud providers must be able to assist customers to meet their compliance requirements via cloud adoption.

In many cases, cloud solution providers (CSPs) will become part of the customer's compliance chain. Consider working closely with your cloud provider to identify your organization's compliance needs and verify how the cloud provider can fulfill your requirements. Also, it's important to verify whether the CSP has a proven record of delivering secure, reliable cloud services while keeping the customer's data private and secure.

> **MORE INFO** For more information on Microsoft's approach to compliance, see *https://www.microsoft.com/en-us/trustcenter/default.aspx.*

Ideally, your cloud security posture management (CSPM) platform will enable you to map the security controls applied to your cloud workloads to the major regulatory compliance standards and allow you to customize your data visualization according to your needs.

Risk management

Cloud customers must be able to trust the CSP with their data. CSPs should have policies and programs in place to manage online security risks. These policies and programs can vary depending on how dynamic the environment is. Customers should work closely with CSPs and demand full transparency to understand risk decisions, how they vary depending on data sensitivity, and the level of protection required.

Identity and access management

Organizations planning to adopt cloud computing must be aware of the identity- and access-management methods available and of how these methods will integrate with their current on-premises infrastructure.

These days, with users working on different devices from any location and accessing apps across different cloud services, it is critical to keep the user's identity secure. Indeed, with cloud adoption, identity becomes the new perimeter—the control panel for your entire infrastructure, regardless of the location, be it on-premises or in the cloud. You use identity to control access to any services from any device and to obtain visibility and insights into how your data is being used.

As for access management, organizations should consider auditing and logging capabilities that can help administrators monitor user activity. Administrators must be able to leverage the cloud platform to evaluate suspicious login activity and take preventive actions directly from the identity-management portal.

Operational security

Organizations migrating to the cloud should evolve their internal processes, such as security monitoring, auditing, incident response, and forensics, according to the needs of their industry. For example, if your organization is working in the financial industry, they have different requirements than for organizations in the health insurance industry. The cloud platform must allow IT administrators to monitor services in real-time, observing the health conditions of these services and providing capabilities to quickly restore interrupted services. You should also ensure that deployed services are operated, maintained, and supported in accordance with the service-level agreement (SLA) established with the CSP.

Endpoint protection

Cloud security is not only about how secure the CSP infrastructure is. It is a shared responsibility. Organizations are responsible for their endpoint protection, so those that adopt cloud computing should consider increasing their endpoint security because these endpoints will be exposed to more external connections and will access apps that different cloud providers may house.

Because endpoints (workstations, smartphones, or any other device that can be employed to access cloud resources) are the devices employed by users, these users are the main target of attacks. Attackers know that the user is the weakest link in the security chain. Therefore, attackers will continue to invest in social engineering techniques, such as phishing emails, to entice users to perform actions that can compromise an endpoint.

One important approach to enabling the end-to-end visibility of your endpoint protection and cloud workloads is the integration of your CWPP with your endpoint detection and response (EDR) solution.

Data protection

When it comes to cloud security, your goal when migrating to the cloud is to ensure that data is secure no matter where it is located. Data might exist in any of the following states and locations:

1. **Data at rest in the user's device**   In this case, the data is located at the endpoint, which can be any device. You should always enforce data encryption at rest for company-owned devices and in BYOD scenarios.

2. **Data in transit from the user's device to the cloud**   When data leaves the user's device, you should ensure that the data is still protected. There are many technologies that can encrypt data—such as Azure Rights Management—regardless of its location. It is also imperative to ensure that the transport channel is encrypted. Therefore, you should enforce the use of transport layer security (TLS) to transfer data.

3. **Data at rest in the cloud provider's datacenter**   Your cloud provider's storage infrastructure should ensure redundancy and protection when your data arrives at its servers. Make sure you understand how your CSP performs data encryption at rest, who is responsible for managing the keys, and how data redundancy is performed.

4. **Data in transit from the cloud to on-premises servers**   In this case, the same recommendations specified in the second bullet above apply. You should enforce data encryption on the file itself and encrypt the transport layer.

5. **Data at rest on-premises**   Customers are responsible for keeping their data secure on-premises. Encrypting at-rest data at the organization's datacenter is critical to accomplishing this. Ensure you have the correct infrastructure to enable encryption, data redundancy, and key management.

Azure security

There are two aspects of Azure security. One is platform security—that is, how Microsoft keeps its Azure platform secure against attackers. The other is the Azure security capabilities that Microsoft offers to customers who use Azure.

The Azure infrastructure uses a defense-in-depth approach by implementing security controls in different layers. This ranges from physical security to data security, to identity and access management, and to application security, as shown in Figure 1-6.

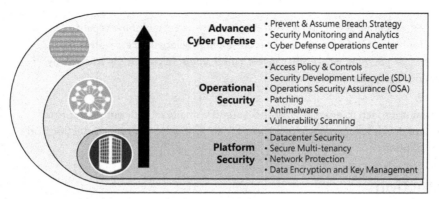

FIGURE 1-6 Multiple layers of defense

From the Azure subscription-owner's perspective, it is important to control the user's identity and roles. The subscription owner, or account administrator, is the person who signed up for the Azure subscription. This person is authorized to access the Account Center and perform all available management tasks. With a new subscription, the account administrator is also the service administrator and inherits rights to manage the Azure portal. Customers should be very cautious about who has access to this account. Azure administrators should use Azure's role-based access control (RBAC) to grant appropriate permission to users.

Once a user is authenticated according to their level of authorization, that person will be able to manage their resources using the Azure portal. The portal is a unified hub that simplifies building, deploying, and managing your cloud resources. The Azure portal also calculates the existing charges and forecasts the customer's monthly charges, regardless of the number of resources across apps.

A subscription can include zero or more hosted services and zero or more storage accounts. From the Azure portal (also through the PowerShell, CLI, or ARM template), you can provision new hosted services such as a new Virtual Machine (VM). These VMs will use resources allocated from compute and storage components in Azure. They can work in silos within the Azure infrastructure, or they can be publicly available on the Internet. You can securely publish resources that are available in your VM, such as a web server, and harden access to these resources using access control lists (ACLs). You can also isolate VMs in the cloud by creating different virtual networks (VNets) and controlling traffic between VNets using network security groups (NSGs).

VM protection

When you think about protecting VMs in Azure, you must think holistically. That is, not only must you think about leveraging built-in Azure resources to protect the VM, you must also think about protecting the operating system itself. For example, you should implement security best practices and update management to keep the VMs up to date. You should also monitor access to these VMs. Some key VM operations include the following:

- Configuring monitoring and export events for analysis
- Configuring Microsoft antimalware or an AV/AM solution from a partner
- Applying a corporate firewall using site-to-site VPN and configuring endpoints
- Defining access controls between tiers and providing additional protection via the OS firewall
- Monitoring and responding to alerts
- Installing a vulnerability assessment tool to have visibility beyond the operating system's vulnerabilities

> **IMPORTANT** For more details about Compute security, see *https:// docs.microsoft.com/en-us/azure/security/security-virtual-machines-overview.*

Reducing network exposure is also a recommended practice for VM hardening. For example, if you don't need constant Internet access to your VM via Remote Desktop Protocol (RDP), why leave it open? A solution for that problem is to use just-in-time VM access, available in Defender for Servers. You can use Azure policies to create enforcement standards for VM deployment based on your organization's needs. You can also use custom images that are already hardened using certain standards to ensure when new VMs are deployed, they are already secure. In Azure Marketplace, you will find hardened images that use the Center for Internet Security (CIS) benchmark (see *https://www.cisecurity.org/cis-benchmarks*).

By leveraging the CIS benchmark's pre-defined images to deploy new VMs, you ensure that your VMs are always hardened based on industry standards. While this is good practice, some organizations might want to go even further and customize their own images, which also is a feasible alternative. When planning to create your custom image, remember that hardening is more than disabling services; it's also about using security configurations in your operating system and applications.

Endpoint protection is also an imperative part of your security strategy, and these days you can't have endpoint protection without an antimalware solution installed on your VM. In Azure, you have the native Azure Antimalware component that you can deploy to all VMs by leveraging Microsoft Defender for Cloud.

Network protection

Azure virtual networks are very similar to the virtual networks you use on-premises with your own virtualization platform solutions. To help you understand this, Figure 1-7 illustrates a typical Azure Network infrastructure.

In Figure 1-7, you can see the Azure infrastructure (on top) with three virtual networks. Contoso needs to segment its Azure network into different virtual networks (VNets) to provide better isolation and security. Having VNets in its Azure infrastructure allows Contoso to connect Azure Virtual Machines (VMs) to securely communicate with each other, the Internet, and Contoso's on-premises networks.

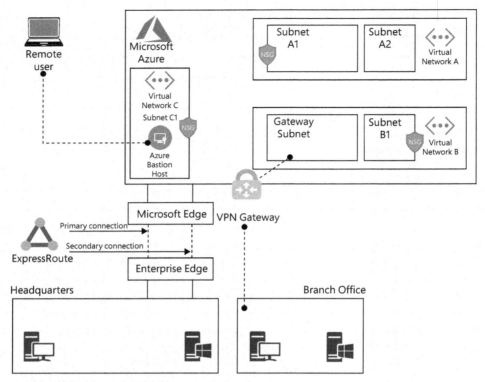

FIGURE 1-7 Contoso network infrastructure

If you think about the traditional physical network on-premises, where you operate in your own datacenter, that's basically what a VNet is but with the additional benefits of Azure's infrastructure, including scalability, availability, and isolation. When you are creating a VNet, you must specify a custom private IP address that will be used by the resources that belong to this VNet. For example, if you deploy a VM in a VNet with an address space of 10.0.0.0/24, the VM will be assigned a private IP, such as 10.0.0.10/24.

Network access control is as important on Azure virtual networks as it is on-premises. The principle of least privilege applies to both on-premises and in the cloud. One way to enforce network access controls in Azure is by taking advantage of network security groups (NSGs). An NSG is equivalent to a simple stateful packet-filtering firewall or router, similar to the type of firewalling done in the 1990s. (We don't say this to be negative about NSGs; instead, we want to clarify that some techniques for network access control have survived the test of time.)

> **IMPORTANT** For more details about Azure network security, see
> *https://docs.microsoft.com/en-us/azure/security/security-network-overview.*

Network segmentation is important in many scenarios, and you need to understand the design requirements to suggest the implementation options. Let's say you want to ensure that hosts on the Internet cannot communicate with hosts on a back-end subnet but can communicate with hosts on the front-end subnet. In this case, you should create two VNets—one for your front-end resources and another for your back-end resources.

NSG security rules are evaluated by their priority, and each is identified with a number between 100 and 4,096, where the lowest numbers are processed first. The security rules use 5-tuple information (source address, source port, destination address, destination port, and protocol) to allow or deny the traffic. When the traffic is evaluated, a flow record is created for existing connections, and the communication is allowed or denied based on the connection state of the flow record. You can compare this type of configuration to the old VLAN segmentation that was often implemented with on-premises networks.

Very useful.

When configuring your virtual network, also consider that the resources you deploy within the virtual network will inherit the ability to communicate with each other. You can also enable virtual networks to connect to each other, or you can enable resources in either virtual network to communicate with each other by using virtual network peering. When connecting virtual networks, you can choose to access other VNets that are in the same or different Azure regions.

Azure DDoS protection

Azure can provide scale and expertise to protect against large and sophisticated DDoS (distributed denial-of-service) attacks. However, when following the share responsibility model used in cloud computing, customers must also design their applications to be ready for a massive amount of traffic. Some key capabilities for applications include high availability, scale-out, resiliency, fault tolerance, and attack surface area reduction. Azure DDoS protection is part of the defense-in-depth defense approach used by Azure networks, as shown in Figure 1-8.

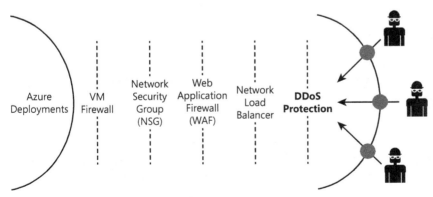

FIGURE 1-8 Azure network defense in-depth approach

By default, Azure provides continuous protection against DDoS attacks as part of DDoS Protection Basic, which is not charged. However, if you want extra metrics for DDoS protection, alerts, mitigation reports, mitigation flow logs, policy customization, and support, you need to go to Azure Protection Standard. You can provision Azure DDoS on a Virtual Network using the Azure portal or PowerShell. If you don't have Azure DDoS Standard enabled on your subscription, Microsoft Defender for Cloud will trigger a recommendation like the one shown in Figure 1-9.

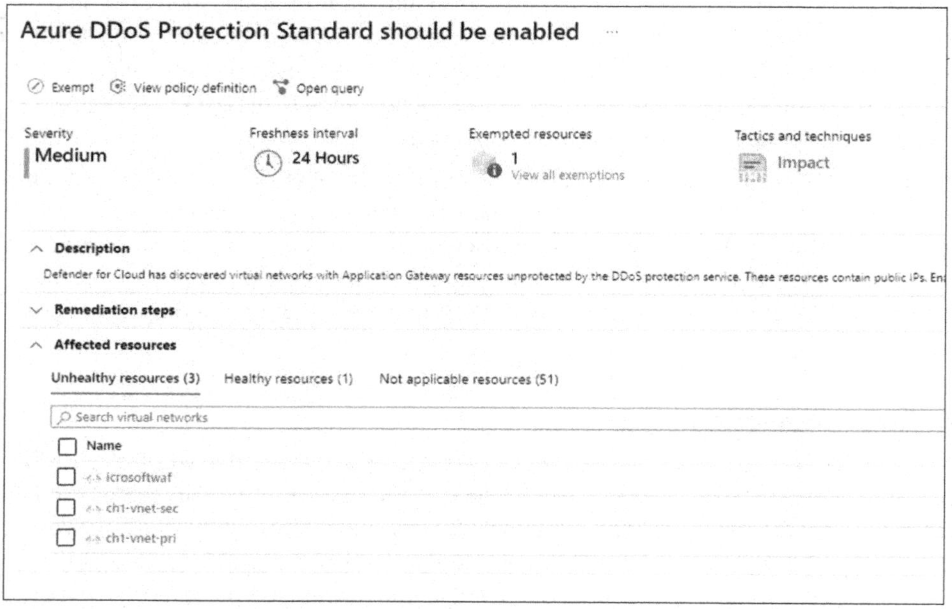

FIGURE 1-9 Microsoft Defender for Cloud recommendation to enable Azure DDoS Standard

> **IMPORTANT** For more details about Azure DDoS Protection, see *http://aka.ms/ ddosprotectiondocs.*

While the basic protection provides automatic attack mitigations against DDoS, some capabilities are only provided by the DDoS Standard tier. The organization's requirements will lead you to determine which tier you will utilize. For example, when your organization needs to implement DDoS protection on the application level, it needs to have real-time attack metrics and resource logs available to its team and create a post-attack mitigation report to present to upper management. These requirements can only be fulfilled by the DDoS Standard tier. Table 1-1 provides a summary of the capabilities available for each tier:

TABLE 1-1 Azure DDoS Basic versus Standard

Capability	DDoS Basic	DDoS Standard
Active traffic monitoring and always-on detection	X	X
Automatic attack mitigation	X	X
Availability guarantee	Per Azure region.	Per application.
Mitigation policies	Tuned per Azure region volume.	Tuned for application traffic volume.
Metrics and alerts	Not available.	X
Mitigation flow logs	Not available.	X
Mitigation policy customization	Not available.	X
Support	Yes, but it is a best-effort approach. In other words, there is no guarantee support will address the issue.	Yes, and it provides access to DDoS experts during an active attack.
SLA	Azure region.	Application guarantee and cost protection.
Pricing	Free.	Monthly usage.

Storage protection

Data encryption at rest is an extremely important part of your overall VM security strategy. Defender for Cloud will even trigger a security recommendation when a VM is missing disk encryption. You can encrypt your Windows and Linux virtual machines' disks using Azure Disk Encryption (ADE). For Windows OS, you need Windows 8 or later (for client) and Windows Server 2008 R2 or later (for servers).

ADE provides operating system and data disk encryption. For Windows, it uses BitLocker Device Encryption; for Linux, it uses the DM-Crypt system. ADE is not available in the following scenarios:

- Basic A-series VMs
- VMs with less than 2 GB of memory
- Generation 2 VMs and Lsv2-series VMs
- Unmounted volumes

ADE requires that your Windows VM has connectivity with Azure AD to get a token to connect with Key Vault. At that point, the VM needs access to the Key Vault endpoint to write the encryption keys, and the VM also needs access to an Azure Storage endpoint. This storage endpoint will host the Azure extension repository and the Azure Storage account that hosts the VHD files.

Group policy is another important consideration when implementing ADE. If the VMs for which you are implementing ADE are domain joined, make sure not to push any group policy that enforces trusted platform module (TPM) protectors. If you want to use BitLocker in a computer without TPM, you need to ensure that the `Allow BitLocker Without A Compatible TPM` policy is configured. Also, BitLocker policy for domain-joined VMs with a custom group policy must include the Configure user storage of BitLocker recovery information -> Allow 256-bit recovery key option.

Because ADE uses Azure Key Vault to control and manage disk encryption keys and secrets, you need to ensure Azure Key Vault has the proper configuration for this implementation. One important consideration when configuring your Azure Key Vault for ADE is that they (VM and Key Vault) both need to be part of the same subscription. Also, make sure that encryption secrets are not crossing regional boundaries; ADE requires that the Key Vault and the VMs are co-located in the same region.

> **IMPORTANT** For more details about Azure Storage security, see *https://docs.microsoft.com/en-us/azure/security/security-storage-overview*.

Another layer of protection that you can include in your Azure Storage is the Storage Firewall. When you enable this feature in Azure Storage, you can better control the level of access to your storage accounts based on the type and subset of networks used. Only applications requesting data over the specified set of networks can access a storage account when network rules are configured.

You can create granular controls to limit access to your storage account to requests from specific IP addresses, IP ranges, or a list of subnets in an Azure VNet. The firewall rules created on your Azure Storage are enforced on all network protocols that can be used to access your storage account, including REST and SMB.

Since the default storage account's configuration allows connections from clients on any other network (including the Internet), it is recommended that you configure this feature to limit access to selected networks.

Defender for Storage

When you enable Defender for Storage, you can be notified via alerts when anomalous access and data exfiltration activities occur. These alerts include detections such as

- Access made from an unusual location
- Unusual data extraction
- Unusual anonymous access
- Unexpected deletions
- Access permission changes
- Uploading the Azure Cloud Service package

You can enable this capability on the Storage Account level, or you can simply enable it on the subscription level in the Defender for Cloud pricing settings. This capability will be covered in more detail in Chapter 6, "Threat detection."

Identity

Azure Identity Protection is part of Azure Active Directory (AD), and it is widely used because of its capabilities to detect potential identity-related vulnerabilities, suspicious actions related to the identity of your users, and the capability to investigate incidents. Azure AD Identity Protection alerts will also be streamed to Defender for Cloud.

> **IMPORTANT** For more details about Azure AD Identity Protection, see *http://aka.ms/ AzureADIdentityProtection*.

Logging

Throughout the years, it has become increasingly important always to have logs available to investigate security-related issues. Azure provides different types of logs, and understanding their distinction can help during an investigation. Data plane logs will reflect events raised using an Azure resource. An example of this type of log would be writing a file in storage. The control plane logs reflect events raised by the resource manager; an example of this log would be the creation of a storage account.

Those logs can be extracted from different services in Azure because Azure provides different layers of logging capability. Figure 1-10 shows the different logging tiers.

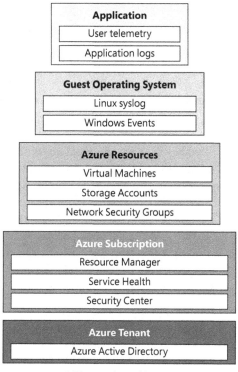

FIGURE 1-10 Different tiers of logging in Azure

It is very important to understand this tier model in order to have a better idea of which areas you should focus on when trying to extract logs. For example, if you want to extract the VM activities (provisioning, deprovisioning, and so on), you need to look at logs at the Azure Resource Manager level. To visualize activity logs about operations on a resource from the "control plane" perspective, you will use Azure Activity Log, which sits in the Azure Tenant layer in the diagram. Diagnostics Logs are located in the Azure Resources layer and are emitted by the resource itself. It provides information about the operation of that resource (the data plane).

Because this book focuses on Microsoft Defender for Cloud, it is important to highlight a common scenario that comes up often: the need to visualize actions performed in the Microsoft Defender for Cloud configuration. Let's use a very simple example: Say you just noticed that you only have one email address for security contact instead of three like before. You can use Azure Activity Log to investigate when this change occurred. For this particular case, you should see an entry similar to the one shown in Figure 1-11.

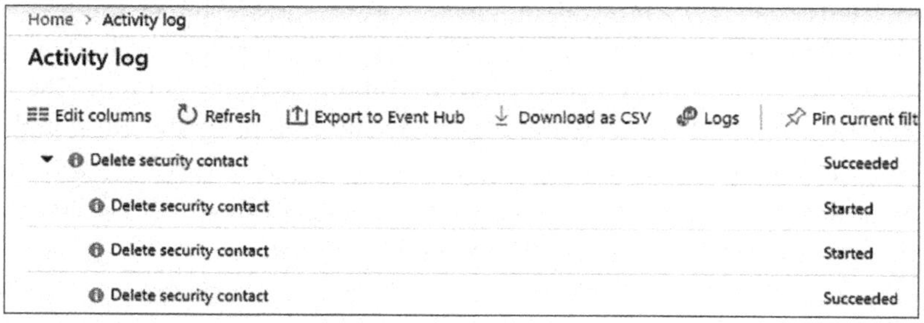

FIGURE 1-11   Azure Activity Log

If you click the successful **Delete Security Contact**, you will have access to the JSON content, and there you will be able to see more info regarding who performed this action and when it was done.

Container security

The utilization of containers is growing substantially in different industries, which makes containers a target for potential attacks. Because a container is a lightweight, standalone, and executable package that includes everything needed to run an application, the threat vectors are very diverse. To avoid exposure, it is critical that containers are deployed in the most secure manner.

Containers in Azure use the same network stack as the regular Azure VMs; the difference is that in the container environment, you also have the concept of the Azure Virtual Network container network interface (CNI) plug-in. This plug-in is responsible for assigning an IP address from a virtual network to containers brought up in the VM, attaching them to the VNet, and connecting them directly to other containers.

One important concept in containers is called a *pod*. A pod represents a single instance of your application and, typically, it has a 1:1 mapping with a container, although there are some unique scenarios in which a pod may contain multiple containers. A VNet IP address is assigned to every pod, which could consist of one or more containers. Figure 1-12 shows an example of what an Azure networking topology looks like when using containers.

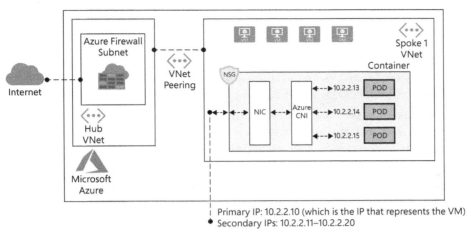

FIGURE 1-12   Container network in Azure

Notice that a virtual network IP address is assigned to every pod (which could consist of one or more containers). These pods can connect to peered virtual networks and to on-premises VNets over ExpressRoute or a site-to-site VPN. You can also configure a virtual network service endpoint to connect these pods to services such as Azure Storage and Azure SQL Database. In the example shown in Figure 1-12, an NSG was assigned to the container, but it can also be applied directly to the pod. If you need to expose your pod to the Internet, you can assign a public IP address directly to it.

Following the defense-in-depth approach, you should maintain network segmentation (nano-segmentation) or segregation between containers. Creating a network segmentation might also be necessary to use containers in industries that are required to meet compliance mandates.

Azure Kubernetes Service (AKS) network

AKS nodes are connected to a virtual network and can provide inbound and outbound connectivity for pods using the kube-proxy component, which runs on each node to provide these network features.

AKS can be deployed in two network models: kubenet networking (default option), where the network resources are usually created and configured during the AKS cluster deployment, and Azure CNI, where the AKS cluster connects to an existing VNet.

You can use NSG to filter traffic for AKS nodes. When you create a new service, such as a LoadBalancer, the Azure platform automatically configures any needed NSG rules. Do not manually configure NSG rules to filter traffic for pods in an AKS cluster. Define the required ports and forwarding as part of your Kubernetes Service manifests, and let the Azure platform create or update the appropriate rules. Another option is to use network policies to apply traffic filter rules to pods automatically. Network policy is a Kubernetes capability available in AKS that allows you to control the traffic flow between pods.

Network policies use different attributes to determine how to allow or deny traffic. These attributes are based on settings such as assigned labels, namespace, or traffic port. Keep in mind that NSGs are suitable for AKS nodes, not pods. Network policies are more suitable for pods because pods are dynamically created in an AKS cluster. In this case, you can configure the required network policies to be automatically applied.

There are two main types of isolation for AKS clusters: logical and physical. You should use logical isolation to separate teams and projects. A single AKS cluster can be used for multiple workloads, teams, or environments when you use logical isolation.

It is also recommended that you minimize the number of physical AKS clusters you deploy to isolate teams or applications. Figure 1-13 shows an example of this logical isolation.

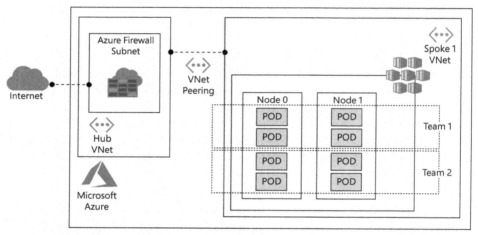

FIGURE 1-13 AKS logical isolation

Logical isolation can help minimize costs by enabling autoscaling and running only the number of nodes required at one time. Physical isolation is usually selected when you have a hostile multitenant environment where you want to fully prevent one tenant from affecting the security and service of another. The physical isolation means that you need to physically separate AKS clusters. This isolation model assigns teams or workloads their own AKS clusters. While this approach usually looks easier to isolate, it adds additional management and financial overhead.

There are many built-in capabilities in AKS that help ensure your AKS cluster is secure. Those built-in capabilities are based on native Kubernetes features, such as network policies and secrets, with the addition of Azure components, such as NSG and orchestrated cluster upgrades.

These components are combined to keep your AKS cluster running the latest OS security updates and Kubernetes releases, secure pod traffic, and provide access to sensitive credentials. Figure 1-14 shows a diagram with the core AKS security components.

When you deploy AKS in Azure, the Kubernetes master components are part of the managed service provided by Microsoft. Each AKS cluster has a dedicated Kubernetes master. This master is used to provide API Server, Scheduler, and so on. You can control access to the API server using Kubernetes RBAC controls and Azure AD.

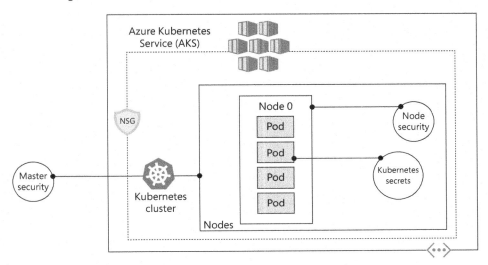

FIGURE 1-14　Core AKS security components

While the Kubernetes master is managed and maintained by Microsoft, the AKS nodes are VMs you manage and maintain. These nodes can use Linux OS (optimized Ubuntu distribution) or Windows Server 2019. The Azure platform automatically applies OS security patches to Linux nodes on a nightly basis. However, Windows Update does not automatically run or apply the latest updates on Windows nodes. This means if you have Windows nodes, you need to maintain the schedule around the update lifecycle and enforce those updates.

From the network perspective, these nodes are deployed into a private virtual network subnet with no public IP addresses assigned to it. SSH is enabled by default and should only be used for troubleshooting purposes because it is only available using the internal IP address.

Chapter 2

Planning Microsoft Defender for Cloud adoption

Given the threat landscape presented in Chapter 1, it is clear that there is a need for a system that can both unify security management and provide advanced threat protection for workloads running in Azure, on-premises, and on other cloud providers.

Microsoft Defender for Cloud gives organizations complete visibility and control over the security of cloud workloads located in Azure, on-premises, or another cloud provider. By actively monitoring these workloads, Defender for Cloud enhances the overall security posture of the cloud deployment and reduces the exposure of resources to threats. Defender for Cloud also uses intelligent threat detection to assist you in protecting your environment from rapidly evolving cyberattacks.

Defender for Cloud also assesses the security of your hybrid cloud workload and provides recommendations to mitigate threats. In addition, it provides centralized policy management to ensure compliance with company or regulatory security requirements.

In this chapter, you will learn more about Defender for Cloud architecture, use cases, and key considerations for adoption.

Deployment scenarios

As enterprises start their journey to the cloud, they will face many challenges trying to adapt their on-premises tools to a cloud-based model. In a cloud environment, where there are different workloads to manage, it becomes imperative to have ongoing verification and corrective actions to ensure that the security posture of those workloads is always at the highest possible quality. Defender for Cloud has a variety of capabilities that can be used in two cloud solution categories:

- **Cloud Security Posture Management (CSPM)** Enables organizations to assess their cloud infrastructure to ensure compliance with industry regulations and identify security vulnerabilities in their cloud workloads.

- **Cloud Workload Protection Platform (CWPP)** Enables organizations to assess their cloud workload risks and detect threats against their Server (Infrastructure as a Service [IaaS]), containers, databases (Platform as a Service [PaaS]), and storage. It also allows organizations to identify and remediate faulty configurations with security best-practice recommendations.

It is always recommended to start your cloud security journey by ensuring that you have visibility across all workloads, and once you have this visibility, you want to understand the security state of these workloads. With the free tier of Microsoft Defender for Cloud enabled on the subscription, you can obtain this information and start working on remediating security recommendations that will improve your overall security posture. That's the scenario for CSPM.

After improving the security hygiene of the environment, you also want to be aware of potential threat actors trying to compromise your workloads, and that's where CWPP capabilities will come into play. An important factor of threat detections that were tailored specifically for a particular workload is that you are only monitoring threats that are truly relevant for that workload. Microsoft Defender for Cloud has different plans that will vary according to the supported workloads.

> **TIP** You can also follow along with the implementation steps of this book by provisioning a trial Azure subscription and following the labs available at *http://aka.ms/MDFCLabs*.

Understanding Defender for Cloud

Because Defender for Cloud is an Azure service, you must have an Azure subscription to use it, even if it's just a trial subscription.

When you enable Defender for Cloud in an Azure subscription, you will initially experience the benefits of the free tier. This free tier provides security policy, security assessment, security recommendations, and Secure Score. In addition to the free tier, Defender for Cloud offers an option to upgrade to enhanced security. This option offers a complete set of security capabilities for organizations that need more control and threat detection. The capabilities will vary according to which plan you enabled. For example, if you enable Defender for Servers, you will get the following features:

- Security event collection
- Network Map
- Just-in-time VM Access
- Adaptive application controls

- Adaptive network hardening
- Regulatory compliance reports
- File integrity monitoring
- Security alerts
- Integration with Microsoft Defender for Endpoint (MDE)
- Multi-cloud support for Amazon Web Services (AWS) and Google Cloud Platform (GCP)
- Capability to monitor on-premises resources
- Vulnerability assessment integration with Qualys and Microsoft Threat and Vulnerability Management (TVM)

In addition to Defender for Servers, you have other plans that offer tailored threat detection for specific workloads. The list below provides the other plans available:

- Defender for Storage
- Defender for SQL
- Defender for Open Relational Database
- Defender for Azure Comos DB
- Defender for Key Vault
- Defender for DNS
- Defender for App Services
- Defender for Resource Manager
- Defender for Containers

When you upgrade to a Defender for Cloud plan, you can use it free for 30 days. This is a good opportunity to evaluate these features, see how your current environment will benefit from them, and decide whether they're worth the investment.

> **TIP** For the latest information about pricing, see *http://aka.ms/ascpricing*.

Defender for Cloud architecture

To better understand how Defender for Cloud communicates with different resources, it is important to understand its core architecture. Figure 2-1 shows the Defender for Cloud architecture and how it interacts with external components.

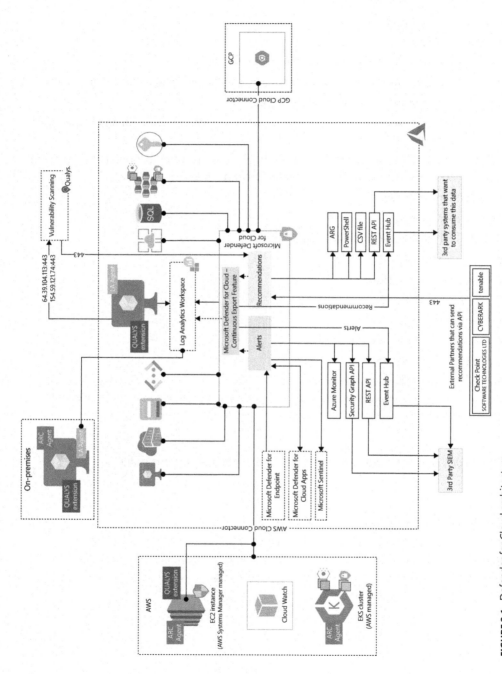

FIGURE 2-1 Defender for Cloud architecture

In Figure 2-1, if you look at the core diagram representing Defender for Cloud, you will see three major boxes: Recommendations, Alerts, and Continuous Export. The recommendations are an important component of the CSPM scenario because it is via the remediation of these security recommendations that you will enhance your security posture. Alerts contain the security alerts that are triggered when suspicious activities are identified. Alerts are based on a variety of threat detections, which are enabled when you enable a Defender for Cloud plan. Recommendations and alerts can be streamed to the Log Analytics workspace of your choice using the Continuous Export feature, and they can also be streamed to an Event Hub to be consumed by a third-party Security Information and Event Management (SIEM) system.

Recommendations can also be received based on the connectivity with other cloud providers such as AWS and GCP, which you will learn how to onboard in the next chapter. Another form of ingesting external recommendations is via third-party partners, which usually sends those recommendations via the Application Program Interface (API). By the time this chapter was written, the partners available were Tenable, Cyberark, and Checkpoint.

Defender for Cloud uses the Log Analytics Agent, which is configured to send information to a particular Log Analytics workspace. Regardless of the VM location (in Azure or not), the agent must always be installed to enable Defender for Cloud to have more visibility about the machine's security events. In Windows systems, Defender for Cloud installs the Log Analytics Agent. In addition to the agent for Linux, Defender for Cloud also creates the `omsagent` daemon, which runs under the `omsagent` account. This account is automatically created during agent installation.

In Linux systems, Defender for Cloud collects audit records from Linux machines using the `auditd` framework. (It doesn't require the `auditd` daemon to be running.) The `auditd` system consists of two major components:

- First is a set of user-space utilities offering a wide collection of operations allowing administrators to better adjust rules, analyze audit log files, or troubleshoot if things are misconfigured.

- Second is a kernel-level subsystem that is responsible for monitoring system calls, filtering them by a given rule set, and writing match messages to a buffer.

Both components are communicating through a `netlink` socket. Auditd records are collected, aggregated into events, and enriched using the latest version of the Log Analytics Agent for Linux.

In Windows systems, the Log Analytics Agent scans for various security-related configurations and events in Event Tracing for Windows (ETW) traces. Also, this agent collects the following:

- Operating system logs, such as Windows events

- Operating system type and version

- Running processes

- Machine name
- IP addresses
- Logged in user (username)
- Tenant ID
- User mode crash dump created by Windows Error Reporting (WER)

This information is sent to your workspace, which is an Azure resource used as a container to store your data. A workspace provides a geographic location for data storage, granularity for billing and data isolation, and helps you to better scope the configuration.

If you are using Azure Log Analytics, and you already have a Log Analytics workspace, this workspace can be used by Defender for Cloud to store data coming from the agent. If you are not using Azure Log Analytics, a new workspace will be automatically created when you start using Defender for Cloud. When using the default workspace provisioning configuration, the location of the workspace created by Defender for Cloud is based on the geolocation of the VM.

If you are a global company and need to store data in specific regions for data sovereignty or compliance reasons, you might consider creating multiple workspaces. Another scenario that might call for multiple workspaces is if you want to isolate various users. For example, you might want each customer, department, or business group to see its own data but not the data of others. There will also be scenarios where you may want to utilize a centralized workspace, for example when all subscriptions want to consolidate the recommendations and alerts exported by the continuous exported feature in a single location.

> **TIP** You need to use Log Analytics to create multiple workspaces. If you need to perform this operation, see *https://aka.ms/ascworkspaces*.

By default, only VM-Based alerts are stored in the workspace; in other words, only alerts generated by Defender for Servers are stored in the workspace. This means even if you have multiple Defender for Cloud Plans enabled, such as Defender for Storage and Defender for Key Vault, the alerts generated are not stored in the workspace. If you need to store the alerts in the workspace, you need to use the Continuous Export feature.

An important point shown in Figure 2-1 is the vulnerability assessment integration with Qualys. When you enable this integration, the agent installed in the VM needs to have access (TCP 443—the default for HTTPS) to Qualys data centers in the United States and Europe (hence the IP addresses shown in the diagram). Another important point about this architecture is the integration with Azure Arc. Figure 2-1 shows some examples of the scenarios where Azure Arc is needed, such as when you are onboarding VMs and Kubernetes located in AWS, GCP, or on-premises infrastructure.

> **TIP** For more information about Azure Arc, see *https://azurearcjumpstart.io*.

Defender for Cloud dashboard

To access the Defender for Cloud dashboard, sign in to the Azure portal (*https://portal.azure.com*) and click the **Microsoft Defender For Cloud** icon in the left pane. What happens the first time you open the Defender for Cloud dashboard may vary according to the types of workloads that you have on your Azure subscription. For the purposes of this example, the dashboard is fully populated with resources, recommendations, and alerts, as shown in Figure 2-2.

FIGURE 2-2 Overview page in Defender for Cloud dashboard

By default, the **Overview** page is highlighted when you open the Defender for Cloud dashboard. This page brings a comprehensive layout that enables you to quickly see important indicators. From the top down, you will see which cloud providers you are connected with (Azure subscriptions, AWS account, and GCP Projects), followed by the number of assessed resources, the total of active recommendations, and security alerts.

Below that are a series of tiles; the first one is the **Security Posture**, which you will learn more about in Chapter 5, "Strengthening your security posture." This tile lets you quickly see the Secure Score for your Azure subscription. In addition, if you are connected with AWS and GCP, you will also see the Secure Score for those cloud providers.

The next tile is **Regulatory Compliance**, which shows some statistics about your journey to compliance with different industry standards. The main statistic is the Azure Security Benchmark, which is the foundation of Defender for Cloud recommendations. Besides that, you also see the lowest compliance based on different industry standards.

Below the **Regulatory Compliance** tile is the **Firewall Manager** tile, which brings a summary of Azure network security-related products that are enabled on this Azure subscription. The content of this tile may vary according to the available Azure network security products that are currently in use on the selected subscription. If multiple subscriptions are selected, this tile will show the aggregated result.

Below the **Security Posture** tile is the **Workload Protections** tile, which contains a brief description of the current number (in percentage format) of resources covered in the selected subscription and a timeline chart with the alerts by severity. The entire right side of the page contains dynamic content that will be refreshed as necessary. This includes insights about alerts, quick access to see which workloads are not protected, and top recommendations.

Planning adoption

When planning to adopt Defender for Cloud, you first need to consider the adoption scope; in other words, are you going to adopt this product to be the centralized dashboard for cloud security in Azure only, or do you plan to connect with other cloud providers? One of the challenges of multi-cloud adoption is ensuring that you have security posture visibility for all clouds in a single dashboard—and that is a big advantage of using Defender for Cloud.

Once you define the scope of the adoption, you need to start thinking about the use-case scenario. Are you planning to use Defender for Cloud as your cloud security posture management and workload protection platform? Remember, there are two major use-case scenarios: CSPM and CWPP. If you plan to use Defender for Cloud for both scenarios, you should always start with CSPM because you first need to ensure that you have good security hygiene and a high Secure Score. In this case, a high Secure Score means reaching 100 percent on your score. You should not leave security recommendations open without remediation, and if you intentionally plan not to follow a security recommendation, make sure you have good justification for assuming this risk.

During this initial phase, you should also ensure that you have the right stakeholders for this project. You need to have members of the following teams involved:

- **Cloud security** Some organizations aggregate CSPM-related tasks in a team called *Cloud Security*. Other organizations refer to this team as the *CSPM team*, so make sure you have the right team that is responsible for managing the cloud's security hygiene.

- **Cloud governance** Often, the team responsible for establishing security policies and adding guardrails at the beginning of the pipeline are part of the Governance team. Therefore, make sure you have representatives from this area.

- **Security Operations Center (SOC)** The SOC Team will need data from Defender for Cloud when it comes to alerts related to threat detection for the different workloads. You need to ensure that this team knows how to interpret the alerts generated by Defender for Cloud and how they will consume these alerts. Usually, they will stream the alerts to their preferred Security Information and Event Management (SIEM) platform.

- **Compliance** Because Defender for Cloud maps to many regulatory compliance standards, it is very common for the compliance team to want to know the level of compliance of the workloads located in different cloud providers. Make sure to have representatives of this team so that you better understand which regulatory standard is more important to them and how they want to consume this information. You can send them a compliance report in PDF format or provide access to the dashboard or a compliance workbook.

While these are the most common teams that should be engaged in this initial conversation to establish the adoption plan, you might need to add other teams or individuals according to your organization's needs. Therefore, you should use those as a starting point and adjust as needed.

Before enabling Defender for Cloud in your subscription, you must also ensure you have the proper privilege level. Review the roles and permissions requirements in Chapter 3, "Onboarding Microsoft Defender for cloud."

Considerations for CSPM

One of the challenges that many organizations face when trying to improve the security hygiene of their cloud workloads is the lack of privileges available to harden workloads based on the recommendations provided by Defender for Cloud. For example, let's use a scenario where the Contoso CSPM team is reviewing the security recommendations for a SQL Database, and they identify the recommendation shown in Figure 2-3, which has a list of unhealthy resources that needs attention.

FIGURE 2-3 Security recommendations for SQL databases

When the Contoso CSPM team tried to remediate the recommendation, they received a message saying that they didn't have the necessary privileges to remediate this resource. Now the questions are: Who should they contact to remediate this resource? Who is the owner of this resource? Is the owner the same person who maintains this database? That's when the CSPM team starts putting aside recommendations they can't remediate and focuses on the ones they can remediate. The problem with this approach is that the recommendations are not prioritized by level of criticality or potential improvement to the Secure Score.

For this reason, it is imperative to establish a workflow of actions that must be followed to ensure that the workload owner is notified when there are open security recommendations that must be remediated. Consider the following actions (in this order) as part of your plan:

1. Identify the workload owners.

2. Train the workload owners to learn how to use Defender for Cloud (100-level basic training is enough). The goal is to help them at least navigate through the recommendations and follow the remediation steps.

3. Create governance rules for these owners and establish a timeline for remediation. This is an important step to ensure accountability.

4. Create automations to notify workload owners that new recommendations are open.

As you continue this journey to improve your security hygiene, you will notice that the Secure Score will continue to grow. To avoid sudden drops in Secure Score, ensure the CSPM team relates closely with the cloud governance team. The goal is to ensure that all recommendations that can be implemented at the beginning of the pipeline to enforce compliance are in place, even before a resource is provisioned, as shown in Figure 2-4.

FIGURE 2-4 Governance and security monitoring working together

In Figure 2-4, two users are provisioning new resources. User 1 provisioned a storage account that is not compliant with the policies established by the cloud governance team. As a result, the resource won't be allowed to be provisioned. User 2 provisioned a VM that is fully compliant with the established policies. This VM will be successfully provisioned and will appear in the Defender for Cloud dashboard as healthy.

Now, let's look at a scenario in which the cloud governance team doesn't have the right guardrails in place, and they are learning from the findings exposed by Defender for Cloud. For example, let's say the Contoso CSPM team determined that every time a new storage account is provisioned, the Secure Score drops. They determined this happens because the **Secure transfer to storage accounts should be enabled** recommendation is triggered, as shown in Figure 2-5.

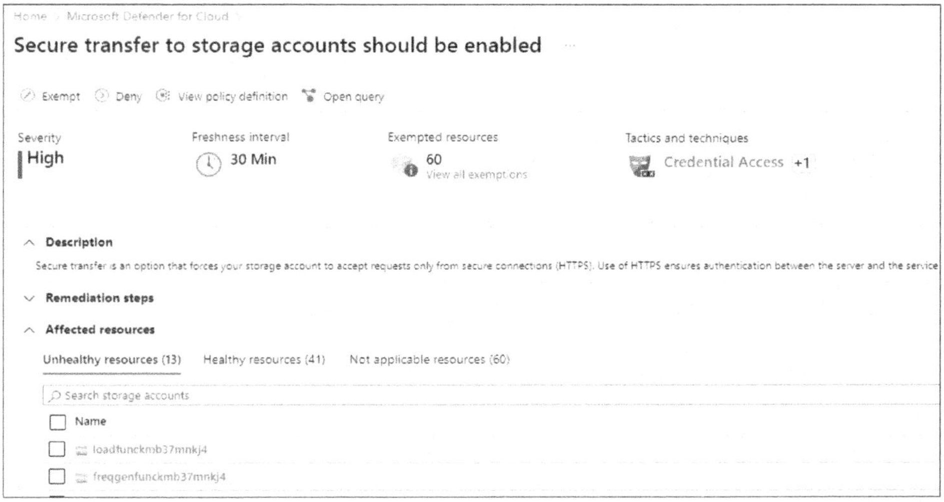

FIGURE 2-5 Security recommendations for storage account

During the weekly meeting, a member of the Contoso CSPM team asked the Contoso cloud governance team lead to create a Deny rule in Azure Policy to prevent new storage accounts from being created if they are not using Secure Transfer. By implementing this rule at the beginning of the pipeline, the cloud governance team ensured that users will not provision a storage account that doesn't follow this recommendation.

That's why the cloud governance team must be engaged in the project from the beginning, so they have a fundamental role in keeping the environment secure by default. While the synchronization of these teams is imperative for the project, you also need upper-management sponsorship to ensure that the entire organization is working toward improving the overall security posture. Based on our observations over the years, the companies that saw a bigger increase in their Secure Score were the ones that had upper-management sponsorship.

To finalize the CSPM considerations, ensure that you have a clear answer to the following questions:

- Do we have upper-management approval for this project?
- Which teams are involved?
- What are the measurements of success?
- Who is going to manage Defender for Cloud?
- Who is the subscription owner?
- Who has administrative privilege at the tenant level?
- Who are the workload owners?
- Which team manages the overall cloud governance?
- Is the governance team effectively using Azure Policy for governance?

- Who has the privileges to change those policies?
- Does the governance team have preventative measures to avoid provisioning new resources that don't comply with pre-established standards?
- Does the cloud governance team partner with the CSPM team to improve their controls?
- What's the current level of Defender for Cloud knowledge across all workload owners?
- Does the company have security awareness training?
- How are workload owners trained to maintain the security of their resources?
- Does the company have any ongoing security campaigns to educate employees?
- How do you triage recommendations to decide which ones will be included at the beginning of the pipeline as policy enforcement?
- What's the process for feeding the governance team with lessons learned from the CSPM team?
- How are you revisiting changes in the environment to adjust the security policies?
- How are you controlling exemptions for those policies?

Good advice

Considerations for CWPP

At this point, you should have a good idea about which workloads are available and need active monitoring. The next step is to plan the enablement of the appropriate Defender for Cloud plan to provide threat detection capabilities for the workload.

Let's use the following scenario as an example: In a meeting between the cloud security and SOC teams, it was agreed that it is imperative to have threat detection for storage accounts because of the growing number of attacks against cloud-based storage. The SOC team wants visibility if threat actors try to scan storage accounts and perform any suspicious operation. The cloud security team knows the price for Defender for Storage is based on transactions, and they want an estimate of how much it will cost to enable this plan.

In this scenario, they can use the Defender for Cloud GitHub repository at *http://aka.ms/ MDFCWorkbooks* and import the Microsoft Defender for Storage Price Estimation Workbook. This will help them calculate how much it will cost to enable Defender for Storage at the sub-scription level and cover all storage accounts. In Chapter 6, "Threat detection," we will cover each Defender for Cloud plan in more detail.

It is very important to emphasize that each Defender for Cloud plan has a 30-day free trial, which means you can enable the plan in the subscription, perform a proof of concept (PoC) to validate the use-case scenarios, and then decide if you want to keep the plan enabled. You can use the **Workload Protections** dashboard in Defender for Cloud to see which workloads have the plan enabled, as shown in Figure 2-6.

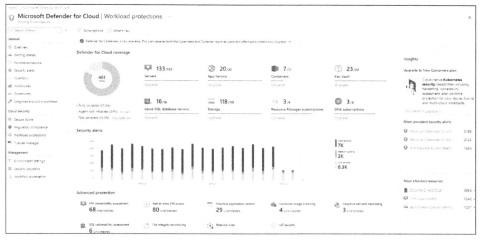

FIGURE 2-6 Workload Protections dashboard with the overall coverage

> **NOTE** You can use the guidelines from the article at *http://aka.ms/MDFCPoC* to prepare a PoC that fits your needs.

Another important point to consider is how the SOC team currently ingests and aggregates the alerts. Most likely, they are using a SIEM solution, such as Microsoft Sentinel, which means you need to consider how the plans you enabled for Defender for Cloud will stream those alerts to the SIEM. In Chapter 7, "Better together," you will learn how to integrate Defender for Cloud with Microsoft Sentinel.

To finalize the CWPP considerations, ensure that you have a clear answer to the following questions:

- Which team handles alerts?
- How are alerts ingested now?
- Which tools are utilized to aggregate alerts?
- Which tools are utilized to orchestrate and automate response to alerts?

Considerations for multi-cloud

Multi-cloud deployments continue to grow as many organizations start to adopt different cloud providers to store different workloads. Defender for Cloud supports integration with AWS and GCP, which allows the CSPM team to have full visibility of the security posture of Azure, AWS, GCP, and on-premises resources in a single dashboard.

When planning for multi-cloud adoption, you need to ensure that you have the right teams engaged because in many organizations, the team that manages Azure is not the same as that of AWS and GCP. If this is the case, you need to make sure everyone is on the same page regarding security posture management across different cloud providers. In Chapter 3 you will learn how to connect with AWS and GCP.

To finalize the multi-cloud considerations, ensure that you have a clear answer to the following questions:

- What are the current cloud providers that are used in the organization?
- Who manages each cloud provider account?
- Who owns the workloads on each cloud provider?
- Which workloads are deployed on each cloud provider?
- Is there any tool currently in use that provides centralized management of all cloud providers?

Considerations for vulnerability assessment

Vulnerability assessment (VA) is another key area for security posture improvement, and the only reason this was not covered in the CSPM section of this chapter is that large organizations usually will have a separate team that handles vulnerability assessment across endpoints and servers. This means the CSPM team needs to engage with the VA Team to ensure that they can take advantage of Defender for Cloud–native VA solutions, which can be either based on Qualys or Microsoft Threat Vulnerability Management (TVM).

Suppose the organization is already using Qualys as its main VA solution. In that case, it can also use the bring your own license (BYOL) model to deploy the Qualys agent to all VMs in Azure via Defender for Cloud. However, suppose the organization wants to use its current Qualys VA to monitor only endpoints and take advantage of the free VA integration for servers enabled by Defender for Cloud. In that case, it will have to manage two different dashboards. This is because the results for Qualys VA in Defender for Cloud are exposed as security recommendations and will not integrate with the Qualys VA dashboard used by the endpoints. Figure 2-7 shows an example of how the vulnerability assessment is presented in a recommendation.

As shown in Figure 2-7, the results presented in the recommendation will list the findings, and once you click a finding—ID 91785—another blade opens up on the right side showing more details about that finding, which VA found it (Qualys or TVM), and the vulnerable machines.

If the organization does not already have a VA solution, the decision will be between deploying Qualys or TVM. Both are fully integrated with Defender for Cloud, though one major difference is that TVM doesn't require an additional agent because it is part of MDE (in other words, it requires MDE), while Qualys does require the installation of an additional agent. However, the deployment experience is similar because Defender for Cloud will flag machines that don't have a VA installed. From there, you can deploy the desired solution, as shown in Figure 2-8.

FIGURE 2-7 Recommendation to remediate vulnerability found by Qualys

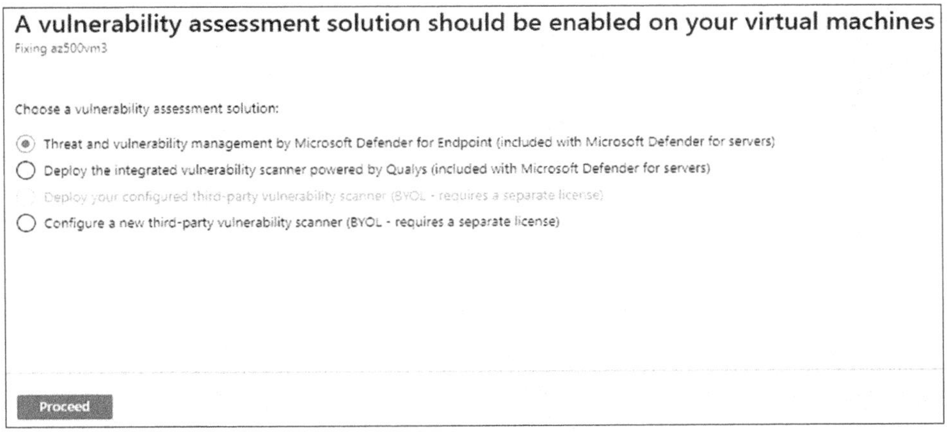

A vulnerability assessment solution should be enabled on your virtual machines
Fixing az500vm3

Choose a vulnerability assessment solution:

- ◉ Threat and vulnerability management by Microsoft Defender for Endpoint (included with Microsoft Defender for servers)
- ◯ Deploy the integrated vulnerability scanner powered by Qualys (included with Microsoft Defender for servers)
- ◯ Deploy your configured third-party vulnerability scanner (BYOL - requires a separate license)
- ◯ Configure a new third-party vulnerability scanner (BYOL - requires a separate license)

Proceed

FIGURE 2-8 Selecting the appropriate VA solution to deploy

While the example shown in Figure 2-8 shows the deployment for just one VM, you can select multiple VMs and deploy them simultaneously. If you plan to deploy at scale for the entire subscription, you can also use Azure Policy. In Chapter 5 you will learn more about the deployment and operations of VA.

To finalize the VA considerations, ensure that you have a clear answer to the following questions:

- Is there any VA solution already deployed and operational in the company?
- Which team manages the current VA solution?
- Which VA solution is in use today?
- Is it a constraint to have another agent installed on the VM?
- Do you need to deploy the VA at scale?

Considerations for EDR

Defender for Cloud has native integration with Microsoft Defender for Endpoint (MDE) on Windows and Linux Servers. This means that if you use the default setting, MDE will be automatically deployed to your Servers, and with that, you will also have an endpoint detection and response (EDR) solution installed on your server. In the list below, you have the main advantages of this integration:

- No additional charges for MDE because the Defender for Server plan already includes MDE integration
- Automatic deployment of MDE across all supported servers in the subscription
- Synchronization of alerts, meaning the alerts generated by MDE will appear in the MDE dashboard, as well as in the Defender for Cloud Security Alerts dashboard

One important consideration in this integration is whether the servers you will onboard already have an EDR solution installed. For example, some organizations want to keep a single EDR solution across client endpoints and servers, so they might not want to have MDE automatically deployed to their servers residing in Azure. If that's the case, you need to disable MDE integration at the subscription level, as shown in Figure 2-9.

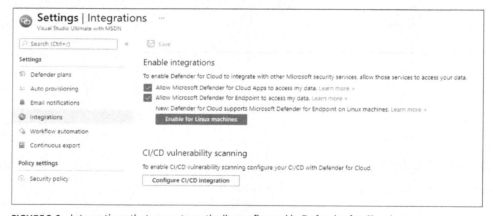

FIGURE 2-9 Integrations that are automatically configured in Defender for Cloud

In Chapter 6 you will learn more about MDE deployment for Windows and Linux via Defender for Servers.

Considerations for multi-tenant

Defender for Cloud is an Azure subscription-based service, which means that the deployment and configuration are always done at the subscription level. This means that if you have multiple subscriptions under a single tenant, each subscription will have its own settings and deployment options by default.

When you need to centralize the deployment for the entire tenant, you can create a management group (MG) in Azure, move your subscriptions to this MG, and assign a single policy to this MG. You will learn more about this scenario and its considerations in Chapter 10.

When you need centralized visibility across multiple tenants, you must first configure Azure Lighthouse to grant multi-tenant access. Once you do that, the Defender for Cloud dashboard will seamlessly show the results for all selected tenants and subscriptions.

> **NOTE** For more information about Azure Lighthouse, see *https://docs.microsoft.com/en-us/azure/lighthouse/overview.*

Chapter 3

Onboarding Microsoft Defender for Cloud

To plan first and act second is one of the most important aspects of enabling Microsoft Defender for Cloud in an environment. While it seems easy, some considerations need to be made before actually starting to have your resources and subscriptions properly onboarded to Defender for Cloud. It is a common misconception that Microsoft Defender for Cloud is automatically enabled on all Azure subscriptions. Also, people tend to over-look planning for governance, including management groups, subscriptions, and Log Analytics workspace designs.

In this chapter, we will dive into the technical aspects of onboarding Microsoft Defender for Cloud, and you will learn what it takes to have the right setup in place for your environment.

Planning your Azure environment for Defender for Cloud

Microsoft Defender for Cloud is a subscription-based service. Once enabled, it will cover all supported resources in a particular subscription, provide security recommendations, and calculate the Secure Score. To monitor servers, it needs to have the Log Analytics agent deployed and connected to a Log Analytics workspace. Creating some recom-mendations will leverage guest configuration policies, which demand an extension to be deployed to all machines in question. As an Azure service, Defender for Cloud relies on an Azure resource provider for a subscription that needs to be registered. This is not enough, though, as there also needs to be the Azure Security Benchmark assigned, a Log Analyt-ics workspace deployed, and more. Whenever you create a new subscription, you must ensure it is onboarded to Microsoft Defender for Cloud. There is an automated process that will do the following:

- Register the Microsoft.Security resource provider to the new subscription
- Automatically assign the Azure Security Benchmark initiative, which we will cover in more detail in Chapter 4, "Policy management"
- Deploy one or more default Log Analytics workspaces, depending on your configuration

But this process does not automatically start—it needs to be triggered. For example, this happens when you create a new subscription, select it, and open Microsoft Defender for Cloud with that subscription selected. You will then see the message indicating that Defender for Cloud is getting things ready for your subscriptions, as shown in Figure 3-1.

FIGURE 3-1 A subscription being onboarded to Microsoft Defender for Cloud

While this process runs smoothly whenever you open Defender for Cloud with a new subscription selected, it is important to understand what happens from a technical perspective. This will allow you to plan your deployment at scale and help you understand what design considerations you need to make before starting.

If you don't have a process in place that will automatically onboard your whole environment at scale—a topic which we will cover in Chapter 10, "Deployment at scale"—Defender for Cloud will start with some defaults:

- The onboarding process will register the Microsoft.Security resource provider to the new subscription. This mandatory step will trigger the back-end assessments to analyze your resource configuration, which relies on the Azure Security Benchmark.

- When opening a new subscription in Defender for Cloud for the first time, the Azure Security Benchmark is automatically assigned to the new subscription once the resource provider has been registered. The Azure Security Benchmark is the security policy Defender for Cloud will leverage to create security recommendations for all resources within the new subscription.

- The onboarding process will create one or more default Log Analytics workspaces, one for each region in which your subscription hosts VM resources. These workspaces can be used to connect your machines' Log Analytics agents to them, and Defender for Cloud will use them to store VM-related security alerts once relevant.

As you can see, a lot is happening in the back-end when onboarding Defender for Cloud, so let's take a look at design considerations first.

Designing your environment

While registering the resource provider and assigning the Azure Security Benchmark to a subscription does not require too many considerations (besides the fact that it needs to happen), Log Analytics design is a bit more complex. Since the beginning of Microsoft

Defender for Cloud, it has been relying on monitoring solutions on the workspace to enable data collection from machines based on the Log Analytics agent. That's why the automated onboarding process will create default workspaces whenever you do not leverage an existing one. The process, in this case, will create one default workspace for each Azure geolocation that you have machines deployed to, using the `DefaultWorkspace-<subscriptionId>-<regionShortName>` name schema.

For example, if you have virtual machines in West Europe and North Europe, you might get one workspace in West Europe and machines from both regions connected to it. Figure 3-2 shows an example of two default workspaces that have been created in the Central US and East US because this particular subscription had machines deployed to both regions before enabling Defender for Cloud.

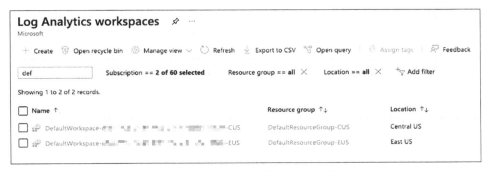

FIGURE 3-2 Default workspaces created by Microsoft Defender for Cloud

The advantage of leveraging default workspaces is that they will automatically have the security solution enabled. However, using them comes with a lot of disadvantages, too, including but not limited to the following:

- Using one or several default workspaces per subscription will quickly become hard to manage.
- Default workspaces do not align with your organization's naming schema.
- Default workspaces might not adhere to your (regulatory) compliance standards.
- Default workspaces cannot be used for Microsoft Sentinel.

From a management perspective, it is best to only use a single Log Analytics workspace for all resources in your organization, while from a governance and data cost perspective, you might want to use one workspace per Azure region. If it comes to leveraging Microsoft Sentinel as your SIEM/SOAR solution, you might even want to divide security logs from performance logs and then end up with two workspaces per region or geolocation, such as Europe, Asia, or America. There are many considerations, and later in this chapter, you will learn how to leverage both the default and custom workspaces with Microsoft Defender for Cloud.

The next aspect to focus on is your role-based access control (RBAC) model. Who should be able to manage Microsoft Defender for Cloud? Who is supposed to review recommendations and security alerts? Who is allowed to change your security policy or add or remove regulatory compliance standards from your subscriptions? Microsoft Azure comes with a variety of different built-in role definitions, some of which are relevant for Microsoft Defender for Cloud:

- Security Reader and Reader roles can be used to view security alerts and recommendations. While the Reader role will allow a user to view anything within the role assignment's scope (resource group, subscription, or management group), the security reader role is limited to security-related information. Viewing security alerts and recommendations is part of all additional roles we will cover below.

- The Security Admin role allows you to dismiss security alerts, enable/disable Microsoft Defender for Cloud plans, and edit the security policy that has been assigned to a subscription.

- The Contributor and Owner roles assigned to a particular resource let you apply and remediate security recommendations for this resource. When assigned to the subscription, these roles also allow you to dismiss alerts, enable or disable Defender for Cloud plans, edit an existing security policy, or create and assign additional policy initiatives, including regulatory compliance standards.

While Defender for Cloud is a subscription-based service, assigning roles to resources or resource groups only will provide a subset of information for this particular scope. For example, if you have one subscription with several resource groups—and each resource group is a representation of a service or project—you might want to grant access rights to resource owners on the resource group only, not on the whole subscription. In this case, these resource owners will only be able to see security alerts and recommendations for their resources, while your subscription's security admin might be able to see the Secure Score, alerts, and recommendations for all resources in this particular subscription.

> **NOTE** Secure Score is calculated per subscription. If an account only has access rights granted to a scope below a subscription, such as a single resource or resource group, this account will not see a Secure Score calculation in Microsoft Defender for Cloud.

When it comes to the advanced capabilities of Microsoft Defender for Cloud, you need to enable Defender for Cloud plans, such as Microsoft Defender for Containers or Microsoft Defender for Storage. We will provide more details about these plans in Chapter 6, "Threat detection," but two of these plans are special within the scope of the Log Analytics workspace and the subscription design: Microsoft Defender for Servers and Microsoft Defender for SQL on machines.

There is a common misconception that enabling Defender for Servers (or SQL on machines) on a Log Analytics workspace, not on the subscription (or the other way round), is enough. However, in order to get the full feature coverage these plans need to be enabled on both your subscription and the Log Analytics workspace to which your machines' agents are reporting. As long as you intend to enable these plans for all servers and SQL installations across your whole estate, this is not a big deal, but it becomes a challenge when you only want a subset of resources to be covered, or if you if you not only connect servers to your Log Analytics workspace but also to user devices, such as Windows 10/11 machines.

Once you enable Defender for Servers on your subscription, it is enabled for all Azure VMs and non-Azure machines that are connected to this subscription. For example, if it is enabled on the Log Analytics workspace, it will cover all agents that are connected to this workspace (regardless of the OS). That said, some cases might influence your subscription and workspace design. These considerations apply to both Microsoft Defender for Servers and Microsoft Defender for SQL on machines:

- **You want to connect Windows 10/11 devices to a Log Analytics workspace** In this case, you should consider working with two different workspaces, one that is being used by Microsoft Defender for Cloud and one that does not have the security solution enabled. This applies to any situation in which you want to connect agents that are not supposed to be protected by Defender for Servers. Be aware that if you connect these machines to a subscription that has Defender for Servers enabled, charges will still apply.

- **You want to connect Windows 10 devices to an Azure subscription via Azure Arc** In this case, you should consider providing a separate subscription for these devices on which you do not enable Microsoft Defender for Servers. This applies to any situation in which you want to connect machines that are not supposed to be protected by Defender for Servers.

- **You want to connect Windows 10 devices through Azure Arc and connect them to Log Analytics** In this case, you should consider using two workspaces and two subscriptions to make sure these devices are not considered for Defender for Cloud billing.

After you decide on your design, you can start onboarding your subscription(s) to Defender for Cloud.

Onboarding VMs from an Azure subscription

Once Defender for Cloud has been enabled on a subscription, it will assess your resources for security (mis)configurations and then provide recommendations on how to remediate them. With PaaS resources such as Storage Accounts, there is nothing you need to do. However, Azure VMs and non-Azure machines require additional steps so that Defender for Cloud can assess the operating systems.

In general, you need to make sure these machines have a Log Analytics agent installed that is connected to a Log Analytics workspace that at least has the SecurityCenterFree solution enabled. While this solution is automatically enabled on a default workspace created by Defender for Cloud, you might need to manually enable it on a custom workspace. This is why Defender for Cloud recently got two new recommendations that give you visibility into this type of misconfiguration. To enable Defender for Cloud solutions on your Log Analytics workspace, follow these steps:

1. Navigate to *https://portal.azure.com* and log in with a user account that has Contributor access rights on the subscription that contains your Log Analytics workspace.

2. In the search bar on top of the portal, enter **Defender** and click **Microsoft Defender For Cloud**.

3. In the left navigation pane of Microsoft Defender for Cloud, click **Environment Settings**. Navigate to the subscription that hosts your Log Analytics workspace and select the workspace.

4. In the **Defender plans** section, set **Security Posture Management** to **On** to enable the **SecurityCenterFree** solution, as shown in Figure 3-3.

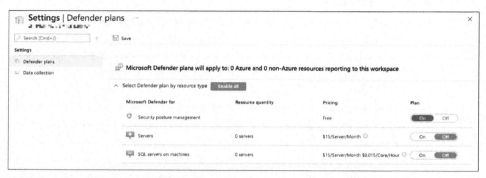

FIGURE 3-3   Enabling Defender for Cloud on a Log Analytics workspace

5. Then click **Save**.

> **TIP**   If you want to enable Microsoft Defender for Servers and Defender for SQL servers on machines instead, you can do so by selecting the Enable all button, or by switching either plan to **On**.

You can confirm that your workspace has been Defender for Cloud-enabled by following these steps:

1. In the Azure portal's top search bar, enter **Log Analytics** and select **Log Analytics Workspaces**.

2. Click the workspace you have just enabled for Defender for Cloud.

3. In the left navigation pane, select **Solutions**.

4. The **Solutions** overview will appear and show **SecurityCenterFree(<yourLogAnalytics WorkspaceName>)**, as shown in Figure 3-4.

FIGURE 3-4   Microsoft Defender for Cloud has been enabled on a custom Log Analytics workspace

> **TIP** If you have enabled Microsoft Defender for Servers and Defender for SQL on machines instead of switching enhanced security off on your workspace, it will have the solutions Security (Defender for Servers), SQLAdvancedThreatProtection, and SQLVulnerabilityAssessment enabled.

After enabling Microsoft Defender for Cloud on your custom Log Analytics workspace, you can now go ahead and connect your Log Analytics agents to it. You can either manually install the agent on your machines and connect them to your workspace, or you can leverage Defender for Cloud's auto-provisioning capability, which we will cover in the following section.

Understanding auto-provisioning

Once enabled, Microsoft Defender for Cloud will start assessing all resources in your Azure subscription. However, in order to provide recommendations and security alerts from both an Azure resource view and from inside the operating system, you must have the Log Analytics agent installed and connected to the Defender for Cloud-enabled Log Analytics workspace. Also, there are other agents and machine extensions that need to be deployed to enrich the experience with Microsoft Defender for Cloud. This is when auto-provisioning comes into play.

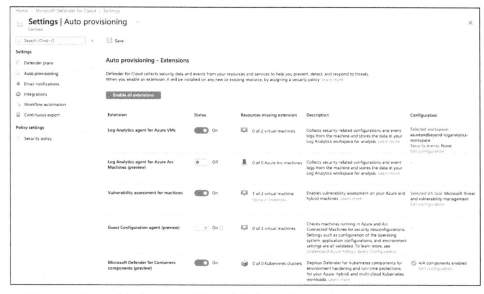

FIGURE 3-5 Auto-provisioning view in Microsoft Defender for Cloud

With auto-provisioning, Microsoft Defender for Cloud helps you easily deploy and configure mandatory and optional agents to Azure VMs and non-Azure machines connected through Azure Arc. Also, it leverages Azure policy definitions and assignments to ensure all relevant resources are automatically covered once they are created in or connected to the subscription on which you configure auto-provisioning.

Auto-provisioning provides deployment and configuration options for the agents and extensions discussed in the following sections.

Auto provision the Log Analytics agent for Azure VMs

The Log Analytics agent creates security recommendations and alerts for servers. The Log Analytics agent has always been an important part of Microsoft Defender for Cloud because it allows you to analyze the operating system configuration and processes. Microsoft Defender for Cloud offers an auto-provisioning capability that allows you to automatically deploy the Log Analytics extension to all Azure VMs in a subscription and connect them either to their default workspaces or to a custom workspace that you can configure for each subscription. When using a custom workspace, this workspace can (but does not need to) be the same across all subscriptions. However, it's a subscription-based configuration that needs to be enabled on each subscription separately.

Follow these steps to configure the auto-provisioning of the Log Analytics extension for Azure VMs:

1. Log in to the Azure portal with a user account that has Security Admin, Contributor, or Owner access rights on your subscription, and then open **Microsoft Defender For Cloud**.

2. In the left navigation pane, select **Environment Settings** and select the subscription from your environment hierarchy on which you want to enable auto-provisioning.

3. In the **Settings** section, select **Auto-Provisioning**. The **Auto-Provisioning** window appears, as shown in Figure 3-5.

4. Switch the toggle for **Log Analytics Agent For Azure VMs** to **On**. Then, in the configuration column, click the **Edit Configuration** link. The **Extension Deployment Configuration** window opens, as shown in Figure 3-6.

5. You can choose either **Connect Azure VMs To The Default Workspace(s) Created By Defender For Cloud** or **Connect Azure VMs To A Different Workspace**. If you select the second option, as shown in Figure 3-6, the dropdown allows you to see all Log Analytics workspaces in your tenant (which means all workspaces in all subscriptions you have access to).

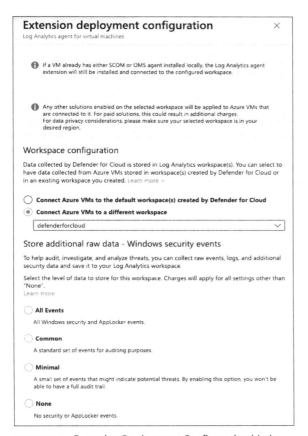

Extension deployment configuration ×

Log Analytics agent for virtual machines

ℹ️ If a VM already has either SCOM or OMS agent installed locally, the Log Analytics agent extension will still be installed and connected to the configured workspace.

ℹ️ Any other solutions enabled on the selected workspace will be applied to Azure VMs that are connected to it. For paid solutions, this could result in additional charges. For data privacy considerations, please make sure your selected workspace is in your desired region.

Workspace configuration

Data collected by Defender for Cloud is stored in Log Analytics workspace(s). You can select to have data collected from Azure VMs stored in workspace(s) created by Defender for Cloud or in an existing workspace you created. Learn more >

○ **Connect Azure VMs to the default workspace(s) created by Defender for Cloud**

◉ **Connect Azure VMs to a different workspace**

defenderforcloud ⌄

Store additional raw data - Windows security events

To help audit, investigate, and analyze threats, you can collect raw events, logs, and additional security data and save it to your Log Analytics workspace.

Select the level of data to store for this workspace. Charges will apply for all settings other than "None". Learn more

○ **All Events**

All Windows security and AppLocker events.

○ **Common**

A standard set of events for auditing purposes.

○ **Minimal**

A small set of events that might indicate potential threats. By enabling this option, you won't be able to have a full audit trail.

○ **None**

No security or AppLocker events.

FIGURE 3-6 Extension Deployment Configuration blade

6. If you select a Log Analytics workspace that has the security solution registered to it (meaning Microsoft Defender for Servers Plan 2 has been enabled on that workspace), you can choose to store additional raw event information from the Windows Security Event Log on this Log Analytics workspace.

> **TIP** Raw event logging is not mandatory for Microsoft Defender for Servers to create security alerts for protected machines, and it never was. You can set this setting to **None** and still get all the value from Microsoft Defender for Cloud and Microsoft Defender for Servers. This option, however, can be useful if you connect Microsoft Defender for Cloud with Microsoft Sentinel or another SIEM solution, so you can bring security alerts into context with raw event information coming from protected servers.

7. Click **Apply**.

8. At the top of the page, click **Save**.

Microsoft Defender for Cloud will now leverage a back-end process to deploy the Log Analytics agent extension to all Azure VMs in this particular subscription and connect these agents to the workspace you selected. As mentioned before, this process is not based on an Azure policy, but there are two built-in policy definitions that you can leverage for the same purpose:

- Enable Security Center's Auto-Provisioning Of The Log Analytics Agent On Your Subscriptions With Default Workspace

- Enable Security Center's Auto-Provisioning Of The Log Analytics Agent On Your Subscriptions With Custom Workspace

By assigning one of these policy definitions to a subscription, you will achieve the same result as turning on auto-provisioning in the UI, but the advantage is that with the policy, you can deploy the same setting to a particular subscription, or you can scale your configuration across all subscriptions in your management group. To assign the policy that will connect agents to a custom workspace, follow these steps:

1. Log in to the Azure portal with a user account that has Resource Policy Contributor, or Owner access rights on your subscription, enter **Policy** in the search bar at the top of the portal, and then click **Policy**.

2. In the left navigation pane, select **Definitions**.

3. At the top of this page, select **Security Center** as the **Category**, and in the **Search** field, enter **auto-provisioning**.

4. Choose the Enable Security Center's Auto-Provisioning Of The Log Analytics Agent On Your Subscriptions With Custom Workspace definition.

5. You will now see the policy definition, including its JSON representation. At the top of that page, click the **Assign** button.

6. On the **Basics** page, select the **Scope** (**Subscription** or **Management Group**) for your assignment and click **Parameters**.

7. In the **Parameters** section, select the Log Analytics workspace to which you want your machines to connect. If you selected a subscription or management group on the previous page and your workspace resides in a different subscription, make sure to click the **[...]** button to select the workspace's subscription first, followed by your workspace of choice.

8. If you want to remediate existing machines and not only future VMs, you need to create a remediation task. You can do so by navigating to the **Remediation** tab and selecting the corresponding check box.

9. Click **Review + Create** and then click **Create**.

The policy definition will now be assigned to your selected scope and, depending on your configuration, auto-remediate all existing or future VMs only.

In addition to deploying the extension to Azure VMs, you can also leverage auto-provisioning for Azure Arc-connected servers, a process we will cover in the next section.

Deploy the Log Analytics agent to Azure Arc machines

Azure Arc-connected servers are the vehicle Microsoft Defender for Cloud leverages to treat and manage non-Azure machines similar to Azure-native virtual machines. It allows the use of Azure Policy, RBAC, and other governance features provided by the platform and, therefore, is Microsoft's tool of choice when it comes to managing and protecting non-Azure machines.

> **MORE INFO** We do not cover Azure Arc onboarding to your machines in this book. For more information on Azure Arc-enabled servers, see *https://docs.microsoft.com/azure/azure-arc/servers/overview*.

In order to deploy the Log Analytics agent to your Azure Arc-enabled servers, follow these steps:

1. Log in to the Azure portal with a user account that has Owner access rights on your subscription, and then open **Microsoft Defender For Cloud**. Other than deploying the Log Analytics agent to Azure VMs, deploying it to Azure Arc-enabled servers will leverage Azure Policy-based deployments and, therefore, needs another level of access.

2. In the left navigation pane, select **Environment Settings** and select the subscription on which you want to enable auto-provisioning from your environment hierarchy.

3. In the **Settings** section, select **Auto-Provisioning**. The **Auto-Provisioning** window will appear.

4. Switch the toggle for **Log Analytics Agent For Azure Arc Machines (Preview)** to **On**. Then, in the **Configuration** column, click the **Edit Configuration** link. The **Extension Deployment Configuration** window opens, as shown in Figure 3-7.

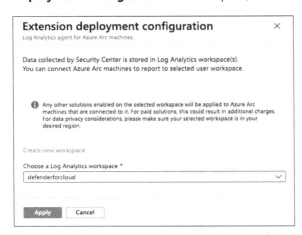

FIGURE 3-7 Log Analytics extension deployment configuration for Azure Arc-enabled servers

5. You can either create a new workspace by clicking the **Create New Workspace** link or selecting an existing workspace from the **Choose A Log Analytics Workspace** dropdown menu.

6. Once done, click **Apply**.

7. At the top of the page, click **Save**.

8. Microsoft Defender for Cloud will now assign two built-in policy definitions to the subscription you selected:

   - `Configure Log Analytics Extension On Azure Arc Enabled Linux Servers`
   - `Configure Log Analytics Extension On Azure Arc Enabled Windows Servers`

As shown in Figure 3-8, the following two policy assignments will be created: `ASC Provisioning LA Agent Linux Arc` and `ASC Provisioning LA Agent Windows Arc`, as shown in Figure 3-8.

FIGURE 3-8 Policy Assignments for Log Analytics auto-provisioning on Azure Arc machines

Next, let's take a look at the auto-provisioning of vulnerability assessment solutions.

Auto-provisioning of vulnerability assessment solutions

With Microsoft Defender for Servers Plan 2, you can leverage two integrated vulnerability assessment solutions for your machines: Microsoft Defender for Endpoint's Threat and Vulnerability Management (TVM) or the integrated Qualys Vulnerability Assessment solution. While we will cover these solutions in more detail in Chapter 5, "Strengthening your security posture," they need to be mentioned in this section because they can be auto-provisioned. Similar to Log Analytics extensions for Azure VMs and non-Azure machines connected through Azure Arc-enabled servers, provisioning for vulnerability assessment solutions is configured in the **Auto-Provisioning** window.

After you have logged in with an account that has Owner permissions on a particular subscription and navigated to the **Auto-Provisioning** view in Microsoft Defender for Cloud, follow these steps to enable auto-provisioning for a vulnerability assessment solution of your choice:

1. Toggle the **Vulnerability Assessment For Machines** switch to **On,** and then click the **Edit Configuration** link in the **Configuration** column.

2. Choose the desired vulnerability assessment solution.

3. Click **Apply**.

4. At the top of the page, click **Save**. See Figure 3-9.

FIGURE 3-9 Extension Deployment Configuration blade for vulnerability assessment solutions

Once applied, Microsoft Defender for Cloud will assign the `Configure Machines To Receive A Vulnerability Assessment Provider` policy definition to your subscription.

Auto-deployment of guest configuration agent

The guest configuration agent is a rather new development that is being used for Azure Policy's guest configuration capability. Historically, Microsoft Defender for Cloud has leveraged the Log Analytics agent to gather information about processes and system configuration that could be transformed into recommendations, such as an operating system security baseline recommendation. The guest configuration offers a more modern option to retrieve information from inside the OS and check it for OS misconfigurations, application configuration, or environment settings. The Microsoft Defender for Cloud development team has already created some preview recommendations that leverage this new agent, with more to come.

To automatically deploy the guest configuration agent to your Azure VMs and your non-Azure machines connected through Azure Arc-enabled servers, follow these steps:

1. Log in with an account that has Owner permissions to your Azure subscription and navigate to Microsoft Defender for Cloud's **Environment Settings** page, as explained in the previous set of steps.

2. Select the subscription on which you want to deploy the guest configuration agent.

3. In the left navigation pane, select **Auto-Provisioning**.

4. Toggle the **Guest Configuration Agent (Preview)** status to **On**.

5. At the top of the page, click **Save**.

Microsoft Defender for Cloud will now create two policy assignments that will take care of deploying the guest configuration agent to all existing and future Azure VMs and Azure Arc-connected servers: `ASC Provisioning Machines With No MI For GC Agent` and `ASC Provisioning Machines With User Assigned MI For GC Agent`.

Deploy Microsoft Defender for Containers components

Microsoft Defender for Containers is one of the latest additions to Microsoft Defender for Cloud. While we cover it in-depth in Chapter 6, it comes with some components that can be automatically deployed to all Kubernetes clusters in Microsoft Defender for Cloud's scope.

Microsoft Defender for Containers has two main categories of components:

- A daemon set running inside a Kubernetes cluster that replaces the Log Analytics agent at the host level
- An Azure Policy add-on for Kubernetes that allows you to extend Gatekeeper v3 so that it is integrated with Azure policy

Both components can be deployed to Azure Kubernetes Services (AKS) and non-Azure Kubernetes clusters that are connected by Azure Arc-enabled Kubernetes, which makes a total of four different settings.

Follow these steps to configure auto-provisioning for these components:

1. Log in with a user account that has Owner access rights on your subscription, and then navigate to the Microsoft Defender for Cloud's **Auto-Provisioning–Extensions** page, as explained in the previous steps.

2. Toggle the **Microsoft Defender For Containers Components (Preview)** status to **On**, and then click the **Edit Configuration** link in the **Configuration** column.

3. In the **Advanced configuration** blade, toggle each switch that applies to your environment to **On**, as shown in Figure 3-10.

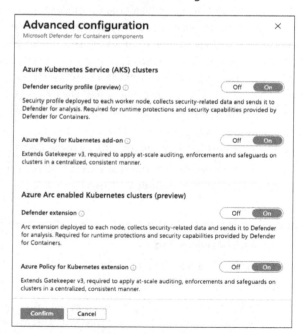

FIGURE 3-10 Advanced configuration for Microsoft Defender for Containers components

4. Click **Confirm**.

5. At the top of the page, click **Save**.

Microsoft Defender for Cloud will now automatically assign up to four Azure Policy definitions to your subscription, with the following assignment names:

- Defender for Containers provisioning AKS Security Profile
- Defender for Containers provisioning Azure Policy Addon for Kubernetes
- Defender for Containers provisioning ARC k8s Enabled
- Defender for Containers provisioning Policy extension for Arc-enabled Kubernetes

Connecting to Amazon Web Services (AWS)

Microsoft Defender for Cloud offers Cloud Security Posture Management (CSPM) for Azure resources or on-premises machines, and it can also connect to Amazon Web Services (AWS) and Google Cloud Platform (GCP). While there have been multi-cloud capabilities in Defender for Cloud as of Microsoft Ignite 2020, Microsoft recently changed the experience to agent-less, native connectors. Once a connector has been created, Microsoft Defender for Cloud will start assessing resources and provide recommendations based on its findings. In addition, you can enable one of the Microsoft Defender for Servers plans and Microsoft Defender for Containers on top of the connector to enable threat detection for virtual machines and Kubernetes clusters running in the other cloud environment.

To start with onboarding your AWS accounts to Microsoft Defender for Cloud, follow these steps:

1. Log in to the Azure portal with a user account that has Owner access rights. Then navigate to **Microsoft Defender For Cloud**.

2. In the left navigation pane, open **Environment Settings**.

3. In the top navigation bar, click **+ Add Environment**, and then select **Amazon Web Services (Preview)**, as shown in Figure 3-11.

4. Enter a **Connector Name** for the AWS connector and decide if you want to onboard a **Single Account** or a **Management Account** (see Figure 3-12). Using a management account, you can onboard all subordinary AWS accounts at scale.

5. Select the **Subscription**, **Resource Group**, and **Location** in which you want to store the connector resource.

6. Enter your **AWS Account ID**.

FIGURE 3-11   Creating a new Amazon Web Services connection

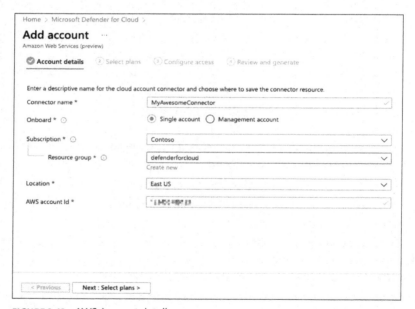

FIGURE 3-12   AWS Account details

7. Click **Next: Select plans >**.

8. **Security Posture Management** is automatically enabled on your connector, which ensures that all AWS resources in your particular account will be assessed and security recommendations are created. Optionally, you can switch the **Servers** and **Containers** plans to **On** to enable threat detection for EC2 instances and EKS clusters.

9. Click **Next: Configure Access >**.

FIGURE 3-13 Select Defender for Cloud plans to be enabled on AWS resources

10. On the **Configure Access** tab, you can download a **CloudFormation** template. Then click the **Go To AWS** button.

11. In AWS, click **Choose File** and select the downloaded template.

12. Click **Next** > **Create Stack**.

13. Once done, back in Defender for Cloud, click **Next: Review And Generate >**.

FIGURE 3-14 Configure access to your AWS account

14. Confirm all settings and click **Create**. See Figure 3-15.

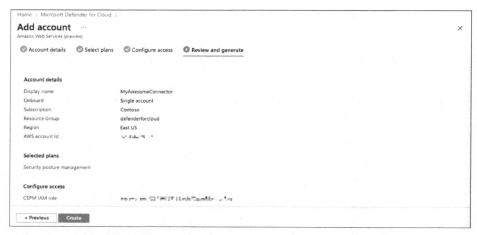

FIGURE 3-15 Configuration summary

Microsoft Defender for Cloud will now onboard your AWS account(s) and enable plans according to your configuration.

Onboard AWS VMs

As mentioned earlier, Microsoft Defender for Cloud leverages Azure Arc-enabled servers for connecting non-Azure machines to Azure, which also applies to AWS EC2 instances. To onboard these machines, you need to enable one of the Microsoft Defender for Servers plans on your AWS connector.

> **TIP** In order to connect non-Azure machines to Microsoft Defender for Cloud, one of the Microsoft Defender for Servers plans (Plan 1 or Plan 2) needs to be enabled. For on-premises machines, you will enable the plan on the Azure subscription to which you connect these machines. For AWS (and GCP), this is done on the corresponding multi-cloud connector.

To connect AWS EC2 instances, you either must have already created a connector on which you then enable Defender for Servers, or you enable the plan during the connector creation process that is explained in the previous section. To enable the Defender for Servers plan on an existing connector, follow these steps:

1. Log in to the Azure portal with a user account that has Owner access rights, and then navigate to **Microsoft Defender For Cloud**.

2. In the left navigation pane, open **Environment Settings**.

3. Select your **AWS Connector**.

4. Toggle the **Servers Plan** to **On**.

5. In the **pricing** column, click the **Select tier** link, then select one of the two Defender for Servers plans to be enabled and click **Confirm**.

6. In the **Configurations** column, click the **Configure >** link for the **Servers Plan**.

7. Make sure to switch the **Azure Arc Agent** toggle to **On**. Also, in the **Additional Agents For Arc Connected Machines** section, enable the **Log Analytics Agent**, and, if you want to integrate your EC2 instances with the Microsoft Defender for Endpoint Agent, switch the corresponding toggle to **On**.

8. Click **Save**.

9. Click **Next: Configure Access >**, then click **Next: Review And Generate >** and **Update**.

Microsoft Defender for Cloud will now automatically onboard your EC2 instances to Azure Arc-enabled servers, deploy the Log Analytics extensions, and, depending on your configuration, onboard your machines to Microsoft Defender for Servers.

How to onboard subscriptions at scale

As you already learned throughout this chapter, there are several technical aspects that need to be considered when onboarding resources and subscriptions to Microsoft Defender for Cloud. In general, there are four steps that need to be taken (or at least considered):

1. Register the Microsoft.Security resource provider.
2. Assign the Azure Security Benchmark policy initiative.
3. Configure auto-provisioning.
4. Optionally, enable Microsoft Defender for Cloud plans.

Because registering the resource provider happens when enabling Defender for Cloud plans, we cover both topics in the following section.

Registering the Microsoft.Security resource provider

The Microsoft.Security resource provider needs to be registered on a subscription to "enable" Microsoft Defender for Cloud. While this happens automatically when you open Defender for Cloud for the first time after creating a new subscription, it is *not* automatically registered on *any* new subscription before doing so. That means that, as long as you do not open that subscription in Defender for Cloud, no recommendations will apply to its resources, and no security alerts will be created.

For enabling Microsoft Defender for Cloud on a subscription, Microsoft Azure comes with a built-in policy definition called Enable Azure Security Center on your subscription. This policy definition will—once assigned to a subscription—set the Microsoft.Security/pricings setting for VirtualMachines to free, in case no Defender for Cloud plan has been enabled on that subscription. Figure 3-16 shows the corresponding code snippet taken from this definition.

```
"resources": [
  {
    "type": "Microsoft.Security/pricings",
    "apiVersion": "2018-06-01",
    "name": "VirtualMachines",
    "properties": {
      "pricingTier": "free"
    }
  }
],
```

FIGURE 3-16   Enabling the Microsoft.Security resource provider

This built-in definition can be assigned on top of your (root) management group, so it applies to all subscriptions (existing and future ones) in this scope. Also, you can see that the Microsoft.Security/pricing setting is used to register the resource provider. By taking the same code and changing the pricingTier value from free to standard, Microsoft Defender for Cloud plans are enabled. Again, Microsoft Azure has built-in policy definitions that can enable Defender for Cloud plans on all subscriptions within a management group (see Figure 3-17).

Name ↑	Definition location ↑↓	Policies ↑↓	Type ↑↓	Definition type ↑↓	Category ↑↓
Configure Advanced Threat Protection to be enabled on open-source relational datab...		3	Builtin	Initiative	Security Center
Configure Azure Defender for App Service to be enabled			Builtin	Policy	Security Center
Configure Azure Defender for Azure SQL database to be enabled			Builtin	Policy	Security Center
Configure Azure Defender for DNS to be enabled			Builtin	Policy	Security Center
Configure Azure Defender for Key Vaults to be enabled			Builtin	Policy	Security Center
Configure Azure Defender for Resource Manager to be enabled			Builtin	Policy	Security Center
Configure Azure Defender for SQL servers on machines to be enabled			Builtin	Policy	Security Center
Configure Azure Defender for Storage to be enabled			Builtin	Policy	Security Center
Configure Azure Defender for open-source relational databases to be enabled			Builtin	Policy	Security Center
Configure Azure Defender for servers to be enabled			Builtin	Policy	Security Center
Configure Azure Defender to be enabled on SQL Servers and SQL Managed Instances		2	Builtin	Initiative	Security Center

FIGURE 3-17   Built-in policy definitions to enable Defender for Cloud plans

As you will realize when learning more about Defender for Cloud plans in Chapter 6, the list shown in Figure 3-17 is not complete. However, you can build your own definition by taking one of the existing ones and replacing the name value with one from Table 3-1.

TABLE 3-1   Defender for Cloud pricing tier names according to Defender plans

Defender for Cloud plan	Pricing tier name
Defender for Servers:	"name": "VirtualMachines"
Defender for SQL	"name": "SqlServers"
Defender for App Services	"name": "AppServices"
Defender for Storage	"name": "StorageAccounts"
Defender for SQL on machines	"name": "SqlServerVirtualMachines"
Defender for Key Vault	"name": "KeyVaults"
Defender for DNS	"name": "Dns"
Defender for Resource Manager	"name": "Arm"
Defender for OSRDB	"name": "OpenSourceRelationalDatabases"
Defender for CosmosDB	"name": "CosmosDbs"
Defender for Containers	"name": "Containers"

Assign the Azure Security Benchmark

The Azure Security Benchmark is a policy initiative that can be assigned to each subscription or to a management group. By default, Defender for Cloud will automatically assign the initiative to a subscription once it is opened in Defender for Cloud's portal for the first time. However, you can also manually assign the initiative from Microsoft Defender for Cloud to a management group. This is a great way to make sure the benchmark will automatically be assigned to any subscription without having to open it in Defender for Cloud's portal. To manually assign the Azure Security Benchmark to a management group, follow these steps:

1. Log in to the Azure portal with an account that has Contributor or Owner rights on a particular management group.
2. Navigate to **Microsoft Defender For Cloud**.
3. In the left navigation pane, select **Environment Settings**.
4. Select the management group to which you want to assign the Azure Security Benchmark.
5. In the **Default Initiative** section, click the **Assign Policy** button, as shown in Figure 3-18.

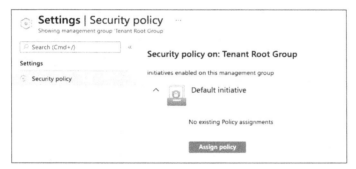

FIGURE 3-18   Assigning the Azure Security Benchmark on a management group

6. If you don't want to create an exclusion or disable a particular recommendation, click **Review + Create**, and then **Create**.
7. The assignment is now being created. If you already had the Security Benchmark assigned to your existing subscriptions before, make sure to remove these assignments now. To do so, select a subscription instead of the management group from the **Environment Settings** page and then, in the left navigation pane, select **Security Policy**.
8. In the **Default Initiative** section, look for the assignment that is assigned on your subscription. Then, on the right side, click **[...]** and **Delete Assignment**.
9. Confirm the **Delete Assignment** dialog by clicking **Yes**.
10. Repeat steps 8 and 9 on all subscriptions in the scope.

Configure auto-provisioning at scale

As you learned earlier in this chapter, when configuring auto-provisioning from the Defender for Cloud portal, the back-end will create policy assignments on a particular subscription. Also, for a Log Analytics agent on Azure VMs, there are built-in policy definitions, too. With that being said, all you need to do is assign these policies to your management group instead of subscriptions, as explained earlier in this chapter.

Chapter 4

Policy management

Policies, guardrails, and definitions. Many ambiguous terms are used synonymously when describing the same topic: a set of rules used to define the boundaries in which an environment can be configured. Since Microsoft Defender for Cloud's beginnings, the Cloud Security Posture Management capability has been built upon Azure Policy, which is a Microsoft Azure service used to technically define a company's governance concept.

In this chapter, you will learn about policies and assessments within the scope of Microsoft Defender for Cloud, and you'll learn about regulatory compliance standards and how to customize the experience in hybrid and multi-cloud environments.

Introduction to Azure Policy

We remember the days when IT environments were made up of server racks within office rooms or corporate datacenters. In those days, IT security mainly meant physical security and security in operations. It was a reactive process that could easily be done as a manual task.

Today, with cloud computing being the most popular operations model, we are facing ever-changing environments, which is both a benefit and a challenge. Cloud environments are meant to be solution-focused instead of resource-focused, which means that once your solution needs more compute power, there ideally is a process in place to spin up new machines once needed (and remove them if they're not needed). Or, if you move one abstraction layer higher, you don't even care about infrastructure resources because you are using PaaS (Platform as a Service) offerings. You can easily create new Storage Accounts or remove Azure Key Vaults from your environments within seconds. But, from an operational perspective, it is impossible to keep track of all these dynamic changes manually.

It is well known that there is no such thing as total security, which means there will always be a chance of being successfully attacked. But, more importantly, without rules, there is no security *at all*! Therefore, rules are important not only for security but also for compliance and governance purposes. In real life, rules are called *laws* defined by a government, and there is an instance to control and enforce these laws, called the *police*. From a technical perspective within Microsoft Azure, this is when Azure Policy comes into play. Azure Policy is that instance to control and enforce the rules that an authority in your company has defined.

Azure Policy is a service that consists of *definitions* and *assignments*, both of which can apply to *policies* and *initiatives*.

1. **Definitions**   Definitions are the configurations that you set up within a policy or initiative. They can be referred to as a *template*, which can later be applied to resources within your environment. Definitions can be compared with your current configuration, and any resources that do not meet the requirements of your policy are determined to be out of compliance. You can then focus on the out-of-compliance assets and bring them into compliance. All policy definitions are created in JavaScript Object Notation, or JSON.

2. **Assignments**   Assignments are definitions that are assigned to a specific scope within your Azure environment. This scope can vary from management groups, over subscriptions, and down to a single resource group. By default, an assignment will be inherited top-down, which means that if you assign a policy definition on a subscription, its settings will apply to all resources within the subscription. However, when creating the assignment, you can also exclude a particular scope from applying your policy or initiative definition. For example, you might use definitions that are supposed to apply to most subscriptions within your Azure environment, but not for particular resources. Let's say you have test resources in one or several resource groups. In this case, you could create an assignment on your management group and exclude this particular resource group so resources within that scope would not apply the definition's settings.

When creating a new definition, you need to be careful with the definition location, which can either be a management group or a subscription. The location will determine to what scope the definition can be assigned later. For example, if you create the definition on a management group, you can assign it to this management group and all child management groups and subscriptions, whereas if you create a definition on a subscription, you can only assign it to this particular subscription and its resources and resource groups.

An *initiative definition* is a collection of *policy definitions* that is tailored toward achieving a singular overarching goal. Initiative definitions simplify the management and assignment of policy definitions by grouping a set of policies into a single item. Each policy definition contains a policy rule that defines in which case the policy definition will assess a resource, and what effect the policy assessment will have. Figure 4-1 shows these components.

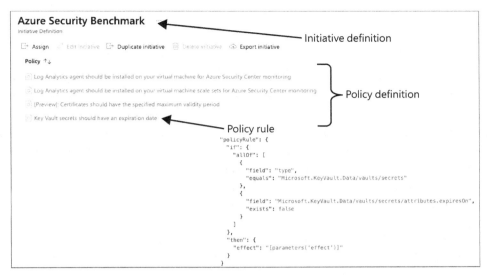

FIGURE 4-1 Azure Policy components

> **IMPORTANT** When working with Azure Policy and automation, you will not find the word *initiative*. You should look for *policy set* instead.

A policy definition can have different effects to the scope it is assigned to. The `append` mode is used to add additional fields to a resource when it is created or updated. For example, you can use `append` to add a list of allowed IP addresses to a storage resource. A policy definition in `audit` mode will report resources that are non-compliant regarding the settings within your definition. For example, if you have an internal agreement that organizational resources are only deployed to Azure regions within Europe, you can use an `audit` policy to report resources that are deployed in a US region. A similar effect is `auditifnotexists`, which will report resources that do not have a particular configuration or setting. For example, you would use `auditifnotexists` if you want to see resources that do not have a particular tag configured.

If you configure a definition in `deployifnotexists` (DINE) mode, once you deploy a resource, a particular setting or configuration is automatically remediated if it has not already been defined when configuring the resource to be deployed. For example, you can use a DINE policy to ensure that the Azure Monitoring Agent is installed on all VMs created within your Azure environment.

A definition that is configured in `deny` mode will prevent the deployment of resources that are non-compliant regarding a particular setting. In the first example with the Azure regions, you can use a `deny` policy to not only audit but also prevent the deployment of resources to a US region. Finally, there is the `modify` mode, which is used to add, update, or remove properties or tags on a resource when it is created or updated. This effect is commonly used to update tags on resources. Also, with `modify`, you can remediate existing resources using remediation tasks.

While having this core understanding of Azure Policy is important, you don't need to create any initiative or policy when using security policy integration with Azure Policy because Defender for Cloud will automatically create it for you. All security controls and recommendations are based on this default policy initiative, called Azure Security Benchmark, which is maintained by Microsoft. This initiative includes a curation of `audit` and `auditifnotexists` policies that are automatically assigned to your subscriptions. If there are changes to existing policy definitions, definitions are removed, or new policy definitions are created and added to the Azure Security Benchmark initiative, these changes will automatically apply to Microsoft Defender for Cloud.

You can also leverage Azure Policy for deployment, remediation, and protection at scale. So, Azure Policy is not only a random governance tool within the Microsoft Azure ecosystem, but it's also an important service you need to understand to implement the best CSPM concept for your organization.

Policy exemptions

Policy exemptions (announced at Microsoft Ignite 2020) are an exciting new feature within the context of Azure Policy. Although it might seem similar to the exclusion scope you can define when assigning a definition, it is *way* more than that. With policy exemptions, you can exclude a management group, subscription, resource group, or a particular resource from an assignment. Additionally, you can configure an expiration date for the exemption or enter a justification for the exemption. You can select `waiver` as the exemption category if you decide to temporarily accept the non-compliance state of a resource, or you can select `mitigated` if the policy's intent was met through a different method or process.

> **MORE INFO**   To learn more about policy exemptions, see *https://docs.microsoft.com/en-us/azure/governance/policy/concepts/exemption-structure.*

When you configure an exclusion scope, you need to do it within the assignment, and doing so is a static decision, whereas when you create a policy exemption, the policy assignment itself is not changed. As you can see in Figure 4-2, there is an **Exemptions** button in the left navigation pane within Azure Policy. This figure shows an exemption that has been created from within Defender for Cloud for the subscription's default assignment.

FIGURE 4-2 Policy exemption in the Azure Policy dashboard

You will learn more about how to create an exemption in Defender for Cloud in the next chapter, though you can also create policy exemptions directly from the Azure Policy dashboard. That is useful if you do not want to create an exemption for the Azure Security Benchmark policy initiative, but you want to do so for other policies that are not necessarily related to Defender for Cloud.

Follow these steps to create a new policy exemption:

1. Open the Azure portal and sign in with a user who has Resource Policy Contributor or Security Admin privileges.

2. In the search bar, type **Policy** and click the **Policy** service; the **Policy** blade appears, as shown in Figure 4-3.

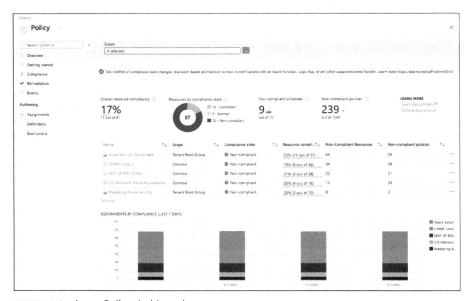

FIGURE 4-3 Azure Policy dashboard

3. The **Exemptions** view, as shown in Figure 4-2, only shows existing exemptions, so to create a new exemption through Azure Policy, visit the **Authoring** section of the **Policy** navigation pane and select **Assignments**.

4. Select the assignment for which you want to create a policy exemption and click the **[...]** menu on the right side. Select **Create Exemption**, as shown in Figure 4-4. The **Create Exemption** window appears.

FIGURE 4-4   Create a new policy exemption

5. In the **Basics** section, define the **Exemption Scope** (**Management Group, Subscription, Resource Group**, or **Resource**), the **Exemption Name**, the **Exemption Category** (**Waiver** or **Mitigated**), and an **Exemption Expiration Setting**, as shown in Figure 4-5. Also, make sure to add a description that helps you understand why the exemption had been created once you come back in the future.

6. If you only want to create an exemption for some policies within an initiative assignment instead of exempting the whole initiative assignment, click **Policies**, set the **Policy Definition Reference** switch to **Off**, and select the policy definitions for which you want to create the exemption. Then, click **Review + Create**, followed by **Create**. Once the exemption has been created, it will show up in the **Exemption** view you saw earlier in Figure 4-2.

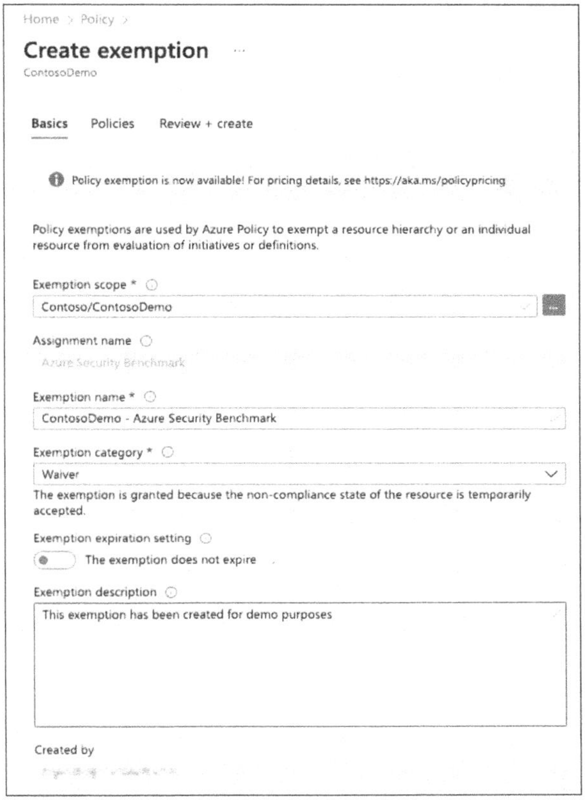

FIGURE 4-5 Create a new policy exemption

Understanding Azure Security Benchmark

Azure Security Benchmark, the default policy initiative that comes with Microsoft Defender for Cloud, contains all security policies. At the time of publication, the default policy initiative contained 205 separate policy definitions. The number of policies will keep growing as the Defender for Cloud engineering team continues adding new services to monitor and creating new recommendations, which will be reflected as new policy definitions. As you learned in Chapter 3, "Onboarding Microsoft Defender for Cloud," the Azure Security Benchmark initiative is either automatically assigned to all subscriptions onboarded to Defender for Cloud or manually assigned to a management group to cover all (existing and future) subscriptions.

> **TIP** Security policies in Microsoft Defender for Cloud can only be assigned at the subscription or management group levels. This is an important observation because if you look at the Azure Policy itself, it can be assigned to a resource group. However, this capability is not available for Defender for Cloud.

The Azure Security Benchmark (ASB) is a curation of security best practices that are aligned with industry-wide security standards, such as those from the National Institute of Standards and Technology (NIST) and the Center for Internet Security (CIS). All policy definitions that are part of the ASB reflect as a recommendation in Defender for Cloud. Also, the ASB will show up as a regulatory standard in Defender for Cloud's Regulatory Compliance view, which we cover later in this chapter. It is important to understand that while the Azure Security Benchmark comprises audit policies, not all are used to assess resource compliance. While Azure Policy can only audit resources and their configuration if information is accessible through Azure Resource Manager (ARM), Microsoft Defender for Cloud and the Azure Security Benchmark contain recommendations for non-Azure settings, such as Azure Active Directory Multi-Factor Authentication (MFA). Because Azure Policy cannot assess these types of settings, Defender for Cloud uses intelligent background assessments and will only reflect the assessment status to Azure Policy.

Also, Azure Policy only has two different compliance states (compliant and non-compliant), while Microsoft Defender for Cloud has three different health states for assessed resources (`Healthy`, `Unhealthy`, `NotApplicable`). That's why assessments will run in Defender for Cloud's back end and then the assessment status code for a particular resource is audited by a particular policy in the ASB. That way, if an assessment status is **Healthy** or not applicable, a resource will be flagged as being compliant in Azure Policy. The resource will show as non-compliant in Azure Policy only if the assessment status code is **Unhealthy**.

Figure 4-6 shows the **Secure Score Recommendations** view in Microsoft Defender for Cloud, including the **Enable MFA** security control. This control contains several recommendations for enabling multi-factor authentication on accounts with access rights to an Azure subscription.

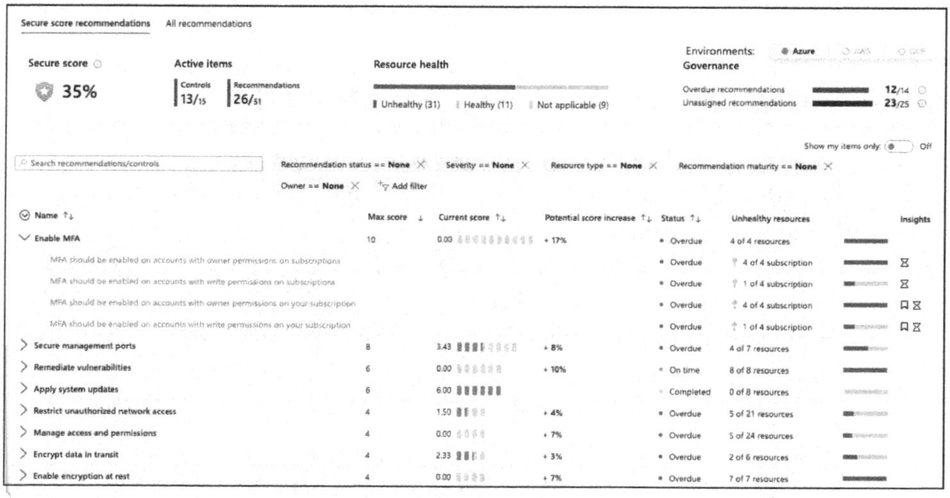

FIGURE 4-6 Secure Score recommendations in Microsoft Defender for Cloud

For these recommendations, the assessed resource type is a subscription, but the setting cannot be checked via ARM, which would be mandatory for Azure Policy to audit a resource. For example, consider the first recommendation in Figure 4-6, **MFA Should Be Enabled On Accounts With Owner Permissions On Subscriptions**. The actual assessment for creating this recommendation on a subscription will run in Defender for Cloud's back end, and the policy definition will then check for each subscription in scope. This check is done to identify whether a `Microsoft.Security/assessments` resource named 94290b00-4d0c-d7b4-7cea-064a9554e681 exists in that subscription, based on the information contained in the Microsoft.Security/assessments/status.code field. As long as the status code is `Healthy` or `NotApplicable`, the subscription that's been assessed will be shown as compliant in Azure Policy's compliance dashboard. Figure 4-7 shows the actual policy rule.

```
"policyRule": {
  "if": {
    "field": "type",
    "equals": "Microsoft.Resources/subscriptions"
  },
  "then": {
    "effect": "[parameters('effect')]",
    "details": {
      "type": "Microsoft.Security/assessments",
      "name": "94290b00-4d0c-d7b4-7cea-064a9554e681",
      "existenceCondition": {
        "field": "Microsoft.Security/assessments/status.code",
        "in": [
          "NotApplicable",
          "Healthy"
        ]
      }
    }
  }
}
```

FIGURE 4-7 Policy rule of a recommendation in Azure Security Benchmark

Each assessment has a unique name that is a Globally Unified Identifier (GUID). This GUID is a unique number that can be used to identify anything in the universe, which makes it a great fit for creating unique names that can be used across different environments. Therefore, the assessment name is predefined and the same in each customer's Azure environment. With that, it's possible to have the same (built-in) policy definition that will audit the same assessment in each environment.

Fine-tuning policies in Defender for Cloud

It is important to have full visibility of your workloads in Azure and ensure that you are using the security best practices available for all resources that you are monitoring. As you already learned, security policies in Azure Security Benchmark reflect Defender for Cloud's security assessments for all monitored resources. Each assessment is a recommendation for a particular resource, and assessment results and recommendations will vary according to the type of resources that a subscription has.

There are situations where a recommendation might not apply to your scenario. For example, Defender for Cloud might recommend that you enable MFA, but this wouldn't be helpful if you are already using a third-party MFA provider in your environment. Because Defender for Cloud doesn't consider the third-party implementation of MFA, this recommendation becomes a false-positive. To completely disable a particular recommendation, follow the steps below:

1. Open the Azure portal and sign in with a user who has Security Admin privileges.

2. Open Microsoft Defender for Cloud.

3. In the left navigation pane, click **Environment Settings**.

4. Depending on the scope to which you have assigned the Azure Security Benchmark, select a management group or subscription. Then, in the left navigation pane, click **Security Policy**.

5. On the **Security Policy** blade, select the policy assignment in the **Default Initiative** section, as shown in Figure 4-8.

FIGURE 4-8   Default initiative assignment in Defender for Cloud

6. After clicking the assignment, the **Edit Initiative Assignment** page appears. Click the **Parameters** tab.

7. Deselect the **Only Show Parameters That Need Input Or Review** checkbox, which makes all parameters appear. These parameters correspond to each recommendation (Azure policies). Look for the recommendation that you want to disable, click the dropdown, and click **Disabled**, as shown in Figure 4-9.

8. After selecting **Disabled** for the recommendation that is not applicable to your scenario, click the **Review+Save** button, which is located at the bottom of the page, and then click **Save**.

9. Once the change is committed, go back to Defender for Cloud's **Overview** page.

FIGURE 4-9 Disabling a recommendation that is not relevant to your scenario

Now that the recommendation has changed, you need to wait for the dashboard to refresh. Changes to the initiative might take up to 48 hours to be re-assessed.

> **MORE INFO** Each recommendation in Defender for Cloud has its own Freshness Interval which indicates how often an assessment will run. If the Freshness Interval is set to 24 hours, the assessment will run once every 24 hours. If you want to know how long it will take for the recent change to your policy to reflect in your recommendations, the Freshness Interval is a good indicator.

Because each subscription has its own policy assignment, there will be scenarios for which you want to deploy a single assignment for multiple subscriptions. When this occurs, you can use Azure management groups. The idea is that you can organize subscriptions into containers (called management groups) and apply your governance conditions to the management groups, as shown in Figure 4-10. For more information on how to manage policy at scale, see Chapter 3 and Chapter 10, "Deployment at scale."

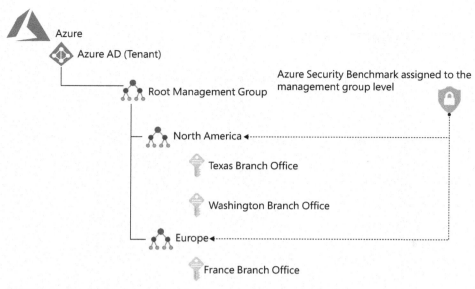

FIGURE 4-10 Security policies assigned at the management group level

Each directory is given a single top-level management group called the Root Management Group. Unlike other management groups, the Root Management Group cannot be moved or deleted. For more information on how to create Azure management groups, see *http://aka.ms/ azuremgroup*.

Creating custom policies in Microsoft Defender for Cloud

Using the built-in policy initiative in your Defender for Cloud deployment has several advantages. Most obvious is the fact that you don't need to care about enabling recommendations because they will automatically apply to every subscription you enroll to Defender for Cloud. Less obvious, but as important nonetheless, both the built-in policy and initiative definitions are maintained by Microsoft. In other words, if there are changes to the resource providers used within these policy definitions, if new definitions are created, or if existing recommendations are changed, these changes will automatically be incorporated into the built-in initiative definition. However, there are cases when you still want to have additional custom policies in your environment, either because you want to tailor an existing policy, or because you want to add more assessments to your environment.

To add a custom policy initiative to Microsoft Defender for Cloud, follow these steps:

1. Open the Azure portal and sign in with a user who has Security Admin privileges.
2. Open Microsoft Defender for Cloud.
3. In the left navigation pane, click **Environment Settings**.

4. Depending on the scope to which you want to assign a custom initiative, select a management group or subscription. Then, in the left navigation pane, click **Security Policy**.

5. At the bottom of the **Security Policy** blade, in the **Your Custom Initiatives** section, click the **Add A Custom Initiative** button. The **Add Custom Initiatives** blade appears, as shown in Figure 4-11.

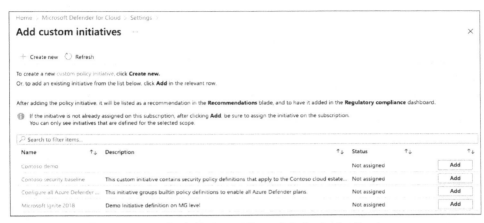

FIGURE 4-11 Adding a custom policy initiative to Microsoft Defender for Cloud

6. You can either click **Add** to assign an existing custom initiative or **+ Create New** to start building a new custom initiative definition from scratch and assign it to your subscription.

7. You can add a combination of existing custom and built-in policy definitions to your custom initiative. Once you've created an initiative, click **Save** and then **Add** to assign it to your subscription.

8. When assigning the custom initiative from Defender for Cloud, you can assign it to a management group, subscription, or a particular resource group within that subscription. (Remember, the Azure Security Benchmark initiative can only be assigned on management groups and subscriptions.) At the same time, you can define an exclusion for either a resource group or a particular resource so the policies won't apply to the excluded scope, as shown in Figure 4-12.

9. Click the **Review + Create** button, and then click **Create**.

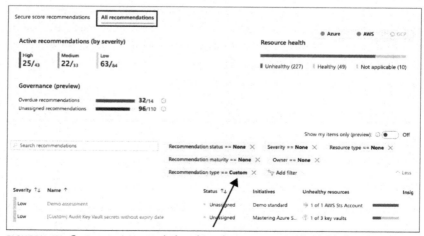

Home > Microsoft Defender for Cloud > Settings > Add custom initiatives >

Contoso security baseline ...
Assign initiative

Basics   Parameters   Remediation   Non-compliance messages   Review + create

Scope
Scope   Learn more about setting the scope *

> Contoso

Exclusions

> Optionally select resources to exclude from the policy ..

Basics
Initiative definition

> Contoso security baseline

Assignment name * ◯

> Contoso security baseline

Description

Policy enforcement ◯
(Enabled) Disabled

Assigned by

> Tom Janetscheck

FIGURE 4-12   Assign a custom policy definition with scope and exclusions

Custom policy definitions within your custom initiative will be shown in Defender for Cloud's **All Recommendations** tab, as shown in Figure 4-13. To narrow down the results, you can filter the **Recommendation Type** for custom recommendations only.

Secure score recommendations | All recommendations |

Active recommendations (by severity)   Resource health   ● Azure   ● AWS   ○ GCP

High   Medium   Low
25/43   22/33   63/84   ▌Unhealthy (227)   ▌Healthy (49)   ▌Not applicable (10)

Governance (preview)

Overdue recommendations   ▬▬▬▬ 32/14 ◯
Unassigned recommendations   ▬▬▬▬ 96/110 ◯

Show my items only (preview): ◯ ●) Off

Search recommendations   Recommendation status == **None** ✕   Severity == **None** ✕   Resource type == **None** ✕

Recommendation maturity == **None** ✕   Owner == **None** ✕

Recommendation type == **Custom** ✕   ⊹ Add filter   ∧ Less

Severity ↑↓	Name ↑		Status ↑↓	Initiatives	Unhealthy resources	Insig
Low	Demo assessment		Unassigned	Demo standard	1 of 1 AWS Sts Account	▬▬▬
Low	[Custom] Audit Key Vault secrets without expiry date		Unassigned	Mastering Azure S...	1 of 3 key vaults	▬▬

FIGURE 4-13   Custom recommendations based on a custom policy initiative

As mentioned before, you can use both custom and built-in policy definitions within your custom initiative definition. If you choose to use built-in policies, they still are maintained by Microsoft, whereas custom policy definitions are not automatically updated. So, if you are using custom policies in a custom initiative, you need to establish a process that helps you keep track of back-end changes related to the policies' intentions and update your custom policies accordingly.

Policy enforcement and governance

With cloud computing, there is no security without governance. Cloud environments are too dynamic to manually make sure that infrastructure and platform resources are protected and configured correctly (whatever that means for your particular environments), so you need a robust end-to-end governance concept which includes Azure Policy as one of its main components.

Governance is defined as the "Establishment of *policies*, and continuous *monitoring* of their proper *implementation*, by the members of the governing body of an organization [...]." That's a great definition, as it contains very important parts.

> **MORE INFO** To read the full definition, see *https://businessdictionary.info/definition/ governance/.*

You already know that policies are rules that apply to your environment. These rules can apply to your organization because of legal restrictions, regulatory compliance, or because your organization simply decides to go one way versus another.

The second part of the definition, monitoring, is a very important one because it applies to rules and policies, as well as to everything in the cloud. Without proper monitoring, you are blind, and being blind means that you will never know what exactly is going on in your cloud environment. If you don't know what is going on, you will never have a chance to react or pro-actively change anything.

And then there is implementation. The definition means "implementation of policies," but you can expand its scope to security implementation and resource deployment. In other words, we need to talk about deployment processes, continuous integration and continuous deployment (CI/CD), DevOps, and so on.

When you take a closer look at Microsoft Defender for Cloud, you will realize that all of the definition's aspects are already incorporated in the product. Defender for Cloud comes with its own security policy initiative, enables visibility (monitoring) into resource compliance and, therefore, the policies' proper implementation. Also, Defender for Cloud helps you to understand which changes are necessary in your deployment processes to be—and stay—compliant.

In Chapter 5, "Strengthening your security posture," we take a closer look at the Secure Score as the main KPI (key performance indicator) to measure your security posture, but it is also important to understand how resource deployments can negatively affect your resources' security within the context of policy enforcement and governance.

The Secure Score is calculated based on resources and their compliance with the Azure Security Benchmark policy definitions, which security recommendations rely on. In short, the higher your Secure Score, the more resources are compliant with your security policies and the more secure your resources are. Figure 4-14 shows an ideal Secure Score trend for a fictive Azure environment. The trend starts low and increases over time, which is an indicator of security and compliance improvements.

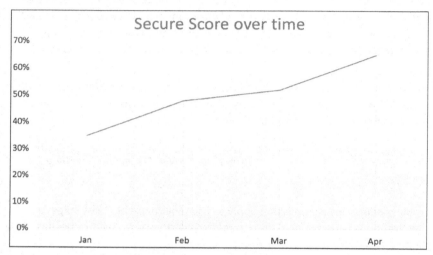

FIGURE 4-14   Azure Secure Score over time improvement

In this scenario, someone has taken care of remediating security recommendations that count toward the organization's Secure Score. Once security issues and recommendations are remediated, the Secure Score will increase. However, this is *reactive* security management. Reactive means that you take care of security once a resource is non-compliant with a given security recommendation, and you will learn why this is not sufficient while continuing with the demo scenario in this chapter. Figure 4-15 shows a similar curve, but in May you see that the Secure Score dropped to an even lower percentage than you saw in January. But why?

As discussed in Chapter 2, "Planning Microsoft Defender for Cloud adoption," when managing security reactively, once new resources are deployed, your Secure Score will drop. This is when your resources are not deployed securely by default. In this case, you would need to take care of remediating configuration issues and security recommendations reactively again. This means on the one hand, it will require a lot of effort after every resource deployment, but on the other hand, your cloud environment will be more vulnerable immediately after new resources have been deployed. So, reactively managing security comes with several drawbacks.

Don't get us wrong: Hands-on mentality is great because it means that people want to roll up their sleeves and get things done, but in this case, the same mentality also needs to be projected onto security management.

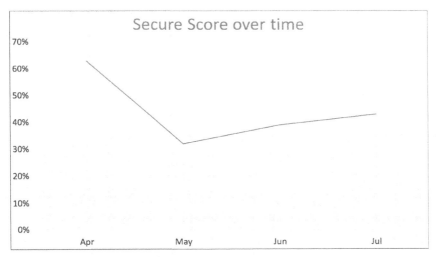

FIGURE 4-15 Secure Score over time when not taking care of governance

How to overcome reactive security management

IT security has always been an important part of IT operations. The problem with that approach is that security comes last—at the end of the deployment process—instead of being integrated into it. With ever-changing cloud environments, increasing sophistication of cyber threats and the lack of security specialists in many organizations, it is no longer enough to react to issues. However, you need to make sure to *proactively* integrate security into the build pipeline and your deployment processes. The earlier you care for security in these processes, the easier it is to align with corporate rules and restrictions.

Once your cloud environment grows, you will automatically want to enforce policies across a broad set of resources, resource groups, or even subscriptions so you can make sure that all these resources will automatically adhere to your corporate rules, instead of having to take care of remediation manually.

Prevent security misconfigurations with Defender for Cloud

Security misconfigurations are one of the main reasons organizations get compromised, and the good news is that Defender for Cloud leverages Azure Policy to *prevent* misconfigurations. With this integration, you can make sure you keep your resources secure and that you have already stabilized your Secure Score when/before resources are deployed (proactively), instead of taking care of security afterward (reactively). You can use Defender for Cloud to enforce a secure configuration with two effects:

1. With the deny effect in Defender for Cloud's recommendations, you can prevent unsecure resources from being created. This effect will use the deny effect from Azure Policy.

2. The enforce effect in Defender for Cloud's recommendations will leverage Azure Policy's DeployIfNotExists effect to automatically remediate resources from an unsecure configuration.

You can create a deny or enforcement recommendation directly from a recommendation's blade in Microsoft Defender for Cloud, following these steps:

1. Open the Azure portal and sign in with an account that has **Security Admin** privileges.

2. In the search bar, type **Defender**, then select **Microsoft Defender For Cloud**.

3. In Defender for Cloud's left navigation pane, click **Recommendations**.

4. Open a security control and select a recommendation within. In this example, you are using the Encrypt data in transit security control and the Secure transfer to storage accounts should be enabled recommendation.

5. Click the **Enforce** or **Deny** button within the recommendation as shown in Figure 4-16.

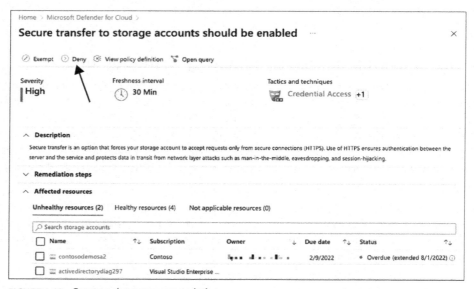

FIGURE 4-16   Create a deny recommendation

6. Select the subscription or subscriptions for which you want to change the policy effect from audit to deny and click the **Change To Deny** button, as shown in Figure 4-17.

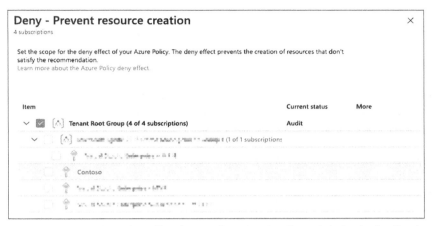

Deny - Prevent resource creation ✕
4 subscriptions

Set the scope for the deny effect of your Azure Policy. The deny effect prevents the creation of resources that don't satisfy the recommendation.
Learn more about the Azure Policy deny effect.

Item	Current status	More
☑ [⌂] **Tenant Root Group (4 of 4 subscriptions)**	Audit	
[⌂] ⌐ ▪ ▪ ▪ (1 of 1 subscription)		
⌐ ▪ ▪ ▪		
Contoso		
⌐ ▪ ▪ ▪		
⌐ ▪ ▪ ▪		

FIGURE 4-17 Change a policy effect from audit to deny in Microsoft Defender for Cloud

7. Be aware that depending on the scope you assigned the Azure Security Benchmark to, you can either create the deny or enforcement policy on a subscription, or on the management group only.

> **MORE INFO**   To learn for which recommendations you can create a deny or enforcement policy, see *https://aka.ms/MDFCEnforceDeny*.

Denying resource creation or enforcing auto-remediation on some subscriptions is good, but wouldn't it be even better to have an option for large-scale deployments, too? Here we go!

Large-scale provisioning with Azure Blueprints

Microsoft Defender for Cloud is a subscription-based service, which means that any configuration you want to enforce, deny, or activate is always done on a particular subscription unless you have assigned the Azure Security Benchmark on a management group. That might be good for existing environments, but what about new subscriptions under the same Azure AD tenant? Or what if your organization has a large cloud estate with more than 1,000 subscriptions?

Azure Blueprints is a service that brings together all the goodness of several important governance services within Microsoft Azure. One could say that with Azure Blueprints, you have a way to automate governance across your entire cloud estate. Similar to policies, Blueprints divide between definitions and assignments, as shown in Figure 4-18.

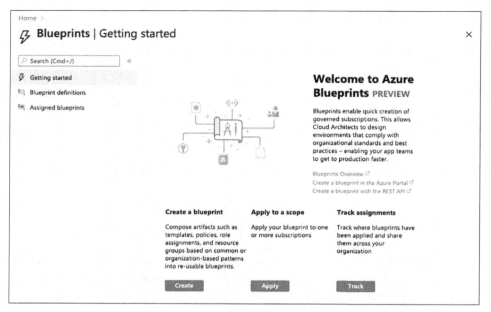

FIGURE 4-18 Getting started with Azure Blueprints

A **Blueprint definition** can be created on management groups and subscriptions. It contains *artifacts* that are supposed to be applied to a particular scope. Artifacts can be policy and initiative assignments, as well as role assignments, resource groups, and even ARM Templates. So, with a Blueprint definition, you can apply policies and initiatives to a subscription, and you can also create resource groups and resources, and grant access rights to users and/or groups. The definition is saved in either a management group or a subscription. The location will determine to which scope the definition can be assigned. For example, if you create a Blueprint in only one subscription, you cannot assign it to another subscription, whereas if you store it in a management group, you can assign it to all subscriptions in that scope (and it will also automatically be assigned to new subcriptions within that management group). Other than policies and initiatives, a Blueprint definition can be stored in a draft before publishing it. Once a definition is published, it will get a new version. With that, you can assign the same definition in different versions to different scopes, such as when you want to test a new Blueprint definition on a small scope before rolling it out to your entire environment.

A **Blueprint Assignment** is similar to a policy or initiative assignment, meaning it's a Blueprint definition assigned to a subscription, but there is an important difference: Blueprint assignments can be locked using the Azure Resource Lock capability. With this option set to **Do Not Delete**, you can make sure that artifacts deployed by the Blueprint assignment cannot be deleted, even by resource or subscription owners. If you set the option to **Read Only**, resources that have been deployed cannot be changed at all, even by the resource or subscription owner.

To start creating and assigning a new Blueprint definition, follow these steps:

1. Open the Azure portal and sign in with an account that has **Owner** privileges on the management group in which you want to save the definition.

2. Select **Blueprints** from the left navigation pane. This will open the **Getting Started** view you saw in Figure 4-18.

3. Click the **Create** button. You can now either select a Blueprint sample from the list or start with a blank Blueprint. For this exercise, select **Start With Blank Blueprint**.

4. Enter a name for the Blueprint definition and decide where to store it. Remember, if you want the definition to be assigned to more than one subscription, store the definition in a management group. Click the **Next: Artifacts >>** button, as shown in Figure 4-19.

FIGURE 4-19   Create a Blueprint definition

5. Click the + **Add Artifact** button and select the artifact type you want to add to your Blueprint definition. Depending on the artifact type, fill in the necessary information and then click the **Add** button to add the artifact to your definition. Repeat this step for every other artifact you want to add to your Blueprint.

> **IMPORTANT**   For some artifact parameters, you will see a **This Value Should Be Specified When The Blueprint Is Assigned** checkbox. If you deselect this checkbox, you define the parameter in the definition, so it is the same value for every assignment. If you select the checkbox, the parameter is set per assignment.

6. Click the **Save Draft** button.

7. You are now redirected to the **Getting Started** page again. Your Blueprint definition is now saved but not published. To publish its first version, click **Blueprint Definitions** in the navigation pane and select the definition you just created from the list.

8. Click **Publish Blueprint**, as shown in Figure 4-20, enter a version, and click the **Publish** button.

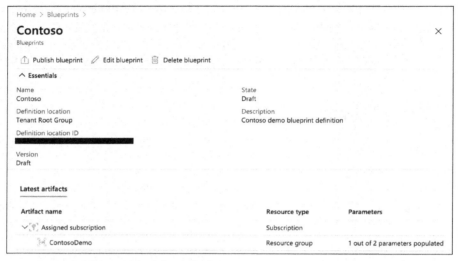

FIGURE 4-20   Publish your Blueprint definition

9. You are now redirected to the **Create Blueprint** page shown previously in Figure 4-18, and you can assign the Blueprint definition to one, some, or all existing subscriptions underneath the management group in which you created the definition. To assign the definition, click **Assign Blueprint**.

10. Fill out all mandatory fields, such as **Subscriptions**, **Assignment Name**, **Location**, and **Blueprint Version**. Also, make sure to enter values for all parameters that have not already been defined in the Blueprint definition. Also, decide if you want to lock your resources with a **Do Not Delete**, or a **Read Only** lock. Then click **Assign**.

> **MORE INFO**   To learn more about Azure Blueprints, see *https://docs.microsoft.com/azure/governance/blueprints/overview*.

Policy deployment and best practices

You have already learned that policies, initiatives, and Blueprints are a great way to make sure your cloud estate will automatically align with your corporate rules. But in order to get the best out of policies, there are some best practices to consider.

1. **Get yourself familiar with ARM Templates, PowerShell, and Azure CLI**   When working with policy definitions, there is no way around JavaScript Object Notation, or JSON. As you learned at the beginning of this chapter, policy definitions are always created in JSON syntax. The good news is that ARM Templates as a declarative deployment language are also based on JSON, so once you know how to create a policy definition, the path to creating an ARM Template is short. ARM Templates are a very efficient way of deploying policies and initiatives versus using the Azure portal. For example, you can use ARM Templates within your building pipeline based on Azure DevOps, but you can also run a deployment using PowerShell and Azure CLI. Also, when running a deployment, you can reference the template file directly from a repository, such as GitHub or Azure Repos.

2. **Assign definitions top-down**   Policy settings are inherited from a higher to a lower scope. In other words, if you assign an initiative definition on your Root Management Group, its policy settings will apply to all subscriptions within that scope. Therefore, the settings you want to apply to all your resources should be assigned on the highest possible scope; settings that only apply to some subscriptions (or resources within them) should be assigned on a lower level of scope. The higher you assign a policy, the less restrictive it usually is, whereas the lower the assignment is created, the more restrictive it might be.

3. **Avoid layering and overriding policy settings**   Although possible, you should not override settings from one assignment by those of another because it might lead to unexpected results. Every resource individually evaluates all policy assignments to make sure that no resource will accidentally bypass the evaluation, and the result of layering assignments is considered to be cumulatively most restrictive. See the following example:

   - **Policy 1:**
     - Assigned to Subscription A
     - Allows resource creation only in the westus Azure region
     - Deny effect
   - **Policy 2:**
     - Assigned to Resource Group B in Subscription A
     - Allows resource creation only in the eastus Azure region
     - Deny effect

The deny effect in Policy 1 will deny all resources which are created in any Azure region other than West US. This setting applies to Subscription A. Policy 2 will deny resource creation in all Azure regions except East US. If you create a resource in Resource Group A in Subscription A, the resource can be created in the West US Azure region. In Resource Group B of Subscription A, any new resource is denied. In other words, with this set of policy assignments, you entirely deny resource creation in Resource Group B because the policy effects are cumulative. In this scenario, you would have to work with notScope, or policy exemptions to make sure that Resource Group B is exempted from the policy setting of Policy 1.

Also, overriding a policy setting with another setting might also lead to unexpected results. See the following example:

- **Policy 1:**
  - Assigned to Subscription A
  - Set the tag `Resource Owner` to the value IT
  - `Modify` effect
- **Policy 2:**
  - Assigned to Resource Group B
  - Set the tag `Resource Owner` to the value SOC
  - `Modify` effect

If you create a resource in Resource Group A of Subscription A, the resource will automatically get the tag `Resource Owner` set to IT. If you create the same resource in Resource Group B, the tag's value could be either IT or SOC, depending on which assignment is evaluated first/last.

> **MORE INFO** To learn more about scopes in Azure Policy, see *https://docs.microsoft.com/azure/governance/policy/concepts/scope.*

Regulatory standards and compliance

Governance might be one of the most important topics when it comes to security hygiene. You already learned that, with Azure Policy, you have a great tool to create guardrails within which your developers and resource administrators are allowed to move when it comes to resource creation.

Also, there might be legal restrictions and regulatory standards that apply to your organization, such as the Payment Card Industry Data Security Standard (PCI DSS) for organizations that handle credit cards, or ISO27001, an international standard on how to manage information security. Azure Policy contains several built-in initiative definitions, which can be used to determine your resources' compliance with particular compliance standards, as shown in Figure 4-21.

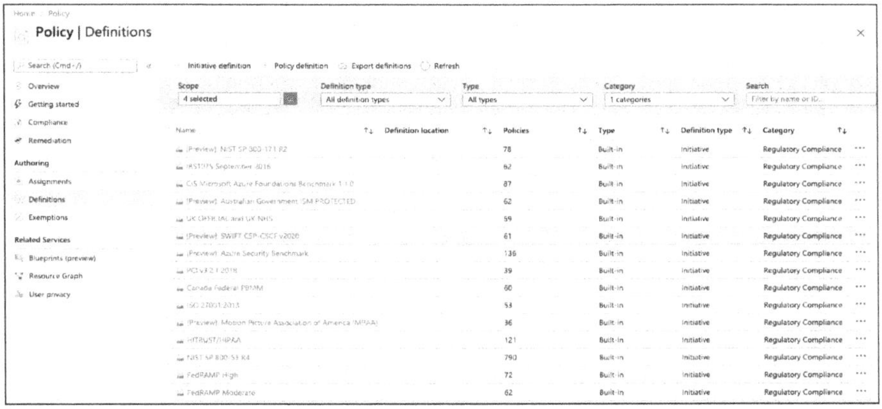

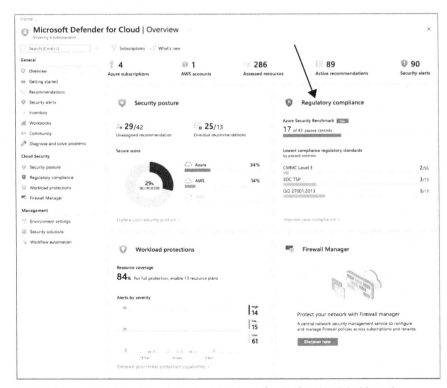

FIGURE 4-21 Regulatory Compliance policy initiatives in Azure Policy

You can assign these definitions directly to your management groups or subscriptions to see the results in the Azure Policy compliance dashboard, or you can leverage Microsoft Defender for Cloud to assess your resources' compliance with the standards that apply to your organization. Figure 4-22 shows the new Defender for Cloud main dashboard, with **Regulatory Compliance** as one of the four main tiles in the upper-right corner.

FIGURE 4-22 Regulatory Compliance in the main Defender for Cloud dashboard

Regulatory compliance in Microsoft Defender for Cloud

Under the hood, Defender for Cloud leverages the built-in policy initiatives to automatically assess resource compliance with a given compliance standard whenever possible. Azure Policy will only show resources as being compliant or non-compliant regarding a particular policy or initiative definition, but there are parts of the compliance standards that cannot automatically be assessed and therefore, are not represented in the respective initiative definition. Defender for Cloud adds more context to these standards, so you see both assessment results and the category in which these assessments belong.

> **TIP** Regulatory Compliance is part of Microsoft Defender for Cloud's enhanced capabilities. In order to get access to it, you need to enable Microsoft Defender for Cloud plans.

Figure 4-23 shows the Defender for Cloud regulatory compliance dashboard. The PCI DSS 3.2.1 standard is selected in this screenshot, and the compliance controls at the bottom of the page reflect this standard.

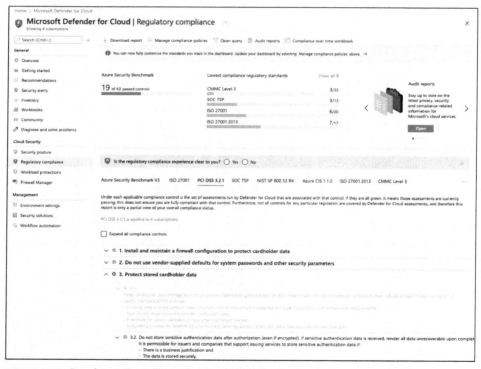

FIGURE 4-23 Regulatory Compliance dashboard in Defender for Cloud

If you open the compliance controls, you will see that each of these controls contains several sub-controls. Compliance controls can have three different states:

1. **Green circle with a checkmark** This state shows that all resources within the scope are compliant with this particular control.

2. **Red circle with a cross** This state shows that resources are non-compliant with regard to this particular control.

3. **Unavailable** Some controls and sub-controls are unavailable (grayed-out). These controls are the ones that currently cannot automatically be assessed and, therefore, Defender for Cloud cannot decide whether a particular rule is met. For instance, this might happen if a compliance control is focused on processes rather than resource configurations.

Moving a step deeper into the sub-controls, you will find the assessments that belong to the control. These assessments are based on the policies that are part of the respective regulatory compliance initiative definition. Figure 4-24 shows an assessment that is part of sub-control 3.2 in the PCI DSS 3.2.1 compliance standard, which is part of the main control 3. Protect stored cardholder data.

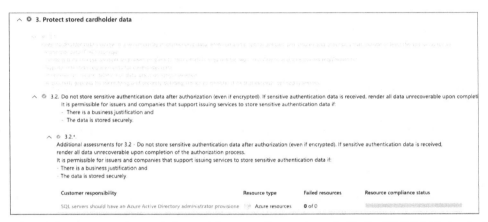

FIGURE 4-24 Assessment as part of a regulatory compliance sub-control in the PCI DSS 3.2.1 standard

If you compare the policies within the built-in compliance initiatives with the policies that are part of the Azure Security Benchmark initiative, you will see that some of these policies are the same, whereas others are different.

The Azure Security Benchmark is a curation of security best practices that will directly influence your Secure Score. In other words, if you take care of remediating recommendations generated based on these policies, your Secure Score will increase.

Regulatory compliance in Defender for Cloud offers another perspective. With regulatory compliance, you get a tool that helps you to focus on remediating findings that block you from achieving a particular compliance certification. If you remediate all findings within a compliance standard, your Secure Score might not even be touched, depending on which findings you are remediating. Also, remediating all findings within a particular compliance standard does not automatically mean that you will receive the respective certification. As you already learned, Defender for Cloud can only determine your environment's compliance if a compliance rule can automatically be assessed. However, the result that Defender for Cloud shows can be taken as evidence for your environment being compliant with the parts of the standard that can be determined automatically.

Defender for Cloud offers an easy way to create a report for any compliance standard that you have activated in your environment. To download the report, follow these steps:

1. Open the Azure portal and sign in with an account with **Security Admin** privileges.

2. Select **Defender For Cloud** from the navigation pane.

3. From the **Defender For Cloud** main dashboard, select **Regulatory Compliance** in the navigation pane. The compliance view you saw previously in Figure 4-23 appears. In the top menu, click the **Download Report** button.

4. Select the compliance standard for which you want to download a report from the list and click the **Download** button, as shown in Figure 4-25.

FIGURE 4-25   Downloading a compliance report from Azure Security Center

Customize your regulatory compliance experience

Microsoft Defender for Cloud will automatically activate the following four compliance standards in every subscription (or management group in case that's the scope of your Azure Security Benchmark assignment):

1. Azure Security Benchmark

2. PCI DSS 3.2.1

3. ISO 27001

4. SOC TSP

The decision has been made to activate these versus others because these four standards apply to most customers' environments. However, what's true for most environments is not necessarily true for your particular environment. That is why you can select the compliance standard(s) that should apply to your subscriptions. To customize this experience, follow these steps:

1. Open the Azure portal and sign in with an account that has **Subscription Owner** privileges.

2. Select **Defender For Cloud** from the navigation pane.

3. From the **Defender For Cloud** main dashboard, select **Environment Settings** in the navigation pane. Select your management group or subscription, then select **Security Policy** in the left navigation pane.

4. Click the **Disable** button for all standards you want to disable. If you want to add more built-in standards, click the **Add More Standards** button, as shown in Figure 4-26.

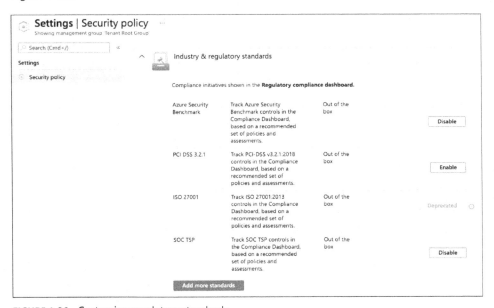

FIGURE 4-26 Customize regulatory standards

5. Select the compliance standard you want to add to your subscription and click the **Add** button, as shown in Figure 4-27.

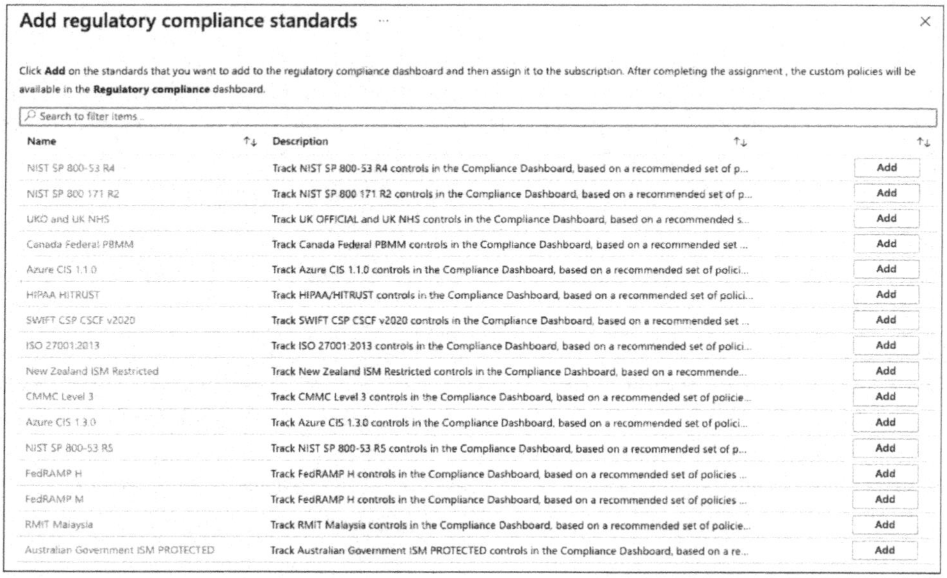

FIGURE 4-27   Select a compliance standard to add to your subscription

6. The **Policy Assignment** window appears. Make sure to fill in all information relevant to your environment, such as exclusions or parameters, and then click **Review+Create** > **Create**.

> **TIP**   It may take a few hours for a new compliance standard to appear in the regulatory compliance dashboard.

Build your own compliance initiative

You already learned how to add a custom policy initiative to Defender for Cloud to generate custom recommendations. This custom initiative will also show up in the regulatory compliance view, enabling you to get a more structured view of your policies. With a custom initiative in regulatory compliance, you can make sure you get a condensed view of only the policies that you want to focus on. Of course, you should always try to enhance your Secure Score by focusing on the most impactful recommendations. (This is covered in more detail in Chapter 5. However, if your governance concept demands further restrictions, building your own custom initiative is a great idea. To do that, follow these steps:

1. Open the Azure portal and sign in with an account that has **Subscription Owner** privileges.

2. In the search bar, type **Policy**, and then select **Policy**.

3. In the **Azure Policy** blade, select **Definitions** in the left pane.

4. From the top menu, click **+ Initiative Definition**.

5. Select the **Initiative Location** button. Remember: The initiative assignment is only available to resources at or below this location in the hierarchy.

6. Provide a **Name** and an informative **Description**, so others can easily figure out what is the purpose of your new initiative.

7. Select a **Category**. It is best practice to create a custom category, such as **Contoso**, so you can easily filter initiative and policy definitions if needed.

8. Set the **Version** of your initiative. Your configuration should now look similar to Figure 4-28. Then click **Policies** in the top menu.

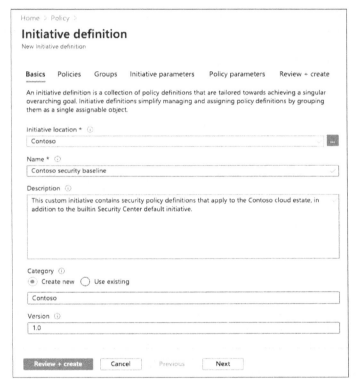

FIGURE 4-28 Basic configuration when creating a new initiative definition

9. Click the **Add Policy Definition(s)** button on the **Policies** page. Select all the policy definitions you want to add to your custom initiative. Once you have added all relevant policy definitions, select **Groups** from the top menu.

10. Groups help you to organize policies within an initiative. Furthermore, groups are used to reflect the different settings in the regulatory compliance dashboard within Defender for Cloud. Create as many groups as you need within your initiative definition. Make sure to use informative names and descriptions because this information is shown in the **Regulatory Compliance** dashboard that helps others understand how you have grouped your policy definitions.

11. Then navigate back to **Policies** in the top menu.

12. Select all policy definitions that you want to add to one group. Then click the **Add Selected Policies To A Group** button and select the particular group(s). You can add every policy definition to one or several groups. Go ahead with the rest of your policy definitions until you have added all of them to at least one group. Your view should now look similar to Figure 4-29.

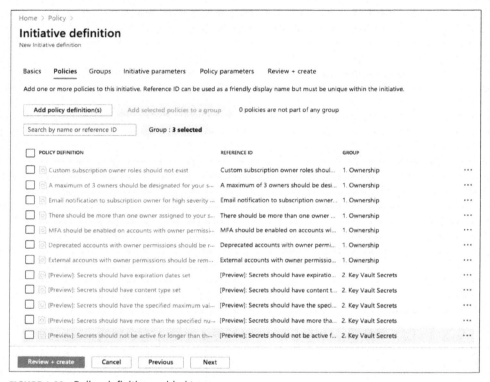

FIGURE 4-29 Policy definitions added to groups

13. You can now add **Initiative Parameters** and **Policy Parameters** by clicking the respective menu if needed, or you can click **Review+Create** > **Create**.

14. Now, you can assign the new initiative in Defender for Cloud, following the steps outlined earlier in this chapter.

The assignment is now created, but it may take a few hours until you will see its results as custom recommendations in the **All Recommendations** blade and as a new compliance standard in the **Regulatory Compliance** dashboard, as shown in Figure 4-30.

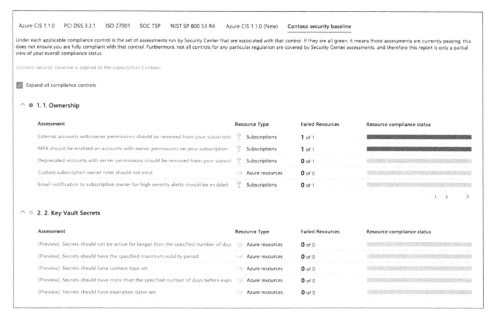

FIGURE 4-30 Your custom initiative in the Regulatory Compliance dashboard

> **MORE INFO** To learn more about custom security policies, see *https://aka.ms/ MDFCCustomPolicies*.

Creating custom assessments for AWS and GCP

Other than Azure resources, AWS and GCP do not rely on Azure Resource Manager. With that, there is no way to leverage Azure Policy for auditing resources from other clouds for resource compliance. That's why the new AWS and GCP connectors have a new capability that lets you build custom assessments via the Azure Resource Graph, which is KQL (Kusto Query Language).

When leveraging Azure Policy to assess Azure resources for compliance, there are three different configurations that need to be created:

1. **Policy definition** A *policy definition* contains one or several rules to define resource compliance.

2. **Initiative definition** An *initiative definition* contains one or several policy definitions.

3. **Initiative assignment** An *initiative assignment* will assign the initiative definition to a scope.

For custom assessments in AWS and GCP, there also are three different configurations that need to exist:

1. **Assessment** An *assessment* contains assessment details, such as name description, severity, the assessment logic in KQL, and information about the standard it belongs to.

2. **Standard** A *standard* groups several assessments.

3. **Standard assignment** A *standard assignment* defines the scope the standard will evaluate, which can be AWS accounts or GCP projects.

As you will see, a standard within the scope of Defender for Cloud's multi-cloud capabilities is similar to an initiative, whereas an assessment will contain the actual "audit rule" to assess a resource for compliance, so it's comparable to a policy definition. Figure 4-31 shows built-in standards for AWS that will automatically be available once you create a new AWS connector.

FIGURE 4-31 Built-in standards for AWS resources

The AWS Foundational Security Best Practices standard is automatically enabled once you create a new AWS connector. It is the standard that is used for creating CSPM recommendations and will influence an AWS account's Secure Score. AWS CIS 1.2.0 and AWS PCI DSS 3.2.1 are regulatory compliance standards that, once enabled, will reflect their status in Defender for Cloud's Regulatory Compliance dashboard.

> **TIP** Compliance standards in AWS and GCP are part of Defender for Cloud's enhanced capabilities. Although they are available once a connector has been created, you need to enable an additional Defender plan besides security posture management on the connector to assign compliance standards.

On a GCP connector, you will find similar default and compliance standards, as shown in Figure 4-32. GCP Default is the standard that is being used similarly to Azure Security Benchmark and AWS Foundational Security Best Practices. It contains all assessments that will create security recommendations and influence Secure Score. GCP CIS 1.1.0 and GCP CIS 1.2.0 are compliance standards that can be assigned to the GCP connector to reflect in Defender for Cloud's Regulatory Compliance dashboard.

FIGURE 4-32   Built-in standards for GCP resources

Besides these built-in standards, which contain a variety of built-in assessments, you can also build your own standards and assessments. To start, follows these steps:

1. Open the Azure portal and sign in with a user who has Security Admin privileges.
2. Open **Microsoft Defender For Cloud**.
3. In the left navigation pane, click **Environment Settings**.
4. Select the AWS account or GCP project you want to create a custom assessment for.
5. In the left navigation pane, select **Standards**.
6. In the top navigation, select **+ Add**, and then select **Assessment**.
7. In the **Add Assessment** view, select the **New Assessment** option button.
8. At the least, you need to enter mandatory information, such as a **Name** and **Severity**. Also, you can select an **Assessment Template**, which will then show the underlying **Query**, as shown in Figure 4-33.
9. You can now adjust the query according to your needs and test it with dummy data in Azure Data Explorer by clicking the corresponding link underneath your query. Once you're done, click **Save**. You will now be back in the **Standards** view.

Add assessment   ✕
Scope 'TomAWSDemo'

Description

This is a demo assessment for our latest Defender for Cloud book project.

Remediation description

Write a remediation description

Severity *

Low   ⌄

Query

Assessment template *

MFA should be enabled for the "root" account   ⌄

Query * ⓘ

let ExtendedSummaryMap = Iam_SummaryMap | extend ConnectorId =   ✓
tostring(RecordProviderInfo.ConnectorId) | extend HealthStatus =
iff(Record.AccountMFAEnabled != 1, 'UNHEALTHY', 'HEALTHY'); Aws_Account |
extend ConnectorId = tostring(RecordProviderInfo.ConnectorId) | join kind=inner
ExtendedSummaryMap on ConnectorId

Azure Data Explorer >

Scope

[Save]   [Cancel]

FIGURE 4-33   A KQL query in a custom assessment

Once your assessment has been created, you can go ahead and add it to a new standard. To do so, follow these steps:

1. In the top navigation pane, select **+ Add**, and then select **Standard**.

2. In the **Add Standard** view, select **New Standard** and enter a **Name** and **Description**.

3. Select the custom assessment you just created from the **Assessments** dropdown.

4. Click **Save**.

5. You can now assign your custom standard to your account/project. To do so, right-click the standard and select **Assign Standard**, as shown in Figure 4-34. Confirm your selection by clicking **Yes**.

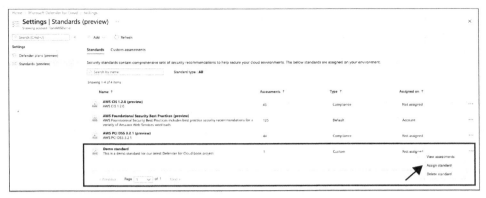

FIGURE 4-34 A custom standard being assigned

Once assigned, all assessments in your custom standard will start to evaluate AWS (or GCP) resources and then create security recommendations in Defender for Cloud. The data source for the underlying KQL query is Azure Data Explorer. When creating the AWS or GCP connector, Microsoft Defender for Cloud will start retrieving information from the third-party cloud's REST APIs and store it in an Azure Data Explorer instance. When creating an assessment query, this query will work against this instance.

> **TIP** To learn more about how to create custom assessments in GCP, see *https://aka.ms/ MDFCGcpCustomAssessments*.

Now that you know how recommendations are created in Defender for Cloud, we will focus on improving your security posture in the next chapter.

Chapter 5

Strengthening your security posture

During the last couple of years, supply chain attacks, such as Solorigate, reinforced both the importance of having a vulnerability-management system and the fact that many computers are not fully updated and do not use the most secure configuration. As you already learned in Chapter 1, "Threat landscape," the COVID-19 pandemic even amplified these observations and presented new challenges. What all these challenges and observations have in common is that security hygiene today is one of the most important topics when it comes to protecting IT resources. A security assessment is critical to identifying the current security state of your assets and what you need to do to improve it. Microsoft Defender for Cloud can perform a security assessment for all major workloads: compute, network, storage, and applications. The result of these security assessments is a set of recommendations that will help you enhance the security posture of your workloads.

In this chapter, you will learn how to use Defender for Cloud to perform a security assessment for major workloads and how to use the result of this assessment to improve your defense system.

Driving security posture improvement using Secure Score

When working in a cloud environment, monitoring the security state of multiple workloads can be challenging. How do you know if your security posture across all workloads is at the highest possible level? Are there any security recommendations that you are not meeting? These are hard questions to answer when you don't have the right visibility and tools to manage the security aspects of your cloud infrastructure.

Microsoft Defender for Cloud reviews your security recommendations across all workloads, applies advanced algorithms to determine how critical each recommendation is, and calculates your Secure Score based on them. Secure Score helps you to assess your workload security posture from a single dashboard. You can view the overall Secure Score in the Defender for Cloud's Overview dashboard, as shown in Figure 5-1.

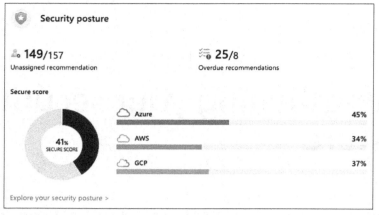

FIGURE 5-1 Overall Secure Score of your workloads assessed by Defender for Cloud

The overall Secure Score shown in the main dashboard's **Security Posture** tile is an accumulation of all your security control scores. Keep in mind that this score can vary because it reflects the subscription that is currently selected and the resources that belong to that subscription. If you have multiple subscriptions selected, the calculation will be for all subscriptions. The active recommendations on the selected subscription also make this score change. For example, as shown previously in Figure 5-1, the current overall Secure Score of this environment is 31 percent, while numbers vary between Azure (45 percent), AWS (34 percent), and GCP (37 percent). To access more details about your Secure Score, click the **Explore Your Security Posture** option in the Security posture tile. This will lead you to the **Security Posture** blade, as shown in Figure 5-2.

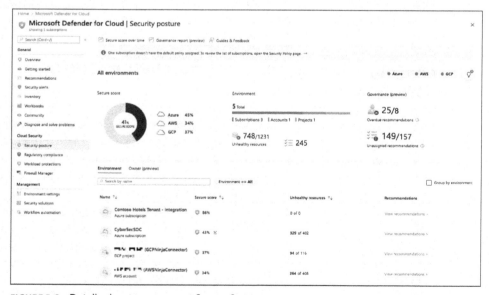

FIGURE 5-2 Details about your current Secure Score

This dashboard provides a better visualization of which Azure subscriptions, AWS accounts, and GCP projects have the lowest scores. Also, this dashboard provides a per-environment breakdown of Secure Scores. From this view, you can see that the Contoso Hotels Tenant—Integration subscription has a Secure Score of 86 percent, whereas other subscriptions have only 34 to 43 percent. Next to the **Environments** tab, you can select the **Owner** (preview) tab, which gives you an overview of recommendations assigned per owner. This capability is part of the new security governance experience we will discuss later in this chapter.

From the **Environment** tab, you can click the **View Recommendations** option to see all recommendations for a particular subscription, account, or project. If you would rather see recommendations and controls for your entire environment, click the **Recommendations** button in Defender for Cloud's main navigation pane, as shown in Figure 5-3.

FIGURE 5-3 Recommendations and controls that have a direct impact on the Secure Score

Secure Score calculation is based on a max score that is assigned to a particular *security control*, in which recommendations are gathered. In Figure 5-3, you see the **Enable MFA** security control with a max score of 10 points and a current score of 1.12 points. These numbers may change when applying an Environment filter. Figure 5-4 shows the same environment with AWS and GCP removed from the view. On the top-right corner, you can see filter buttons to add/remove a particular cloud environment from the overall view.

To increase your Secure Score, *all* recommendations within a security control that apply to a particular resource need to be remediated. For example, let's take a closer look at the **Secure Management Ports** security control of another environment. In Figure 5-5, you can see that it contains several recommendations, some of which already have been remediated as indicated by the Completed flag, whereas others still need to be addressed, such as the **Management Ports Should Be Closed On Your Virtual Machines** recommendation, that applies to four of seven virtual machines in this particular environment.

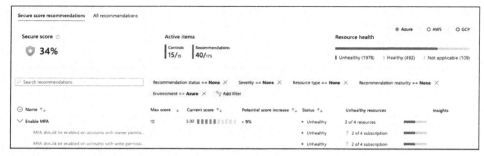

FIGURE 5-4 Secure score when AWS and GCP are removed from the view

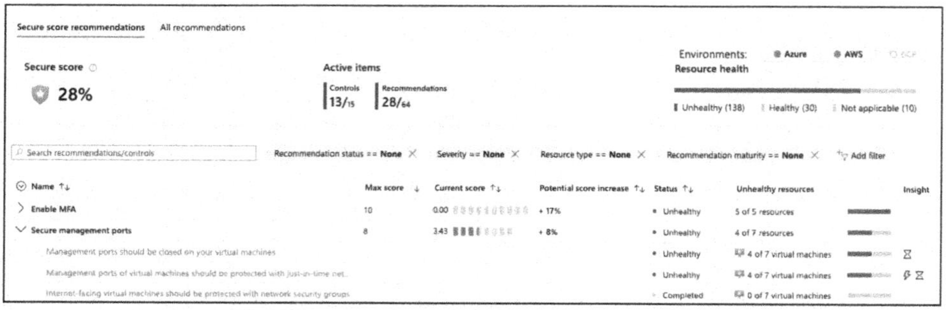

FIGURE 5-5 Recommendations within the Secure Management Ports control

The **Secure Management Ports** security control weighs a total of 8 points toward your Secure Score once all recommendations are remediated. In this particular environment, there is a potential score increase of +8 percent. The total number of points in a control is static, whereas the percentage toward your Secure Score depends on your environment because the total maximum number of points you can receive depends on the type of resources you have deployed to your subscriptions. Figure 5-5 also shows the **Management Ports Of Virtual Machines Should Be Protected With Just-In-Time Network Access Control** recommendation, which is flagged as a preview recommendation (shown by the lightning symbol in the **Insight** column).

Preview recommendations won't affect your Secure Score as long as they are in preview. In other words, if you remediate all the other recommendations from Figure 5-5 and do not take care of the preview recommendation, you will still get 8 points toward your overall Secure Score. But be aware that once this particular recommendation no longer has a preview status, it will count and then your Secure Score will decrease if you do not take care of remediating it. So, preview recommendations should still be remediated wherever possible to ensure they will not negatively impact your Secure Score once the preview period ends.

> **MORE INFO** Microsoft will announce these and other breaking changes in the Defender for Cloud documentation before they apply. To learn more, see *https:// aka.ms/MDFCUpcomingChanges*.

To calculate the Secure Score influence per resource, the maximum total number of 8 points for this particular control is divided by the total number of affected resources. In the example above, there is a total of 8 points to be assigned to seven virtual machines, so every machine counts 1.14 points toward the overall Secure Score if all recommendations in that control are remediated. Therefore the current score shown in Figure 5-5 is 3.43 points (3 x 1.14). If there were eight machines, every resource would count 1 point; if there were 16 machines, each would be worth 0.5 points. Remember that the Secure Score in a control will only increase once you have remediated all recommendations that apply to a particular resource.

> **MORE INFO**   To learn more about Secure Score calculation, see *https://aka.ms/ MDFCSecureScoreCalculation*.

Fine-tuning your Secure Score

While Secure Score can be utilized to support your organization in enhancing its security posture, there will be some scenarios in which not all recommendations are applicable to your environment. It is common to have customers asking to fine-tune those recommendations; they ask because there are items they consider to be false positives.

Organizations commonly use a third-party MFA solution for subscription accounts with access permissions, and the organizations believe they can safely ignore the recommendations within the **Enable MFA** security control. However, because the organizations are not addressing these recommendations, there is a 10-point drop in their Secure Score. How can they safely disable these recommendations?

If you are absolutely sure that this security control's intent has been addressed by implementing an external factor that is not being taken into consideration by Defender for Cloud, you can follow the steps described in Chapter 4, "Policy management," to disable the policies that reflect your desired recommendations.

Using resource exemptions

Disabling a security policy on a subscription or management group is a good way to make sure that recommendations that entirely do not apply to your environment are removed from the Secure Score calculation. However, a frequent customer demand is to have a more granular option for exempting resources from a particular recommendation. For example, you have a test environment for which you accept the risk of being exposed, or if some of your VMs are protected by an endpoint protection solution which Microsoft Defender for Cloud does not track, whereas others are protected by Microsoft Defender for Endpoint. Leveraging *policy exemptions*, an Azure Policy capability you learned about in Chapter 4, Defender for Cloud comes with resource exemptions, which you can use to fine-tune the set of recommendations that apply to your particular environment more granular. You can create a resource exemption in Defender for Cloud when working with recommendations. Figure 5-6 shows the **Storage Account Public Access Should Be Disallowed** recommendation. When you take a closer look at the recommendation, you see there is already one exempted resource.

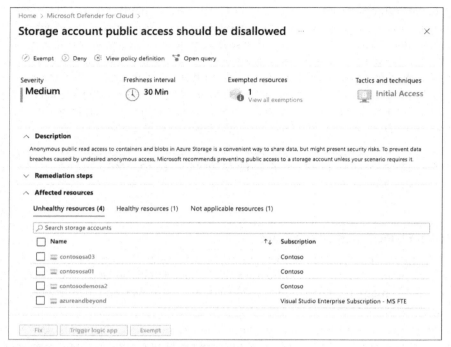

Storage account public access should be disallowed ... ✕

⊘ Exempt ⊘ Deny ⊙ View policy definition ⊸ Open query

Severity	Freshness interval	Exempted resources	Tactics and techniques
Medium	⏱ **30 Min**	**1** View all exemptions	🖥 **Initial Access**

∧ **Description**

Anonymous public read access to containers and blobs in Azure Storage is a convenient way to share data, but might present security risks. To prevent data breaches caused by undesired anonymous access, Microsoft recommends preventing public access to a storage account unless your scenario requires it.

∨ **Remediation steps**

∧ **Affected resources**

Unhealthy resources (4)   Healthy resources (1)   Not applicable resources (1)

🔍 Search storage accounts

☐ Name	↑↓	Subscription
☐ ▦ contososa03		Contoso
☐ ▦ contososa01		Contoso
☐ ▦ contosodemosa2		Contoso
☐ ▦ azureandbeyond		Visual Studio Enterprise Subscription - MS FTE

[Fix] [Trigger logic app] [Exempt]

FIGURE 5-6 Exempted resources in a recommendation

If you look at the **Affected Resources** section, you see that there are four unhealthy resources, one healthy resource, and one not applicable resource. Once you create an exemption for a resource, the resource is moved from unhealthy status to not applicable. To create a new exemption, follow these steps:

1. Open the Azure portal and sign in with a user who has Security Admin privileges.

2. In the top search bar, enter **Defender**, and then click **Microsoft Defender For Cloud**.

3. In the **Defender For Cloud** navigation pane, select **Recommendations**.

4. Open a security control and click the recommendation for which you want to create a resource exemption.

5. In the recommendation's details view, look for the resource for which you want to create an exemption, select the resource, and click **Exempt**.

6. Select the scope you want to create the exemption on—single resource(s), subscription(s), or management group(s)—enter an **Exemption Name**, and define whether and when the exemption will expire. There are two **Exemption Categories**:

   - **Mitigated**   Select **Mitigated** if the policy's intent has been met by a process not tracked by Defender for Cloud.

   - **Waiver**   Select **Waiver** if your organization has decided to (temporarily) accept the risk of not mitigating the recommendation's intent.

7. Finally, enter an **Exemption Description** that explains the reason for creating the exemption. Then, click **Create** to finish creating the exemption, as shown in Figure 5-7.

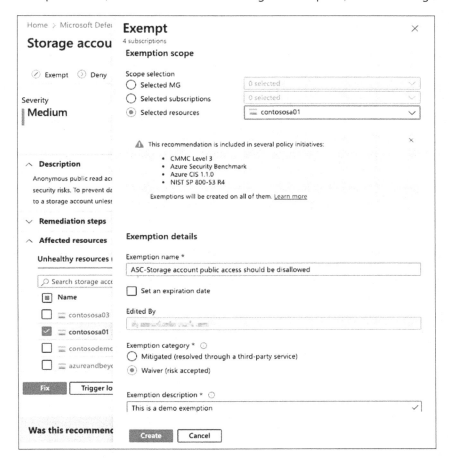

FIGURE 5-7 Create a new resource exemption

In the last section of this chapter, we will take a look at how to build automation artifacts around the resource exemption capability.

Using APIs and Continuous Export to create reports

Secure Score, as it is presented in Microsoft Defender for Cloud, gives you a point in time overview about your current security posture, while customers keep asking for a capability that enables you to keep track of Secure Score changes. You might want to be informed when your Secure Score drops, or you might want to see a progress over time.

Defender for Cloud gives you access to all its information based on the Microsoft.Security REST API provider, and so there is a Secure Score operation group as part of the API provider that lets you pull the Secure Score information for any or all subscription(s) within your environment, anytime you want. What sounds like just another API opens a lot of ways for you to build automations upon. In the following section, you will learn more about some of these automations that you can find in the Microsoft Defender for Cloud Community GitHub.

> **MORE INFO** You can find the Defender for Cloud GitHub repository at *https://aka.ms/MDFCGithub*.

Also, Defender for Cloud offers a *Continuous Export* capability that allows you to regularly export alerts, recommendations, regulatory compliance, and Secure Score information to either an Azure Event Hub or a Log Analytics workspace (or both). Continuous Export will automatically send this information to the respective endpoint (Event Hub or Log Analytics workspace) every time Defender generates a new alert or recommendation for Cloud, a regulatory compliance status changes, or your Secure Score changes. You can use this capability for different purposes. Exporting alerts and recommendations to an Azure Event Hub is a great option if you want to feed your third-party SIEM solution, whereas exporting to a Log Analytics workspace allows you to generate overtime reports to track changes in your environment.

> **MORE INFO** You can find further information about the Continuous Export capability at *https://aka.ms/ContinuousExport*.

In the following section, we cover the configuration of Continuous Export for Secure Score data.

Get Secure Score data

With the `SecureScores` API provider, you can pull Secure Score information for a particular subscription whenever you want. The result will always present the current Secure Score to the particular point in time when pulling the information. Figure 5-8 shows the JSON result when executing a `GET` request against the `Microsoft.Security/secureScores/ascScore` API to get the Secure Score information for a subscription.

```
"id": "/subscriptions/        /providers/Microsoft.Security/secureScores/ascScore",
"name": "ascScore",
"type": "Microsoft.Security/secureScores",
"properties": {
    "displayName": "ASC score",
    "score": {
        "max": 56,
        "current": 17.49,
        "percentage": 0.3123
    },
    "weight": 293
}
```

FIGURE 5-8 Result of pulling Secure Score information from the SecureScores API provider

You can see that the result contains the following information:

- **Maximum points that can currently be achieved, depending on the resource types that are deployed**   56
- **Current points**   17.49
- **Current percentage calculated based on current points divided by total points**   0.3123 (=31.23%)

If you compare these results with the Contoso subscription's Secure Score in Defender for Cloud, you realize that these numbers are the same, as you can see in Figure 5-9.

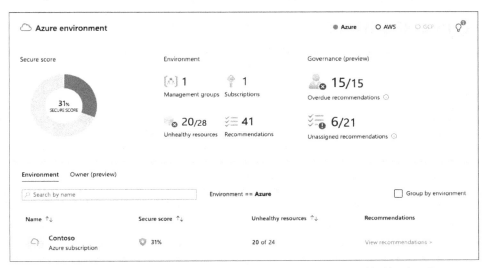

FIGURE 5-9   Secure Score results in Defender for Cloud are the same as provided by the API

Using this API, you can store the current results in an EventHub, Log Analytics workspace, database, and so on. In the Defender for Cloud GitHub, you find a LogicApp called Get-SecureScoreData that will query all your subscriptions for their Secure Score information once a day and store it in a Log Analytics workspace. This Logic App is a great automation artifact for starting other automations built on top of the data stored in Log Analytics.

> **MORE INFO**   You can find the Get-SecureScoreData Logic App at *https://aka.ms/ MDfCGetSecureScoreData.*

Secure Score Continuous Export

With Continuous Export, Defender for Cloud has a built-in capability to export recommendations, alerts, and Secure Score information to either a Log Analytics workspace or an Azure Event Hub (or both), so you can build further automations on top of this data. Continuous

Export is always configured on a subscription level, so you need to create a Continuous Export configuration for all subscriptions for which you want to export security data. To enable Continuous Export of Secure Score data, follow these steps:

1. Open the Azure portal and sign in with a user who has Security Admin privileges.

2. In the search bar, enter **Defender**, and then click **Microsoft Defender For Cloud**.

3. In the left navigation pane, select **Environment Settings**.

4. Select the subscription on which you want to enable Continuous Export, and then click **Continuous Export** in the left navigation pane.

5. Determine if you want to export the data to an existing **Event Hub** or **Log Analytics Workspace** by selecting the respective tab.

6. For the **Exported Data Types**, select **Secure Score**.

7. You can export the **Overall Score**, **Control Score**, or both. When you select **Control Score**, you can choose the **Controls** you want to export, as shown in Figure 5-10.

FIGURE 5-10   Select which Secure Score scope you want to export

8. Make sure to configure **Export Configuration** and **Export Target** as explained in the screen, and then click **Save**.

Once the configuration has been saved, Defender for Cloud will automatically take care of exporting changes in your Secure Score. If you have configured export to a Log Analytics workspace, you can then, for example, start building an Azure Monitor Workbook based on the data stored in the workspace. In the next section, you will learn about a built-in workbook that leverages Continuous Export to show an environment's Secure Score over time.

Secure Score over time report

One of the various built-in workbooks integrated with Defender for Cloud and which you can find in the **Workbooks** tab of Defender for Cloud's main navigation pane is the **Secure Score Over Time** report. The workbook relies on the overall score and control score information, which is stored in a Log Analytics workspace, by leveraging Continuous Export. The workbook enables you to track Secure Score changes over time, overall trends, and trends per security control. Figure 5-11 shows the main Secure Score Summary dashboard.

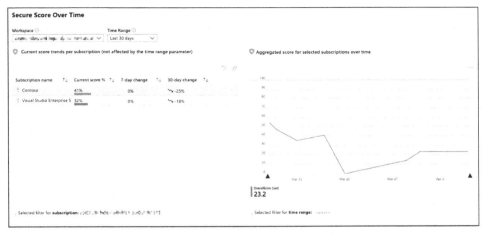

FIGURE 5-11 Secure Score Over Time report summary dashboard

Notify on Secure Score downgrade

Secure Score is the main KPI to express your environment's security status. With the Secure Score Over Time workbook, you have good visibility about your trend, so you can see how you are doing in improving your organization's security posture. However, when it comes to a sudden decrease, as might happen when you deploy insecure resources (resources that are not deployed as secure by default), you might want to be notified in addition to seeing it in a dashboard.

You already know that by using the SecureScores API provider, you can regularly export a subscription's Secure Score. If you compare the latest Secure Score with the score from a previous export, you can react to a decreasing Secure Score and receive a notification using a Logic App that runs once a day. In the Defender for Cloud GitHub repository, you can find a Logic App sample that will send you an email once your Secure Score drops by a configurable percentage (such as 5 percent).

> **MORE INFO** You can find the Logic App sample to get a notification once your subscription's Secure Score decreases in the ASC GitHub at *https://aka.ms/ ASCBook-SecureScoreDrop.*

Remediating recommendations

Misconfigurations, lack of security expertise, and lack of visibility are the most common reasons for being vulnerable to attacks. You already know that Defender for Cloud recommendations are based on security policies which are used to assess your environment. Recommendations are the result of these assessments, they give you an overview of where and why your environment is vulnerable. Grouped by security controls, Microsoft Defender for Cloud will show you the most impactful recommendations at the top of the list, as shown in Figure 5-12.

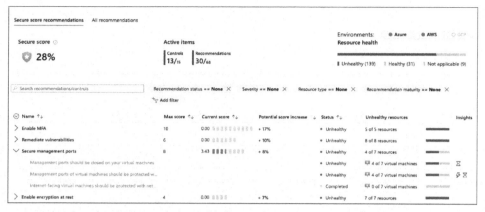

FIGURE 5-12 Security recommendations with filter options, grouped by controls, and ordered by potential Secure Score increase

Also, Defender for Cloud provides you with several filtering options that help you to focus on recommendations and controls that are more important for your environment than others. The following filtering options are available:

- **Control Status**   This option lets you filter for security controls with the following status types: active, completed, not applicable.

- **Recommendation Status**   This option filters for active, completed, or not applicable recommendations.

- **Recommendation Maturity**   This option lets you decide to focus on GA and/or Preview recommendations.

- **Quick Fix Available**   This option lets you select recommendations that only have a Quick Fix capability. Quick Fix helps you easily remediate a particular recommendation for one, some, or all unhealthy resources. This capability uses a built-in remediation process. You will see how to use Quick Fix in action in one of the following sections.

- **Contains Exemption**   This option helps you to filter for recommendations that do or do not contain resource exemptions.

- **Resource Types**   This is a filter to select recommendations that apply to one, several, or all types of resources. This filter will change according to the types of resources you have deployed in your environment.

- **Severity**   This option filters for recommendations with low, medium, or high severity.

- **Initiative**   This filter lets you filter for recommendations that belong to a particular policy initiative, such as Azure Security Benchmark or a custom initiative you have added to your environment.

- **Tactics** Defender for Cloud has added a MITRE ATT&CK Tactics and Techniques mapping to its recommendations. The **Tactics** filter lets you filter for recommendations that are mapped to one, several, or all of the 15 tactics.

- **Environment** The **Environment** filter lets you filter for recommendations that belong to Azure, AWS, and/or GCP, depending on which environment you have connected to your Defender for Cloud estate.

- **Recommendation Type** This option lets you filter for built-in and custom recommendations.

- **Insights** This option lets you filter for recommendations that have additional capabilities, such as Deny, Enforce, or Quick Fix.

- **Resource Group** This filter helps you to focus on resources that belong to a particular resource group.

- **AWS Account** and **GCP Project** These filters help you to only show recommendations that belong to a particular AWS account or GCP connector.

Microsoft Defender for Cloud groups recommendations into 15 controls that make up a total maximum Secure Score of 58 points, which equals 100 percent. Table 5-1 shows all 15 security controls with their maximum scores.

TABLE 5-1 Security Controls and their maximum Secure Score impact

Control	Max score
Enable MFA	10
Secure management ports	8
Apply system updates	6
Remediate vulnerabilities	6
Enable encryption at rest	4
Encrypt data in transit	4
Manage access and permissions	4
Remediate security configurations	4
Restrict unauthorized network access	4
Adaptive application control	3
Enable endpoint protection	2
Protect application against DDoS attacks	2
Enable auditing and logging	1
Enable enhanced security features	Not scored
Implement security best practices	Not scored

The higher the potential Secure Score impact, the more important it is to remediate recommendations within a particular control. In order to start remediating recommendations and controls, it is a good idea to start with the recommendations at the top of the list; doing so will make the biggest difference between secure and insecure configurations. In the following sections, you will learn more about the ideas and recommendations behind these security controls.

Enable multi-factor authentication (MFA)

Back when servers were only installed in your own datacenters, it was a good approach to protect your network and physical boundaries from unauthorized access. Today, however, organizations are no longer providing IT access only from their own offices to their own datacenters. Data is shared across organizations, resource access is allowed from home, the airport, or a restaurant, and identities are stored in the cloud. Today, most security incidents start with an identity-based attack. Just one compromised account is enough for attackers to get access to your environment, and once they're in, they start moving laterally, elevating their access, and doing what they've come for.

Passwords are one of the main problems with identity-based attacks. And while no one likes passwords, attackers sure do because it's relatively easy to use them as the weakest link in an attack chain. Unique and complex passwords are hard to memorize for hundreds of applications, so users tend to reuse their passwords and create them based on personal information they can easily remember, such as names of dear people or favorite sports teams. All of these make passwords an easy way for attackers to steal user identities.

The use of multifactor authentication for Azure Active Directory-based accounts is an easy but powerful step toward protecting your corporate identities from unauthorized access. Nearly all (99.9 percent) of successful identity-based attacks can be prevented by enabling MFA. That's why the Enable MFA is the only security control with a maximum Secure Score impact of 10 points, making it the most impactful control of all. The control contains several recommendations that relate to Azure MFA, not a third-party MFA provider. However, if you're absolutely sure that the control's intent has been met by a third-party solution that Defender for Cloud is not tracking, you can disable the corresponding security policies, as you've already learned in "Fine-tuning your Secure Score" earlier in this chapter. Also, you will see MFA recommendations for multi-cloud environments once you onboarded them to Defender for Cloud, as shown in Figure 5-13.

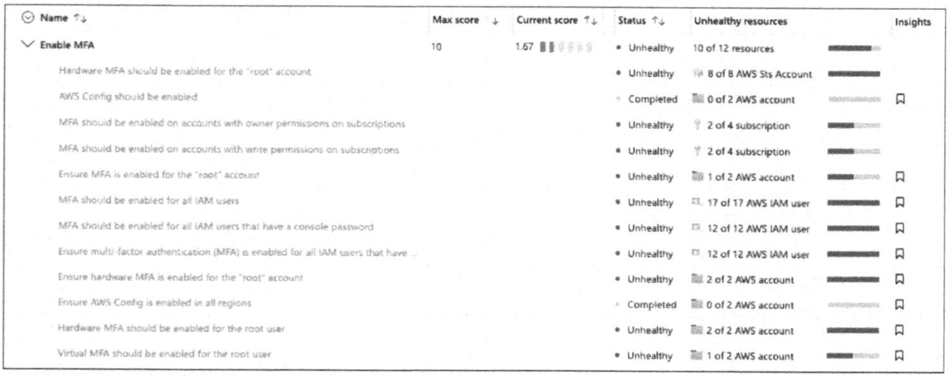

FIGURE 5-13 Enable MFA contains recommendations for Azure subscriptions and AWS accounts

Defender for Cloud will assess all subscriptions within its scope for accounts that have either read, write, or owner permissions. If one account with subscription-wide access does not have

MFA enabled, the whole subscription's recommendation will appear as Unhealthy. Today, Defender for Cloud looks at Conditional Access policies and Security Defaults to determine whether an account is MFA-enabled.

Security Defaults is a set of free identity-security protections for your Azure AD tenant, including the following settings:

- Require all users to register for Azure AD Multi-Factor Authentication
- Require administrators to perform multi-factor authentication
- Block legacy authentication protocols
- Require users to perform multi-factor authentication when necessary
- Protect privileged activities, such as access to the Azure portal

To activate Security Defaults, follow these steps:

1. Open the Azure portal and sign in with a user who has **Azure AD Global Administrator** privileges.
2. In the search bar, enter **Azure Active Directory**, and then click the respective option.
3. In the Azure AD navigation pane, select **Properties**. Click the **Manage Security Defaults** link.
4. Move the **Enable Security Defaults** toggle switch to **Yes** and click **Save**.

> **MORE INFO**   To learn more about Security Defaults, see *https://aka.ms/MDfCSecurityDefaults*.

Conditional Access policies help you to fine-tune the MFA behavior within your organization. Conditional Access is a premium Azure AD Identity Protection feature, which requires Azure AD Premium P2 licenses. It is important to understand that you can only use one of the two mentioned ways (Security Defaults and Conditional Access) to enforce the usage of MFA within your organization. Once you activate Security Defaults, you'll no longer be able to configure Conditional Access policies, and once you have configured a Conditional Access policy, you cannot activate Security Defaults.

> **MORE INFO**   To learn more about Conditional Access, see *https://aka.ms/ASCBook-ConditionalAccess*.

Once you have enforced MFA on all accounts that have access rights to a subscription, it can take up to 12 hours for the change to reflect in Defender for Cloud's recommendations.

Manage access and permissions

In addition to making sure your identities are protected from credential theft attacks, you should also keep in mind that with great power comes great responsibility. Accounts with elevated and far-reaching access rights are valuable targets for bad actors and, therefore, should be protected in a special way. But security issues can also occur when an account has access rights to resources they should not be allowed to work with. The **Manage Access And Permissions** control is focused on the principle of least privilege, which says that access rights will always reflect the level of necessity. This control counts as 4 points toward your overall Secure Score, as shown in Figure 5-14.

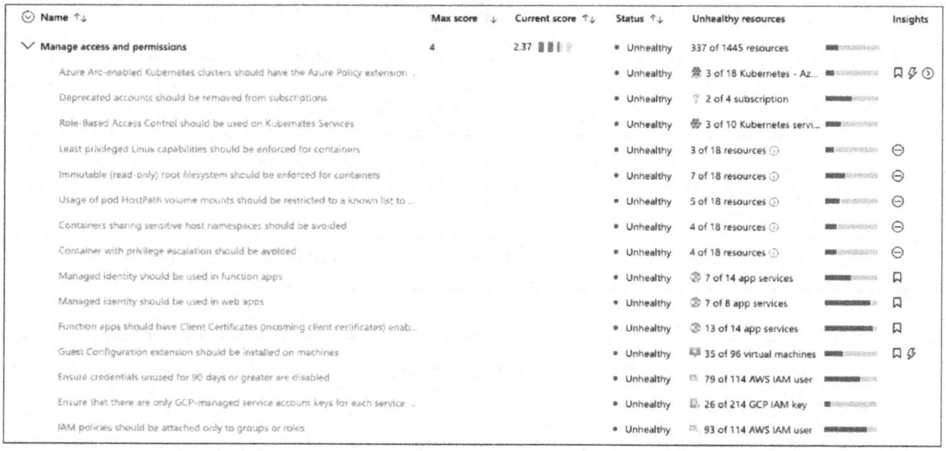

FIGURE 5-14 Manage access and permissions

For security purposes, it is good practice not to give elevated access rights, such as owner or write permissions on the subscription level, to external accounts. External accounts in this context are accounts that are not part of your organization's Azure Active Directory tenant. Also, deprecated accounts should be removed from your subscription's access control list. These are accounts that have been blocked from signing in. These accounts can be targets for attackers looking for ways to access your data without being noticed.

Regarding subscription ownership, it is best practice to have more than one (but not more than three) accounts with owner permissions. If you only have one account with that level of access, that might become an issue if the account is compromised or if the account owner joins another team or leaves your organization. However, you shouldn't have more than three account owners because owner rights are not needed for everyday jobs besides granting access rights.

With the integration of container security and third-party cloud environments, Defender for Cloud also provides recommendations for these environments. For example, it is best practice to avoid privilege escalation in containers, and sensitive host namespaces shouldn't be shared across containers. Using managed identities to access resources and information is another best practice that applies to App Services environments. To reduce your attack surface, you should think about disabling credentials that have not been used for 90 days or more. Depending on your environment, there can be quite a few recommendations that need to be taken care of, and doing so can become overwhelming. This is where security governance comes into play. Security governance is a new capability in Defender for Cloud that we discuss later in this chapter.

Recommendations and controls focused on compute

In Chapter 3, "Onboarding Microsoft Defender for Cloud," you learned about the Log Analytics agent, and how it performs security assessments. As part of your onboarding process, you should make sure to address all recommendations that have a higher impact on your Secure Score. First, evaluate all other recommendations and apply the recommendations according to your environment's needs.

Some recommendations require system downtime, such as applying certain security updates or remediating vulnerabilities that have been found on a machine. This means that after you identify the changes that need to be made in the target system, you may need to start a change-control process to maintain compliance with the security assessment.

> **IMPORTANT** Recommendations are only applicable for operating systems supported in Microsoft Defender for Cloud. Visit the latest version of supported operating systems at *https://aka.ms/MDfCSupportedOS*.

Compute recommendations include a collection of recommendations for Azure VMs, non-Azure computers, Azure Arc machines, App Services, containers, managed clusters such as AKS or Azure SQL, and VM Scale Sets (VMSS).

> **IMPORTANT** Remember, new recommendations may be introduced without previous notice, and they will appear with a Preview tag. However, they will not impact your Secure Score as long as they are in preview state.

In addition to agent-based assessments inside the operating system, Microsoft Defender for Cloud has some recommendations that rely on the Azure Policy Guest Configuration extension, which lets Defender for Cloud assess operating system configuration without relying on Log Analytics.

> **MORE INFO** To learn more about the Guest Configuration feature, see *https://aka.ms/MDfC-GuestConfig*.

Secure management ports

You learned about the Cyber Kill Chain in Chapter 1. Alongside identity-based attacks, exposed management ports are a valuable target for attackers because they can be used to run attacks, such as brute-force or password-spray attacks. They belong to a group of attacks known as *dictionary attacks* because they use lists of usernames and passwords to generate log-in credentials that are then used in an automated process. If these attack campaigns are distributed and slow enough, it can be hard to block them.

The problem with username/password lists is that they often contain valid credentials that have been stolen in a random attack. If only one user in your organization has been affected by such a credential theft, and they are using their usernames and passwords for various services, a brute-force or password-spray attack might be successful. Figure 5-15 shows that the threat is a real threat, not a theoretical one. On February 14, 2022, a machine called `Contoso-Linux-VM` was started with an exposed SSH management port (port 22). Without doing anything else but starting the VM, Microsoft Defender for Cloud fired the `Failed SSH brute force attack` alert because someone had tried (but failed) to get access to our machine!

FIGURE 5-15   Failed brute force attack as a result of exposed management ports

Because of its importance, the Secure Management Ports control counts a total of 8 points toward your overall Secure Score. It contains three different recommendations, as shown in Figure 5-16 and listed below.

Secure management ports	8	3.43	Unhealthy	4 of 7 resources
Management ports should be closed on your virtual machines			Unhealthy	4 of 7 virtual machines
Management ports of virtual machines should be protected with just-in-time networ...			Unhealthy	4 of 7 virtual machines
Internet-facing virtual machines should be protected with network security groups			Completed	0 of 7 virtual machines

FIGURE 5-16   Recommendations in the Secure management ports control

- Management Ports Should Be Closed On Your Virtual Machines
- Management Ports Of Virtual Machines Should Be Protected With Just-In-Time Network Access Control
- Internet-Facing Virtual Machines Should Be Protected With Network Security Groups

The third recommendation (Internet-Facing Virtual Machines Should Be Protected With Network Security Groups) is essential for the other two because network security groups (NSGs) are used on both network interface cards (NICs) and subnet configurations to restrict communications between resources that are connected to Azure Virtual Networks (VNets). Defender for Cloud will verify whether an NSG exists on either the VM's NIC or subnet and then create a recommendation accordingly.

The two other recommendations help you focus on closing exposed management ports on your machines. If an NSG exists on either the NIC or subnet, Defender for Cloud will assess whether there's a rule that denies external access to management ports such as 22 for SSH or 3389 for RDP. If external access to your machine is allowed, you'll see this particular machine listed as unhealthy regarding both recommendations. Now you have two options: You can either manually create an NSG rule that completely denies external access, or you can configure just-in-time VM access for that machine, a feature that we will cover in Chapter 8, "Enhanced security capabilities." Whichever way you choose, once you have made sure that external access to your management ports is blocked, both recommendations will show the machine as healthy.

To manually create a rule that prevents external resource access, follow these steps:

1. Open the Azure portal and sign in with a user who has Security Admin privileges.
2. In the search bar, enter **Defender**, and then click **Microsoft Defender For Cloud**.
3. In the Defender for Cloud navigation pane, select **Recommendations**.
4. Look for the **Secure Management Ports** control and select the **Management Ports Should Be Closed On Your Virtual Machines** recommendation.
5. Click the name of a VM to which you want to block access. You are now redirected to the VM's network configuration.
6. You can either remove an existing allow rule for your management port (which will remove all management access), make the existing rule less permissive by restricting access to only a range of source IP addresses, or click the **Add Inbound Port Rule** button to create a new rule that will block external access to your machine's management ports.
7. For the **Source**, select **Service Tag**, and for the **Source Service Tag** select **Internet**. For the **Destination Port Range**, make sure to enter your machine's management port(s), either as a range (such as 1024-65000) or as a comma-separated list. Set the **Action** to **Deny**, and make sure to enter a higher **Priority** than you have for an existing allow rule, as shown in Figure 5-17.

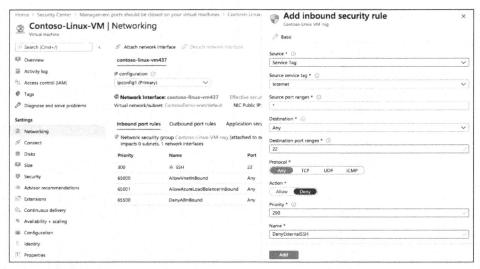

FIGURE 5-17 Adding an inbound security rule

8. Click the **Add** button. It will now take up to 24 hours for Defender for Cloud to reassess the machine's network configuration and show it as healthy regarding both recommendations.

Apply system updates

System updates are the next important topic to focus on. This control counts an additional 6 points toward your overall Secure Score. Defender for Cloud will use the Log Analytics agent to determine if a machine's operating system is missing updates, or if the machine needs to be restarted in order to apply recently installed updates. Depending on the assessment result, Defender for Cloud will then come up with some recommendations, as shown in Figure 5-18.

FIGURE 5-18 Recommendations within the scope of system updates

For Defender for Cloud to be able to assess your machines' OS states, the Log Analytics agent needs to be installed on any type of server you are monitoring, such as Azure VMs, Azure Arc-enabled machines, and VMSS. Also, the Log Analytics agent needs to properly collect security-related information and send it to the configured Log Analytics work-space. Once the Log Analytics agent is working as expected, Defender for Cloud will scan your machines for outstanding update installations or outstanding reboots and reflect the assessment results in its recommendations. If system updates need to be installed, you will see the missing updates as **Findings**, as shown in Figure 5-19.

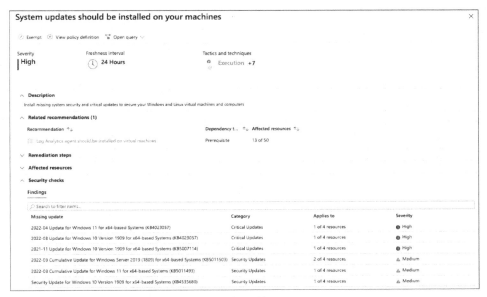

FIGURE 5-19 Missing system updates on several machines

You can click each missing update to see more details about the update, including remediation information.

Remediate vulnerabilities

The remediation of vulnerabilities is another major task to focus on when remediating recommendations that apply to compute resources. The Remediate Vulnerabilities security control counts as a maximum of 6 points toward your overall Secure Score. The collections of recommendations you see within the Remediate Vulnerabilities control will vary depending on the resource types you have deployed to your environment. Figure 5-20 shows the **Remediate Vulnerabilities** control with several recommendations, some of which already are completed and some of which are remediated on some resources.

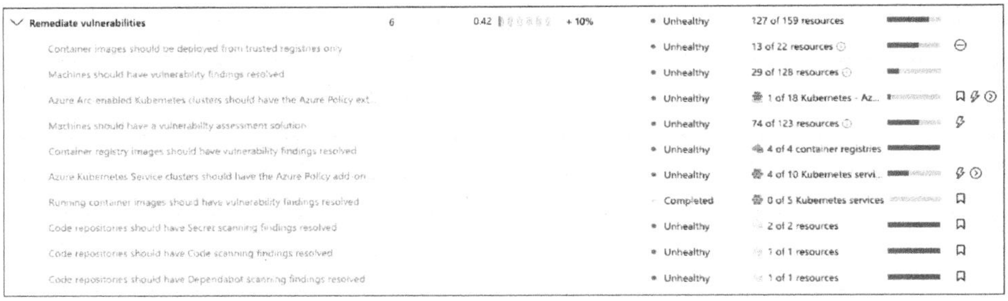

FIGURE 5-20 Recommendations within the Remediate vulnerabilities security control

Vulnerabilities on servers and other compute resources are assessed by an external vulnerability assessment solution. This is when Defender for Cloud's Vulnerability Assessment integrations come into play for the Cloud Security Posture Management scenario. Microsoft Defender for Servers will allow you to either use the integrated Qualys vulnerability assessment solution on your servers, or to leverage Microsoft Defender for Endpoint's Threat and Vulnerability Management (TVM). Also, Microsoft Defender for Containers allows you to scan your container registries for vulnerable images, and Microsoft Defender for SQL will allow you to activate vulnerability assessments on your SQL servers, both of which also are powered by Qualys. For more information about the different Defender for Cloud plans, see Chapter 6, "Threat detection." To enable one of the Defender for Cloud plans, follow these steps:

1. Open the Azure portal and sign in with a user who has Security Admin privileges.
2. Open **Microsoft Defender For Cloud**.
3. In the left navigation pane, click **Environment Settings**.
4. Select the subscription on which you want to activate the Defender for Cloud plan.
5. Switch the Defender for Cloud **Plan** you want to activate to **On**, as shown in Figure 5-21.

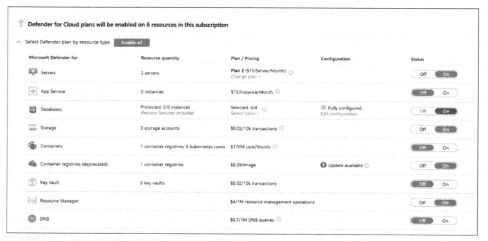

FIGURE 5-21 Select Defender for Cloud Plans

6. Click **Save**.

Once you have activated Defender for Servers, you are eligible for using the integrated Qualys VA solution at no additional cost. Also, you can rely on Microsoft Defender for Endpoint's Threat and Vulnerability Management (TVM). Alternatively, you can deploy an external Qualys VA solution in a Bring-your-own-license (BYOL) scenario if you decide not to use Defender for Servers or if you want to integrate your servers into an existing Qualys environment. The **Machines Should Have A Vulnerability Assessment Solution** recommendation comes with a **Fix** capability that enables you to remediate the recommendation with some easy steps directly from the Recommendations overview in Defender for Cloud. To enable one of the integrated solutions, follow these steps:

1. Open the Azure portal and sign in with a user who has Security Admin privileges. Also, your account needs **Write Permissions** for any VM on which you want to deploy the Qualys VA extension (or enable TVM).

2. Open **Microsoft Defender For Cloud**.

3. In the navigation pane, click **Recommendations**.

4. Open the **Remediate Vulnerabilities** control and click the **Machines Should Have A Vulnerability Assessment Solution** recommendation. You can look at the automated remediation logic that is triggered by the fix capability in the recommendation by opening the **Remediation Steps** section and then clicking **Quick Fix Logic**, as shown in Figure 5-22.

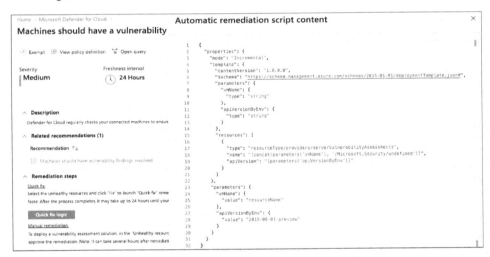

FIGURE 5-22 Remediation logic that is triggered by the Quick fix capability

5. Select one or several machines to deploy a vulnerability assessment solution to and click **Fix**.

6. You can now choose to deploy **Threat and Vulnerability Management By Microsoft Defender For Endpoint** or **Integrated Vulnerability Scanner Powered By Qualys** or configure a new third-party solution, which is the BYOL scenario. Select the desired solution, as shown in Figure 5-23, and then click **Proceed**.

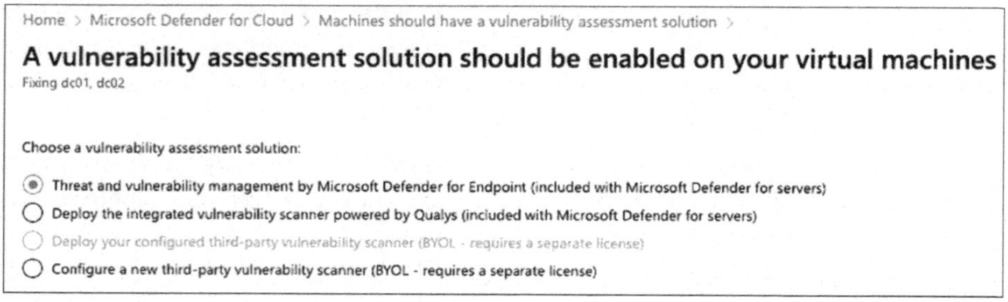

Home > Microsoft Defender for Cloud > Machines should have a vulnerability assessment solution >

A vulnerability assessment solution should be enabled on your virtual machines

Fixing dc01, dc02

Choose a vulnerability assessment solution:

◉ Threat and vulnerability management by Microsoft Defender for Endpoint (included with Microsoft Defender for servers)

○ Deploy the integrated vulnerability scanner powered by Qualys (included with Microsoft Defender for servers)

○ Deploy your configured third-party vulnerability scanner (BYOL - requires a separate license)

○ Configure a new third-party vulnerability scanner (BYOL - requires a separate license)

FIGURE 5-23 Deploy a vulnerability assessment solution to your machines

7. You will see a deployment summary and can start the deployment by clicking the **Fix n Resource(s)** (where *n* represents the number of resources) button.

> **MORE INFO** Learn more about the integrated Qualys VA solution at *https://aka.ms/ MDfCQualysVA*. More information about TVM integration in Defender for Cloud can be found at *https://aka.ms/MDfCTVM*.

If you have remediated all recommendations within the five security controls we have discussed so far, you have already achieved an overall Secure Score of 58.6 percent (10+4+8+6+6/58=0,5862). Congratulations!

Additional recommendations for Container Security

Microsoft Defender for Cloud comes with a bunch of recommendations that are especially focused on container images in Azure Container Registries and containers running on Kubernetes clusters, such as Azure Kubernetes Services (AKS). You have seen some of these recommendations in the preceding sections already, but there are a lot more that you can find using the new filtering option.

To see recommendations that apply to container registries and Kubernetes clusters only, select **Container Registries**, **Kubernetes Services**, and **Kubernetes–Azure Arc** as resource types in the recommendations filter, as shown in Figure 5-24.

Recommendations for containers are either focused on vulnerability management or environment hardening. Defender for Cloud will continuously monitor your Docker configuration and your Kubernetes clusters, and it will create recommendations for workload protection based on Kubernetes admission control. These recommendations are then added to the respective security controls, such as **Remediate Vulnerabilities**, **Apply System Updates**, or **Remediate Security Configurations**.

Container image scanning is one of the advanced capabilities that comes with Defender for Containers. Once you have enabled the Defender for Containers plan on your subscription, container images will be scanned once they are pushed to the Azure Container Registry, whenever they are pulled, and periodically afterward to ensure vulnerabilities that recently have been discovered are also found in existing images. You will learn more about detecting threats in container environments in Chapter 6.

FIGURE 5-24 Recommendations that apply to containers

Enable endpoint protection

After making sure you have protected your organization's identities and closed the management ports on your machines, you have already made a huge step toward securing your environment from unauthorized access. The problem with malware is that it can be installed by both unauthorized actors and inadvertently—or on purpose—by legitimate users within your organization.

Once a machine is compromised, it might start downloading further malware, opening new attack vectors and helping bad actors in other ways to get a foot into your environment. This is when the Enable Endpoint Protection control comes into play. This control will add two more points toward your overall Secure Score once it is taken care of. As you can see in Figure 5-25, this control also includes the same recommendations for the Log Analytics agent that you already know from the apply system updates control.

∨ Enable endpoint protection	2	0.06	• Unhealthy	57 of 162 resources
Log Analytics agent should be installed on virtual machines			• Unhealthy	13 of 56 virtual machines
Endpoint protection health issues on machines should be resolved			• Unhealthy	1 of 97 resources
Install endpoint protection solution on virtual machines			• Unhealthy	21 of 56 virtual machines
Log Analytics agent should be installed on virtual machine scale sets			Completed	0 of 15 virtual machine s...
Endpoint protection health issues on virtual machine scale sets should be resolved			Completed	0 of 15 virtual machine s...
Endpoint protection should be installed on machines			• Unhealthy	1 of 41 resources
Endpoint protection should be installed on machines			Completed	0 of 41 resources
Endpoint protection health issues on machines should be resolved			• Unhealthy	8 of 37 virtual machines
Endpoint protection should be installed on virtual machine scale sets			Completed	0 of 15 virtual machine s...

FIGURE 5-25 Enable endpoint protection

The reason for this recommendation being shown multiple times is that Defender for Cloud will also need the Log Analytics agent for assessing whether an endpoint protection solution has been installed on a machine, and if so, if the endpoint protection solution is working properly. Defender for Cloud will discover the following endpoint protection solutions:

- Microsoft Defender Antivirus for Windows Server 2016 or later
- Microsoft Defender for Endpoint for Linux on Linux Server Family
- System Center Endpoint Protection (Microsoft Antimalware) on Windows Server 2012 R2
- Trend Micro – Deep Security on the Windows Server Family
- Symantec v12.1.1100+ on the Windows Server Family
- McAfee v10+ on the Windows and Linux Server Families
- Sophos v9+ on the Linux Server Family

Microsoft Defender Antivirus is included in the operating system as of Windows Server 2016 and, therefore, does not require further installation. But if there is a Windows Server 2012 R2 machine without an endpoint protection solution installed, you can use Defender for Cloud to install the Microsoft Antimalware directly from the portal. To install the extension to your machines, follow these steps:

1. Open the Azure portal and sign in with a user who has Security Admin privileges. Also, your account needs **Write Permissions** for any VM on which you want to deploy the Microsoft Antimalware extension.

2. Click **Microsoft Defender For Cloud**.

3. In the navigation pane, click **Recommendations**.

4. Open the **Enable Endpoint Protection** control and click the **Endpoint Protection Should Be Installed On Your Machines** recommendation.

5. Select the VM(s) on which you want to install the extension and click **Install**. You will realize that you can only see Windows Server VMs that support installation of the Microsoft Antimalware extension.

6. Select **Install On n VMs** (where n represents the number of resources), and then select **Microsoft Antimalware** and click **Create**.

7. If you wish, you can now exclude files, folders, file extensions, or processes and also define a scheduled scan (see in Figure 5-26). Then click **OK** to start the extension deployment.

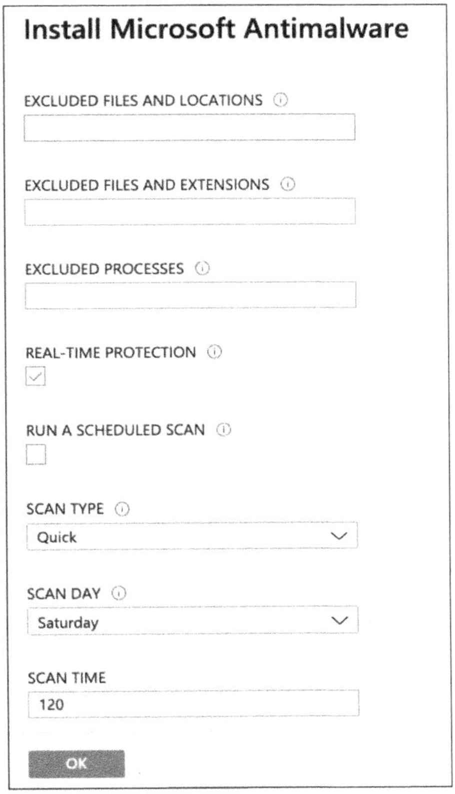

Install Microsoft Antimalware

EXCLUDED FILES AND LOCATIONS ⓘ

EXCLUDED FILES AND EXTENSIONS ⓘ

EXCLUDED PROCESSES ⓘ

REAL-TIME PROTECTION ⓘ
☑

RUN A SCHEDULED SCAN ⓘ
☐

SCAN TYPE ⓘ
Quick ⌄

SCAN DAY ⓘ
Saturday ⌄

SCAN TIME
120

OK

FIGURE 5-26 Configure antimalware settings

> **MORE INFO** For more information and further references, see *https://aka.ms/ MDfCEnableEndpointProtection*.

Networking

An Azure virtual network is a logical isolation of the Azure cloud dedicated to your subscription. Defender for Cloud will identify the Azure virtual networks available in your subscription, and it will provide recommendations to improve the overall security. Besides networking recommendations, Defender for Cloud has some advanced capabilities that are enabled once you enable Defender for Servers. In the Defender for Cloud navigation pane, click **Workload Protections** to open the **Workload Protections** dashboard. In the **Advanced Protection** section, you will find the **Adaptive Network Hardening** and **Network Map** tiles, as shown in Figure 5-27.

FIGURE 5-27 Defender for Cloud advanced protection capabilities

Network map

The **Network Map** appears when you click the respective tile on this page. This option allows you to view the topology of your Azure network and the traffic pattern, as shown in Figure 5-28.

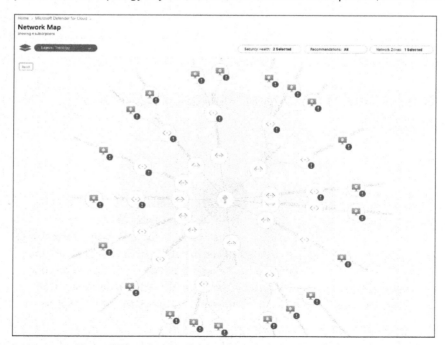

FIGURE 5-28 Network Map showing the Azure network topology for the selected subscription

This map is organized from inside-out, with the subscription shown in the middle, then working outward, you see the Azure VNet, the subnet, and the Virtual Machine (VM) connected to that subnet. The default visualization includes some filters that can be adjusted:

- **Security Health** This is based on severity level (high, medium, low, or healthy) of your Azure resources.
- **Recommendations** These are based on the active recommendations for those resources.
- **Network Zones** These are based on internal or Internet-facing resources (or both).

If you hover the mouse over each icon, you will see more information about that object, and if you click one of those VMs, you will see more details about the VM itself, as shown in Figure 5-29.

FIGURE 5-29 Properties in the Network Map

On this blade, you have important information about the selected VM, and a list of relevant recommendations is shown at the bottom of the page. On the right side, you can switch to the **Allowed Traffic** tab. On this tab, you have two tables with the list of TCP and UDP ports open for inbound and outbound traffic. This provides better visibility of the traffic allowed for that specific machine. If you want a broader view of the current possible traffic between your resources, you can switch to the network map view to show not only the network topology, but also possible allowed traffic between resources by selecting **Allowed Traffic** in the **Layer** selection in the upper left corner. By switching to this view, you see the same map, but now it shows your configured rules, defining which resources can communicate with other resources.

Adaptive network hardening

The intent of this feature is to enable you to easily harden your network traffic by using Network Security Group (NSG) rules. Defender for Cloud will use machine learning to gather information about the network traffic from/to a machine. After learning about the traffic pattern, Defender for Cloud will suggest a list of rules for hardening the network environment.

When you click the **Adaptive Network Hardening** tile in Defender for Cloud's **Workload Protections** blade, you will see the **Adaptive Network Hardening Recommendations Should Be Applied On Internet Facing Virtual Machines** recommendation, as shown in Figure 5-30.

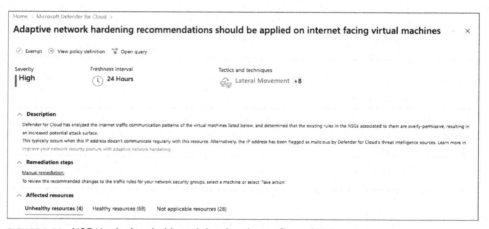

FIGURE 5-30 NSG Hardening dashboard showing the configured VMs

Unhealthy Resources shows the number of VMs with network-hardening recommendations that should be applied. You can click each VM and see the current rules and alerts, as shown in Figure 5-31.

Under the **Rules** tab, you see the rules automatically created by the Adaptive Network Hardening capability based on the learning process. You can click the **Add Rule** button to create a new rule, or you can select the suggested rule and click the **Enforce** button. To see the alerts, you can click the **Alerts** tab and select the alert itself.

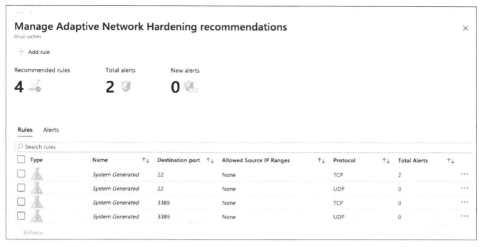

FIGURE 5-31 Hardening policy with visibility for alerts and rules

There will be some cases in which the Adaptive Network Hardening algorithm won't be able to run, and the **Unscanned Resources** tab will appear. Following are the scenarios under which the Adaptive Network Hardening algorithm won't be able to run:

- **VMs are Classic VMs** Only Azure Resource Manager VMs are supported.
- **Not enough data is available** To produce accurate traffic-hardening recommendations, Defender for Cloud requires at least 30 days of traffic data.
- **VM is not protected by Defender for Servers** This feature is only available in the Microsoft Defender for Servers P2 plan.

The following section includes examples of recommendations that can be remediated directly through the Defender for Cloud dashboard.

Data and storage

One of the ultimate goals of an attacker is to gain access to a target's data. Therefore, it is important to address all security recommendations for storage (where the data is located) and for the data itself.

Defender for Cloud meets these requirements by providing security recommendations for databases, storage accounts, Redis, Data Lake Analytics, and Data Lake storage. Storage and data recommendations vary depending on the environment. To see a list of data and storage recommendations that apply to your environment, select all respective resource types in the recommendations filter. The following sections cover the implementation of some of these recommendations.

Secure transfer to storage accounts should be enabled

Secure transfer is an option that enforces a storage account to only accept requests that are using secure connections (HTTPS). Using HTTPS for all connections enforces authentication between the storage account and the requesting service and makes sure that data in transit is always encrypted and protected from network layer attacks, such as man-in-the-middle, or session-hijacking. You can deny the creation of unsecure storage accounts directly from this recommendation, and you can also auto-remediate existing accounts using the Quick Fix capability, as shown in Figure 5-32.

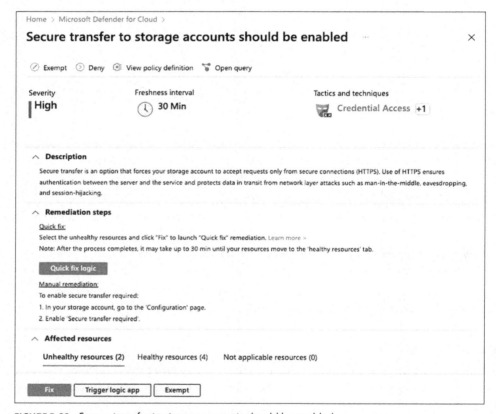

FIGURE 5-32 Secure transfer to storage accounts should be enabled

Enable auditing on SQL server

Defender for Cloud can perform a security assessment to verify whether you are leveraging Azure SQL auditing and threat detection security capabilities. Auditing and threat detection can assist you with the following tasks:

- Maintaining regulatory compliance
- Understanding database activity

- Gaining insight into discrepancies and anomalies
- Identifying security violations

Because of this integration with Azure SQL, this recommendation enables you to apply the remediation directly from Defender for Cloud. Follow these steps to address this recommendation:

1. From the **Recommendations** blade, open the **Enable Auditing And Logging** control, and choose **Auditing On SQL Server Should Be Enabled**.

2. On the **Auditing On SQL Server Should Be Enabled** blade, you will see the detailed explanation about this recommendation, **Remediation Steps**, and **Affected Resources**, as shown in Figure 5-33.

FIGURE 5-33 Details about the advantages of enabling auditing on the SQL server

3. Click the **Unhealthy Resources** tab at the bottom of this page to see the SQL servers affected by this recommendation.

4. Click the SQL server for which you want to remediate this recommendation, and the **Auditing** blade will open, as shown in Figure 5-34.

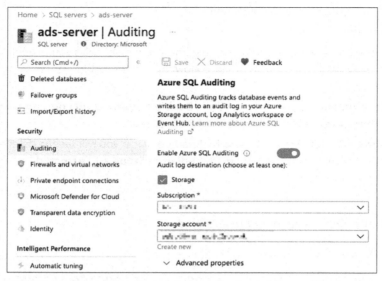

FIGURE 5-34   Remediating the recommendation by enabling auditing

5. Under **Auditing**, toggle the switch to **On** and select the **audit log destination**, and then click the **Save** button.

6. After the save has finished, close this blade.

Using workflow automation to remediate security recommendations

In Chapter 4 you learned that remediating security recommendations is more of a returning process than a one-time job and that it's not enough to only cover existing resources. Besides using Deny- or Deploy if not exists-policies, Defender for Cloud offers a lot of automation capabilities that help you to auto-remediate recommendations or to remediate at scale.

Workflow automation is a capability that helps you to automatically react to either a new alert or a new recommendation. It leverages Azure Logic Apps as the automation artifact, and within the Logic App, you are offered almost unlimited possibilities to automate processes. The workflow automation feature brings additional trigger types to Logic Apps:

■ **Recommendation**   The Recommendation trigger will start a Logic App Playbook in the following conditions:

  ■ A resource has been added to a recommendation as a result of an assessment

  ■ A resource status has changed within a recommendation as a result of an assessment, while the resource status can be healthy, unhealthy, or not applicable

  ■ A Logic App is manually triggered from a recommendation within Defender for Cloud

- **Security Alert** The *Security Alert* trigger will start a Logic App Playbook in the following conditions:
  - A new security alert is created in Microsoft Defender for Cloud
  - From an alert, the Logic App is manually triggered
- **Regulatory Compliance Standards** The Regulatory Compliance Standards trigger is triggered when a compliance control's status within a standard is changed. The status in this case can be `failed`, `passed`, `skipped`, or `unsupported`

The first trigger type will help you to create several types of automation artifacts. For example, you could let the Logic App create a JIRA or ServiceNow ticket if a new recommendation is created, or notify stakeholders about new resource exemptions. You could also auto-remediate or quarantine resources if they were part of a recommendation. Every time Defender for Cloud triggers the Logic App, it will send a bunch of information that you can use for further steps:

- Name of the assessment as a GUID
- Assessment ID
- The recommendation's display name
- Metadata information for the recommendation, including a description, remediation steps, and severity
- Resource details, including the resource ID
- Status code (`healthy`, `unhealthy`, or `not applicable`)
- A deep link to the assessment result in the recommendations blade

This information can then be used within the Logic App, either for storing it or notifying someone but also to retrieve further information from other APIs, such as the different Microsoft Defender for Cloud REST API providers. Figure 5-35 shows a sample result that is sent from Defender for Cloud to the Logic App trigger.

```
"body": {
    "name": "bc303248-3d14-44c2-96a0-55f5c326b5fe",
    "id": "/subscriptions/<subscriptionID>/resourceGroups/Contoso/providers/Microsoft.Compute/virtualMachines/Contoso-VM/providers/Microsoft.Se
    "type": "Microsoft.Security/assessments",
    "properties": {
        "displayName": "Management ports should be closed on your virtual machines",
        "metadata": {
            "description": "Open remote management ports are exposing your VM to a high level of risk from Internet-based attacks. These attack
            "remediationDescription": "We recommend that you edit the inbound rules of some of your virtual machines, to restrict access to spe
            "severity": 4
        },
        "resourceDetails": {
            "source": "Azure",
            "id": "/subscriptions/<subscriptionID>/resourceGroups/Contoso/providers/Microsoft.Compute/virtualMachines/Contoso-VM"
        },
        "status": {
            "code": "Unhealthy"
        },
        "links": {
            "azurePortalUri": "https://portal.azure.com/#blade/Microsoft_Azure_Security/RecommendationsBlade/assessmentKey/bc303248-3d14-44c2-9
        }
    }
}
```

FIGURE 5-35 Information sent from Defender for Cloud to a Logic App within the scope of workflow automation

If you want to auto-remediate a resource, the information about the resource and the assessment/recommendation help you to determine the next steps. In the next section, you will find examples for manually and automatically triggered Logic Apps as a reaction on recommendations. Once you have built your Logic App, you need to create a workflow around it so Defender for Cloud can automatically trigger the Logic App without manual interaction. To create a workflow, follow these steps:

1. Open the Azure portal and sign in with a user who has Security Admin privileges. Also, your account must have write permissions for the target resource.

2. In the search bar, enter **Defender**, then open **Microsoft Defender For Cloud**.

3. In the navigation pane, select **Workflow Automation**, and then click **+ Add Workflow Automation**.

4. Enter a **Name**, and select the **Subscription** and **Resource Group** in which the workflow configuration will be stored.

5. From the **Defender For Cloud Data Types** dropdown, you can choose between **Security Alert**, **Recommendation**, or **Regulatory Compliance Standards**. This setting will determine the trigger type on which the workflow will react. Notice that the blade will change depending on your selection.

6. Select **Recommendation**.

7. Select the recommendations to react on, the severity, and the recommendation state on which to trigger your workflow, as shown in Figure 5-36.

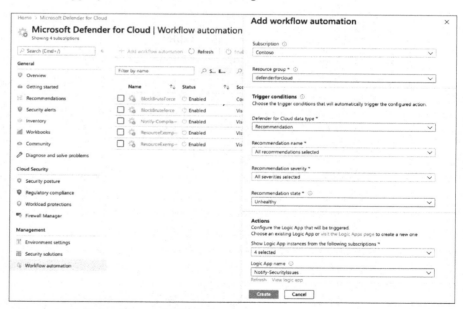

FIGURE 5-36 Add a workflow to Defender for Cloud

8. Select the **Subscription** in which you have created your Logic App and then select the **Logic App** from the dropdown. Click **Create**.

9. Once the workflow automation has been created, it will trigger the Logic App you've selected whenever the trigger condition is true. In Figure 5-36, this means that every time a resource is flagged as unhealthy in any assessment, the Logic App will be triggered.

Resource exemptions and automation

Workflow automation and the capability to manually trigger Logic Apps directly from the Defender for Cloud blades offer a variety of options to enrich your ASC experience. In this chapter's last section, we give you some ideas about what is possible with different connectors and API providers.

In order to create resource exemptions, a capability that we have discussed earlier in this chapter, your account needs to have elevated access rights: Security Administrator or Resource Policy Contributor. However, often users whose job it is to remediate security findings might have resource access rights so they can change the resources they are responsible for, but not administrative rights on subscriptions or governance aspects. In this case, they might want to but cannot exempt a resource from a recommendation because of the lack of access rights. With the Trigger Logic App capability, you can use a Playbook for them to request a resource exemption directly from the recommendation's blade. Once the **Trigger Logic App** button is clicked and the Logic App is selected, Defender for Cloud will send information about the recommendation and the resource, which is enough to generate an email that is sent to the subscription's security contact. Figure 5-37 shows an email body in the Logic App Designer, that contains dynamic values from the recommendations trigger.

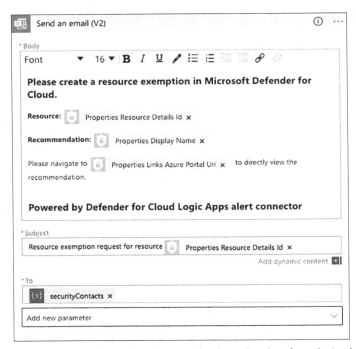

FIGURE 5-37 Email template that contains dynamic values from the Logic App trigger

To retrieve the security contacts that are used as the email recipients, the Logic App will pull the information from the `Microsoft.Security/securityContacts` API provider, as shown in Figure 5-38.

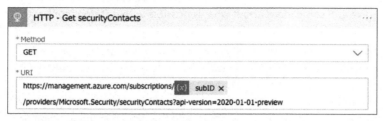

FIGURE 5-38 API connection in a Logic App

While this Logic App is not very difficult to create, it still offers a great benefit toward remediating security recommendations as it allows you to directly request an exemption without leaving Defender for Cloud at any time.

> **MORE INFO** You can find more information about this Logic App and download it from the Defender for Cloud GitHub in our article at *https://aka.ms/ MDfCRequestResourceExemption*.

Another automation within the scope of resource exemptions is the notification once a new exemption has been created. This artifact is a bit more complex because it demands to retrieve information from the Defender for Cloud trigger, as well as several API providers, including Azure Policy APIs.

Although resource exemptions are based on policy exemptions and, therefore, do not belong to either alerts or recommendations, we can still use the recommendations trigger to automatically react on them. This is because once you create a resource exemption, the resource status will change from unhealthy to not applicable.

Also, creating a resource exemption will add an `exempt` value to the `cause` attribute in the information that is sent to the Logic App. Figure 5-39 shows the properties coming from Defender for Cloud once a new exemption has been created.

With that being said, every time the Logic App is triggered, we first need to check if both conditions (status is `NotApplicable` and cause is `Exempt`) are true. If so, the Logic App will continue to pull information from the `Microsoft.Authorization/policySetDefinitions` and `Microsoft.Authorization/policyExemptions` API providers. Once you create a resource exemption, this exemption is created in Azure Policy and can then be retrieved from the policyExemptions API. It will contain information about the person who has created the exemption, so it is worth looking at. Unfortunately, there is no direct way of using the information coming from Defender for Cloud to pull exactly the one exemption that has been created and triggered the Logic App, so you need to take a detour over the `policySetDefinitions` provider.

This provider will retrieve the Defender for Cloud Policy Initiative with all of its policy definitions (and their IDs), so we can compare the policy definition IDs from the initiative with the ID we get from the Logic App trigger. In Figure 5-39, you can see this information as `policyDefinitionID` in the `metadata` section.

```
"properties": {
    "resourceDetails": {
        "source": "Azure",
        "id": "/subscriptions/<subscriptionID>/resourceGroups/Contoso/providers/Microsoft.Compute/virtualMachines/Contoso-VM"
    },
    "displayName": "Adaptive network hardening recommendations should be applied on internet facing virtual machines",
    "status": {
        "code": "NotApplicable",
        "cause": "Exempt",
        "description": "Exempt Mitigated"
    },
    "metadata": {
        "displayName": "Adaptive network hardening recommendations should be applied on internet facing virtual machines",
        "assessmentType": "BuiltIn",
        "policyDefinitionId": "/providers/Microsoft.Authorization/policyDefinitions/08e6af2d-db70-460a-bfe9-d5bd474ba9d6",
        "description": "Azure Security Center has analyzed the internet traffic communication patterns of the virtual machines listed below
        "remediationDescription": "To harden the Network Security Group traffic rules, enforce the recommended rules by following the steps
        "categories": [
            "Networking"
        ],
        "severity": "High",
        "userImpact": "Moderate",
        "implementationEffort": "Moderate",
        "threats": [
            "MaliciousInsider",
            "DataSpillage",
            "DataExfiltration"
        ]
    },
```

FIGURE 5-39 Assessment properties after a recommendation has been created

Once there is a match, the corresponding Policy Definition Reference ID from the initiative can be compared with the reference ID from the policy exemptions. Once there is another match, you know you have found the exemption that has just been created. Then you can export the exemption to Log Analytics and take its `createdBy` information together with the information coming from the trigger to send a notification email.

> **MORE INFO**   You can find more information about this Logic App and download it from the Defender for Cloud GitHub in our article at *https://aka.ms/ MDfCNotifyResourceExemption*.

With their capability to work with other Azure resources, but also with APIs and third-party connectors, Logic Apps are a great way to enhance your Defender for Cloud experience. Now, it's your turn to create your own Logic App within the scope of workflow automation. Let us know how it went and get it published at *https://aka.ms/MDfCGitHub*.

Security governance and contextual security

Often, the amount of security recommendations and resources these recommendations apply to becomes overwhelming. For example, when the Log4J vulnerability was disclosed at the end of 2021, you might have seen thousands of vulnerable machines in your environment reported by Defender for Cloud using one of the integrated vulnerability assessment solutions we discussed earlier in this chapter. With thousands of affected machines, you might have wondered where to start your remediations.

Also, we have seen companies struggle with responsibilities. Who owns a resource? Who is responsible for remediating high-severity vulnerabilities? Is there a team that ensures network configurations are in place?

This is why Microsoft implemented the two new concepts of *security governance* and *contextual security* into Microsoft Defender for Cloud.

Using security governance to create responsibility

Security governance is one of the new concepts added to Microsoft Defender for Cloud. Its goal is to create responsibility for remediating recommendations and vulnerabilities on resources in your hybrid and multicloud environments. One of the main aspects with security governance is *ownership* of recommendations. As mentioned before, the overall number of unhealthy resources and open security recommendations can easily become overwhelming in a company's multicloud estate. By assigning owners to recommendations, it creates a responsibility. At the same time, you have a contact to reach out to in case remediation does not take place. Figure 5-40 shows the **Owner** (preview) tab in the **Security Posture** blade you already saw at the beginning of this chapter.

FIGURE 5-40 Different owners assigned to recommendations in Defender for Cloud

When you click the **View Recommendations** link next to a particular owner, you will see only recommendations to which this owner account is assigned.

In addition to ownership, Microsoft introduced the concepts of *due date* and *grace period* with security governance. By assigning a due date to a recommendation, you can make sure that the person who is responsible for its remediation has a defined amount of time to remediate security recommendations. Grace period, in this context, means that as long as the due date has not been reached (in other words, as long as the recommendation is not yet overdue), your Secure Score will not decrease.

Ownership, grace period, and due dates can either be assigned per each recommendation or by using *governance rules*. Figure 5-41 shows the **Management Ports Of Virtual Machines Should Be Protected With Just-In-Time Network Access Control** recommendation with an owner and due date assigned to some resources.

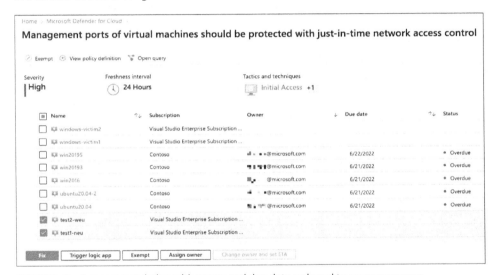

FIGURE 5-41 A recommendation with owner and due date assigned to some resources

As shown in Figure 5-41, there are some resources that do not yet have an owner assigned, but you can manually do so directly from any recommendation by following these steps.

1. In any recommendation's details blade, select the unhealthy resources to which you want to assign an owner, then click the **Assign Owner** button on the bottom, as shown in Figure 5-41.

2. Enter an **Owner**, which should be a valid email address, and a **Due Date**. Optionally, enable the **Apply Grace Period** toggle, as shown in Figure 5-42.

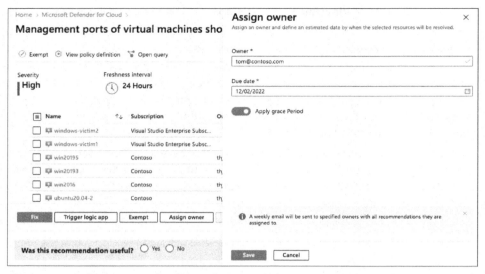

FIGURE 5-42 Assign an owner, due date and grace period

3. Click **Save**. The new owner and due date will be added to the same recommendation for the resources you selected, as shown in Figure 5-43.

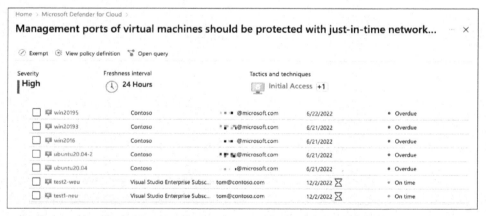

FIGURE 5-43 A new owner and due date have been added to the recommendation

While this manual approach can be a perfect fit for changing existing owners and due dates, or for assigning an owner and date for resources that have not had an owner, yet. A better approach for enterprises at scale is to leverage governance rules. When writing this book, governance rules can only be applied to a subscription, but management groups will be supported in a future release. To assign a governance rule, follow these steps:

1. Log in to the Azure portal with an account that has Contributor, Security Admin, or Owner access rights.

2. In the top search bar, enter **Defender**, then click **Microsoft Defender For Cloud**.

3. In the **Defender For Cloud** navigation pane, select **Environment Settings**, then select the Azure subscription, AWS account, or GCP project for which you want to create a governance rule. Then, in the **Policy Settings** section, select **Governance Rules (Preview)**.

4. Click **+ Add Rule** on the top navigation bar to start creating a new governance rule. The **Create New Governance Rule** dialog box will appear, which allows you to configure a variety of settings. Enter a **Rule Name**, **Description**, and **Priority**. Governance rules with a lower priority will take precedence over rules with a higher priority.

5. Select which recommendations you want your rule to affect. Either select all recommendations by severity, such as all high-severity recommendations in your subscription, or define specific recommendations you want to be addressed by this governance rule. The latter option is perfect in scenarios such as assigning ownership to all MFA-related recommendations to one owner and all network-related recommendations to another one.

6. Select the method to assign an **Owner** to your governance rule. You can either enter a valid **Email Address**, or you can assign an owner **By Resource Tag**. The latter option is the more dynamic one, as it allows you to specify a **Tag Key** used in your environment. For example, in case you use an Owner tag across all your resources and, as a value, you are using a valid email address, the governance rule can leverage this tag to assign ownership. That way, you can use a one-rule-fits-all approach. The governance rule will evaluate resources first, followed by resource groups and subscriptions, until the tag you specified is found. So, in case you assign the specified tag to resource groups or subscriptions instead of resources, the governance rule will assign the specified owner to all resources within this particular scope.

7. Select the remediation timeframe. This is a time range relative to the date on which a governance rule is applied to a resource. As opposed to manually assigning an owner and due date, with a governance rule you can select 7, 14, 30, and 90 days only. For example, when you select 7 days as a remediation timeframe, the due date for each recommendation specified in step 5 will be 7 days after a resource has been flagged as unhealthy.

8. Decide whether you want to apply the grace period feature to your governance rule. If so, enable the **Apply Grace Period** switch.

9. Finally, select whether you want to notify owners and their direct managers weekly about open and overdue tasks. If so, a weekly email similar to the one shown in Figure 5-44 will be sent out.

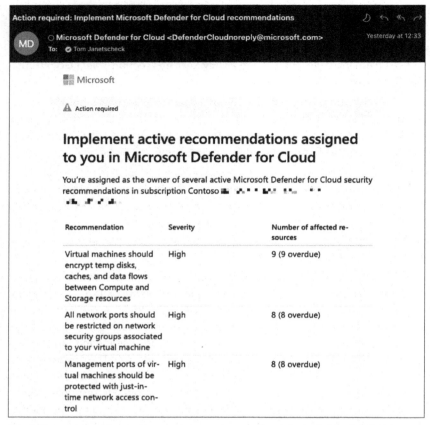

FIGURE 5-44 A weekly governance status report email sent by Defender for Cloud

10. The direct manager is resolved from the corresponding Azure AD attribute.

11. Click **Create**.

Once a governance rule is applied to a subscription, it will cover all recommendations and resources in scope based on the rule's configuration. It will also automatically apply to new future resources.

Find only your own recommendations

As you have learned, the owner is assigned based on a valid email address. Microsoft Defender for Cloud will use this information to find the corresponding user account in Azure AD. If there is a matching account with at least the Security Reader role's access rights, you can use it in Defender for Cloud to only see recommendations for which you are responsible. Follow these steps to see only your recommendations:

1. Log in to the Azure portal with an account that at least has Security Reader access rights.

2. In the top search bar, enter **Defender**, and then click **Microsoft Defender For Cloud**.

3. In the **Defender For Cloud** navigation pane, select **Recommendations**.

4. In the recommendations view, enable the **Show My Items Only (Preview)** switch.

5. Alternatively, if you want to see another owner's recommendations, use the Owner filter, and select the owner you want to track, as shown in Figure 5-45.

FIGURE 5-45   Filter recommendations by Owner

Using Attack Paths to focus on the right resources

Bringing recommendations into context is an important aspect of making educated decisions when it comes to remediating vulnerabilities and security recommendations. For example, when you have thousands of machines that are vulnerable for Log4J, you need to decide which machine to focus on first. Let's assume among all vulnerable machines, you have three different types of machines in your organization:

- Azure VMs that are not connected to the network or that cannot communicate with resources outside of their own VNet

- Azure VMs that are only connected to the Internet but don't have access to any other resources in your environment

- Azure VMs that are accessible from the Internet that can communicate with and access a storage account containing sensitive information

Everybody will agree that machines that belong to the third category will be the most important to remediate and, therefore, should be addressed first. So, the resource's *context* is relevant for the decision. This is where a new concept called *attack paths* comes into play. With attack paths, Microsoft Defender for Cloud can show resources, vulnerabilities, and security recommendations, including their context. The concept knows a variety of pre-defined paths based on the most common attack vectors that attackers use to gain access to information and resources.

> **IMPORTANT NOTE**   When writing this book, the attack paths and cloud security map features were in a private preview and not yet fully implemented in the UI, so while we can explain the concept, the UI might slightly change when the feature is finally released.

Figure 5-46 shows the **Attack Paths** blade in Defender for Cloud with all attack paths that are found in this environment.

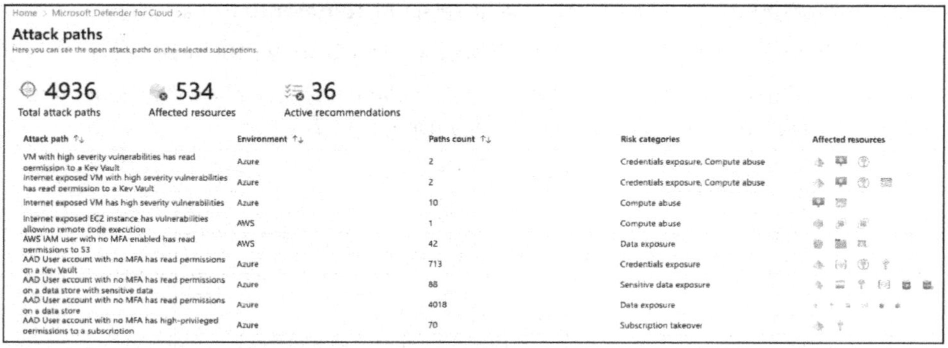

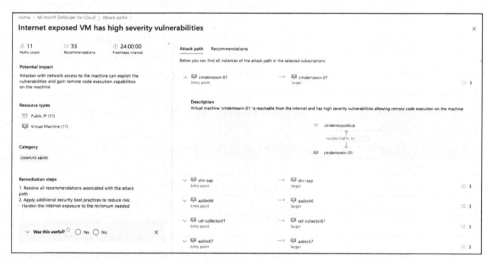

FIGURE 5-46 Attack paths in Defender for Cloud

As mentioned earlier, attack paths are predefined, and you will only see paths relevant to your environment. In other words, if you don't have any Internet-facing virtual machines, you won't see the **Internet Exposed VM Has High Severity Vulnerabilities** attack path in your environment. Let's take a closer look at this particular attack path. Figure 5-47 shows the details when you click the attack path.

FIGURE 5-47 Attack path details

It shows the number of attack paths that belong to the same pattern. In Figure 5-47, this means there are 11 machines that are exposed to the Internet, all of which have high-severity vulnerabilities allowing remote code execution on them. The number of recommendations (33) shows how many security misconfigurations need to be addressed to break the attack path. On the right side, the details page shows two tabs, **Attack Path** and **Recommendations**.

The **Attack Paths** tab shows the attack vector for each machine. Selecting an attack path opens the resource details view. You can click each step in the view to see even more details about the vulnerable resource. In Figure 5-48, you see **Insights** for a virtual machine called **cmdemowin-01**.

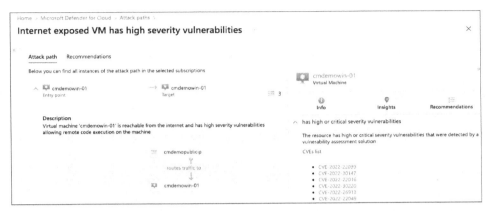

FIGURE 5-48 Attack path insights for a virtual machine

Resource insights in this attack path show high-or critical-severity vulnerabilities as CVE IDs detected on this machine. Defender for Cloud relies on one of the integrated vulnerability assessment solutions you learned about earlier in this chapter.

Besides **Insights**, there is a **Recommendations** view on the **Attack Path** tab that will show all security recommendations detected for the machine you are currently looking at, as shown in Figure 5-49.

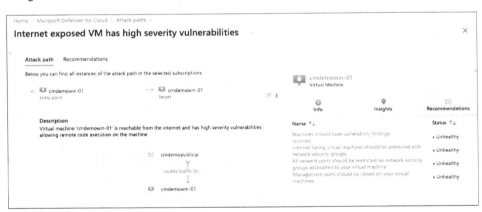

FIGURE 5-49 Security recommendations for an Azure VM in the Attack paths view

While the **Attack Path** tab shows details for one particular attack path, the **Recommendations** tab shows recommendations for all resources affected by the same pattern. As mentioned earlier, the environment used to explain the feature knows 11 machines affected by the same attack vectors. So, in the Recommendations tab, you will see security recommendations for all 11 VMs that are suitable for closing the attack vector, as shown in Figure 5-50.

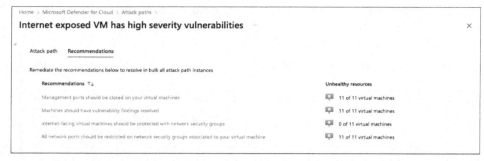

FIGURE 5-50 Security recommendations for all resources affected by the same attack path pattern

If you close the loop to the initial example with Log4J on thousands of servers, you will realize that the new attack path capability will definitely help you make an educated decision about which machines to remediate first. In this example, it's the 11 machines that are highlighted in the **Internet Exposed VM Has High Severity Vulnerabilities** attack path.

Build your own views with Cloud Security Map

Within the scope of Defender for Cloud's contextual security concept, attack paths are important when focusing on the right resources to remediate security issues quickly. However, because they are pre-created by Microsoft based on the most common attack vectors, it's a static concept. Of course, you want to be able to build your own custom views and queries to get the insights you are most interested in.

This is when Cloud Security Map comes into play. Cloud Security Map allows you to either see underlying queries that are used to show attack paths, or you can build your own queries based on all accessible insights in Defender for Cloud. Figure 5-51 shows the Cloud Security Map in the Defender for Cloud portal.

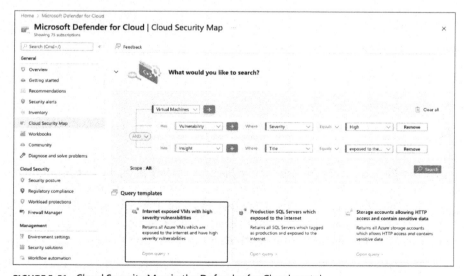

FIGURE 5-51 Cloud Security Map in the Defender for Cloud portal

The query shown in Figure 5-51 is taken from a query template called the **Internet Exposed VMs With High Severity Vulnerabilities** query template. We used this query earlier to create an attack path. You can use the different dropdowns and + buttons to select resources and insights according to your needs. In the example above, the following information is being considered:

- The resource type is Virtual Machines.
- These machines have vulnerabilities with at least high severity.
- These machines are exposed to the Internet.

You can also further narrow down the selection, for example, by adding the exposed network port you want to filter for, as shown in Figure 5-52.

FIGURE 5-52 Cloud Security Map in the Defender for Cloud portal

Once done, you can click the **Search** button to start the query process. You will be presented with all resources to which your filter applies. It's important to mention that the scope includes all Azure subscriptions and AWS and GCP connectors in your environment. With that said, both the attack paths and Cloud Security Map are truly multicloud and multitenant capable, providing a unified overview and bringing into context resources from all your cloud estate.

Chapter 6

Threat detection

U p to now, you've learned how to reduce the attack surface by addressing security recommendations using Microsoft Defender for Cloud, which is part of the overall enhancement of your security posture. However, protection is just one of the pillars of your security posture. You also need to enhance your detection and response, and for that, you need to use different plans available in Defender for Cloud.

On the detection front, Defender for Cloud constantly monitors your assets. When it identifies suspicious activities, it raises an alert, and it does that while reducing the false positives, which is very important for your security operations.

In this chapter, you will learn how to use the different Defender for Cloud plans provide threat detection for different workloads and how to investigate security issues as part of your incident response process.

Methods of threat protection

Defender for Cloud uses advanced security analytics and machine-learning technologies to evaluate events across the entire cloud fabric. The security analytics include data from multiple sources, including Microsoft products and services, the Microsoft Digital Crimes Unit (DCU), the Microsoft Security Response Center (MSRC), and external feeds. This is the core of Defender for Cloud threat detection, and on top of that, there will be different mechanisms of detection according to the plan. For this section, we will explore how Defender for Servers detection works.

Defender for Servers applies known patterns to discover malicious behavior, which is called *behavioral analysis*. It uses statistical profiling to build a historical baseline. An alert can be triggered when Defender for Server detects deviations from established baselines that conform to a potential attack vector. The result will be externalized in the dashboard via a security alert. A security alert contains valuable information about what triggered the alert, the resources targeted, the source of the attack, and suggestions to remediate the threat. Alerts generated by Defender for Server are also called Virtual Machine Behavioral Analysis (VMBA). These types of alerts use behavioral analytics to identify compromised resources based on an analysis of the virtual machine (VM) event logs, such as process-creation events, in memory only (fileless attack), and login events. While these examples were related to Defender for Server, other Defender for Cloud plans use different methods to identify suspicious activity and trigger an alert.

Defender for Servers also identifies suspicious activity in the network layer by collecting security information from your Azure Internet Protocol Flow Information Export (IPFIX) traffic and analyzes it to identify threats and trigger alerts, such as the `Suspicious Incoming RDP Network Activity From Multiple Sources` alert.

Understanding alerts

Before a Defender for Cloud plan triggers an alert, it needs to have a level of certainty that this alert is a true-positive. The intent is to reduce false-positive alerts and provide a high-quality alert level. To accomplish that, the following actions are done during the alert normalization, as shown in Figure 6-1.

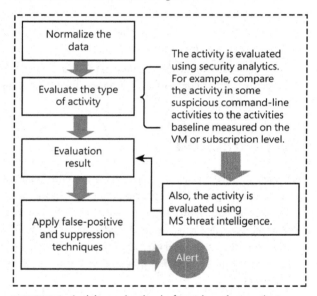

FIGURE 6-1 Activity evaluation before triggering an alert

When an alert is finally triggered, you will be able to answer five main questions that are important for your investigation. The questions are shown in the **Security Alert** blade, as shown in Figure 6-2.

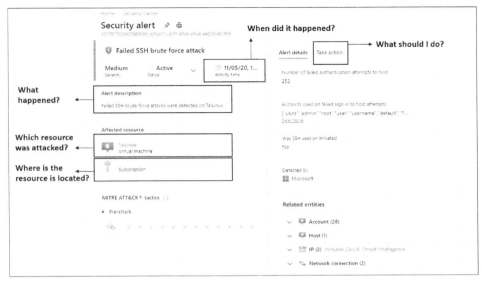

FIGURE 6-2 The Security Alert blade shows the answers to the major investigation's questions.

It is important to emphasize that not all alerts will have the same level of information because it depends on the threat type and the analytics for that threat. Alerts will also differ in the time it takes for them to be triggered. Defender for Servers has three major detection engines that will dictate how long it takes for an alert to be triggered:

1. The event-based detection engine will trigger near-real-time alerts.

2. The query-based detection engine works on different events from different sources before triggering an alert, which, by nature, will take more time.

3. The batch-process detection engine runs massively parallel analytics on large-scale datasets, which can take even longer.

Accessing security alerts

The number of security alerts you see in the Security Alerts dashboard may vary depending on the number of resources that you are monitoring with Defender for Cloud and the business itself. Some organizations receive more attacks than others, and as a result, they have more security alerts. If you don't have any security alerts in your environment, you can simulate an alert using this procedure:

1. Open Azure portal and sign in with a user who has **Security Admin** privileges.

2. In the left navigation pane, click **Microsoft Defender For Cloud**.

3. In the Defender for Cloud left navigation pane under **General**, click the **Security Alerts** option.

4. In the top-right corner, click the **Sample Alerts** option; the **Create Sample Alerts (Preview)** blade appears, as shown in Figure 6-3.

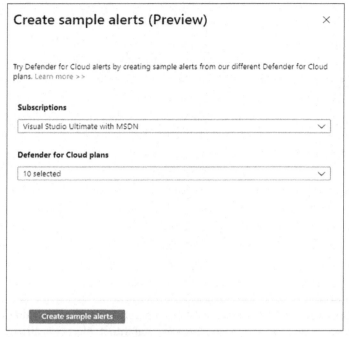

FIGURE 6-3 Creating a sample alert

5. In the **Subscriptions** dropdown menu, select the subscription on which you want to generate the sample alert.

6. Click the **Defender For Cloud Plans** dropdown menu and select only **Virtual Machines**.

7. Click the **Create Sample Alerts** button to generate the sample alerts.

After a few minutes, you will see that five sample alerts appear in the dashboard, as shown in Figure 6-4.

FIGURE 6-4 Security alert dashboard with the sample alerts for VMs

By default, the Security Alerts dashboard presents the alerts indexed by **Severity**, but you can use the filtering options to change the severities you want to see. You can also filter by

- **Subscription** If you have multiple subscriptions selected, you can customize which subscriptions you want to see alerts from.

- **Status**   By default, only **Active** is selected. However, you can change it so you see dismissed alerts.
- **Time**   Allows you to configure the timeline of the alerts you can see for up to the previous three months.
- **Add Filter**   Allows you to add more filters.

In addition to the filters, you can also use the search box to search for **Alert ID**, **Alert Title**, or **Affected Resource**. Once you find the desired alert, you can click it, and the **Alert Details** page appears, as shown in Figure 6-5.

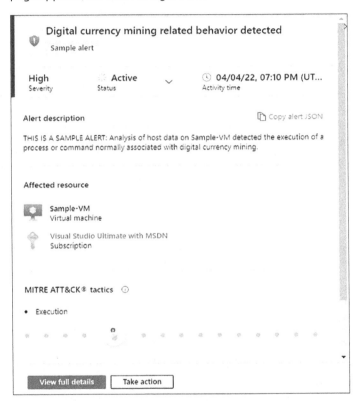

FIGURE 6-5   Alert details page

This page allows you to review the alert's details and change the status from **Active** to **Dismissed**. You also have a graphical representation of where the alerts fit into the **MITRE ATT&CK Tactics** framework.

> **NOTE**   You can learn more about this framework at *https://attack.mitre.org*.

After reviewing the alert's details, you can obtain more granular information by accessing the alert's full details page. To do that, click the **View Full Details** button; the full **Alert Details** page appears, as shown in Figure 6-6.

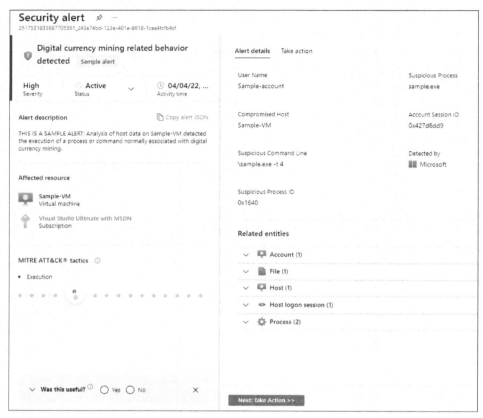

FIGURE 6-6 Full alert page

The right portion of the full alert page shows more details that are relevant for the alert. In the bottom part of the page are the **Related Entities**, which enumerate the relevant entities (**Accounts, Files, Host, Host Logon Session,** and **Process**) that were used during this attack. Keep in mind that the related entities will vary according to the alert type and whether those entities were used. Although the example shown in Figure 6-6 is from a sample alert, the fields shown are the same ones that you would see in a real live alert.

Another important option on this page is the **Take Action** tab, which contains relevant information to mitigate the threat highlighted in this alert (**Mitigate The Threat**), the recommendations that could be remediated to prevent future attacks (**Prevent Future Attacks**), the option to trigger a Logic App automation (**Trigger Automated Response**), and the option to create a suppression rule (**Suppress Similar Alerts**). Figure 6-7 shows the **Take Action** tab.

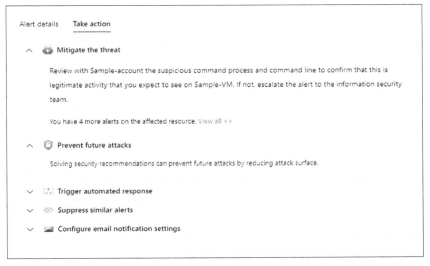

FIGURE 6-7 Take Action tab with the available options for an alert

Alert suppression

There are some scenarios in which you might want to dismiss an alert because it is a false-positive for your environment. A typical scenario is when an organization is going through a pentest (penetration testing) exercise conducted by their red team, and the organization wants to suppress some of the triggered alerts to avoid noise and alert pollution. You can leverage the alert suppression feature for that scenario.

Before configuring alert suppression, you should identify the exact alert you want to suppress and how long the suppression rule should be active. Establishing an expiration date for the rule is important because you don't want to be blind to this alert forever. Usually, those suppression scenarios happen for a reason, and for the most part, they are caused by a temporary circumstance. Follow the steps below to configure an alert suppression rule:

1. Open Azure portal and sign in with a user who has Security Admin privileges.
2. In the left navigation pane, click **Defender For Cloud**.
3. In the Defender for Cloud left navigation pane under **General**, click the **Security Alerts** option.
4. In the **Security Alerts** dashboard, click the **Suppression Rules** option; the **Suppression Rules** page appears, as shown in Figure 6-8.

FIGURE 6-8 Suppression Rules page

5. Click the **Create New Suppression Rule** option; the **New Suppression Rule** blade appears, as shown in Figure 6-9.

FIGURE 6-9 Creating a new suppression rule

6. In the **Rule Conditions** section, click the **Subscription** dropdown menu option and select the subscription on which you want to apply this rule.

7. Under **Alerts**, select **Custom**, and in the dropdown menu, select the alert you want to suppress. For this example, select the **Suspicious PHP Execution Detected** sample alert.

8. For the **Entities** option, you can make the suppression more granular by specifying the specific fields from the alert that should match the suppressed rule. Then, you can click the plus sign button (**+**) to add multiple entities. Just keep in mind that when you do that, the suppression rule will only apply if both conditions are true. In other words, there is an AND between each entity field. For this example, leave this selection as is.

9. In the **Rule Details** section, under the **Rule Name**, type a name for this rule. The name cannot have space. For this example, type **PHPSuppression**.

10. Leave the **State** setting to its default option, **Enabled**.

11. Select the most appropriate option from the **Reason** dropdown menu. For this example, select **Other**, and in the **Comment** field, type **Suppression for red team exercise**.

12. Configure **Rule Expiration** for two months from the day you are configuring.

13. To validate the rule, click the **Simulate** button, and you will see the result right under the **Test Your Rule** option.

14. Click the **Apply** button to commit the change and create the rule.

The next time this alert is triggered, it will be automatically suppressed. It is important to mention that suppressed alerts are still available for you to see. You just need to change the filter in the **Security Alerts** dashboard to see the dismissed alerts. If you are using the **Continuous Export** feature to export all alerts to the Log Analytics workspace, the suppressed alerts will also be available in the workspace; you just need to run a query for dismissed alerts.

Alerts in Azure Resource Graph (ARG)

Starting in the last quarter of 2020, alerts also became available in the Azure Resource Graph (ARG). You can access ARG directly from the **Security Alerts** dashboard by using the **Open Query** option, which will open **Azure Resource Graph Explorer** with a query that represents the visualization you had configured in the Security Alerts dashboard, as shown in Figure 6-10.

FIGURE 6-10 Azure Resource Graph Explorer

You can either click the **Run Query** option to see the results based on the current query, or you can customize the query, which uses the Kusto Query Language (KQL) format.

Defender for Servers

Defender for Servers is the first Defender for Cloud plan available in the price settings for the subscription. In 2022, this plan was split into two tiers called Plan 1 (P1) and Plan 2 (P2):

- P1   P1 was created for scenarios where you only need to deploy Microsoft Defender for Endpoint (MDE) using the native integration of Microsoft Defender for Cloud. In this plan MDE licenses are charged per hour instead of per seat, lowering costs for protected VMs only when they are in use. MDE leverages the Defender for Cloud auto-provisioning capability to automatically deploy to all cloud workloads. Lastly, this plan also offers alerts and vulnerability data from MDE to appear in the Defender for Cloud dashboard.

- P2   P2 does everything that P1 does, but it adds all other Defender for Servers capabilities, such as:
  - Threat detections for the operating system, network layer, and control plane
  - File integrity monitoring
  - Just-in-time VM access
  - Integrated Vulnerability Assessment
  - Adaptive application control
  - Adaptive network hardening
  - Network map
  - Regulatory compliance dashboard
  - 500MB allowance in the Log Analytics workspace for specific data types

When enabling Defender for Server for the first time, you can select whether you want P1 or P2. Also, if you are in an environment that used Defender for Servers before this April 2022 change, the selection will automatically be P2. Follow the steps below to see which plan you are currently using:

1. Open the Azure portal and sign in with a user who has Security Admin privileges.
2. In the left navigation pane, click **Defender For Cloud**.
3. In the Defender for Cloud left navigation pane under **Management**, click the **Environment Settings** option.
4. Click the subscription for which you want to view the pricing settings.
5. On the **Defender Plans** page, under the **Server Pricing**, click the **Change Plan** option, and you will see the **Plan Selection** blade, as shown in Figure 6-11. Here, you can select **Microsoft Defender For Servers P1** or **Microsoft Defender For Servers P2**.
6. Once you finish reviewing, you can click the **Confirm** button.

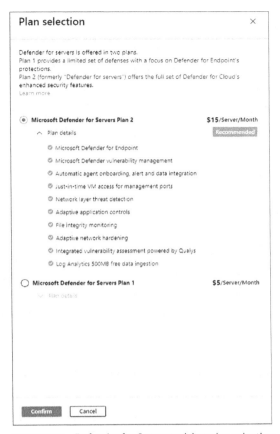

FIGURE 6-11 Defender for Servers pricing plan selection

Figure 6-11 shows the features available on Defender for Servers Plan 2, and while some of these features have already been covered in this book, others are covered in later chapters. The focus of this chapter is to cover the threat detection capabilities for each plan. Defender for Server has different threat detections for Windows and Linux, as shown in the following sections. You will learn more about the integration with MDE in Chapter 7, "Better together."

Windows

Defender for Servers detection in Windows looks at many events, and once it finds something suspicious, it will trigger an alert. For example, if you execute the command below in a VM monitored by Defender for Servers, it will be considered a suspicious activity:

```
powershell -nop -exec bypass -EncodedCommand "cABvAHcAZQByAHMAaABlAGwAbAAgAC0AY
wBvAG0AbQBhAG4AZAAgACIAJgAgAHsAIABpAHcAcgAgAGgAdAB0AHAAcwA6AC8ALwBkAG8AdwBuAGwAb
wBhAGQALgBzAHkAcwBpAG4AdAB1AHIAbgBhAGwAcwAuAGMAbwBtAC8AZgBpAGwAZQBzAC8AUwB5AHMAbQ
BvAG4ALgB6AGkAcAAgAC0ATwB1AHQARgBpAGwAZQQAgAGMAOgBcAHQAZQBtAHAAAXABzAHYAYwBoAG8AcwB0AC4
AZQB4AGUAIAB9ACIA"
```

PowerShell is a very powerful tool, and you can see on the MITRE ATT&CK's techniques (*https://attack.mitre.org/techniques/T1086/*) page that PowerShell has been used in many attack campaigns. When Defender for Servers detects the PowerShell execution with the encoded command, it raises an alert for what the user is trying to hide. In this case, the command below is trying to download the sysmon.zip file from the SysInternals website and save it to the C:\temp folder with the svhost.exe name:

```
powershell -command "& { iwr https://download.sysinternals.com/files/Sysmon.zip -OutFile
c:\temp\svchost.exe }"
```

Using PowerShell encoding to download malware from a command-and-control is a common malicious pattern, so Defender for Servers will raise an alert.

> **TIP** You can test Windows Detections in Defender for Servers using the Playbook available at *https://github.com/Azure/Microsoft-Defender-for-Cloud/tree/main/Simulations*.

Linux

When Linux detections were first released, there was a dependency in AuditD to be installed in the Linux operating system. AuditD is a service that runs in Linux systems to collect and write logs for auditing purposes. While AuditD provides a lot of information that can be used to detect threats, not all Linux distros will have AuditD installed by default. For this reason, the latest change in behavior for Linux detections was to bake the necessary elements that will collect relevant data in the agent (the Log Analytics Agent) itself.

> **TIP** You can test Linux Detections in Defender for Servers using the Playbook available at *https://github.com/Azure/Microsoft-Defender-for-Cloud/tree/main/Simulations*.

Defender for Containers

Defender for Containers provides hardening assessment for Kubernetes clusters running on Azure Kubernetes Services (AKS), Kubernetes on-premises, IaaS, Amazon Elastic Kubernetes Service (EKS) and Google Kubernetes Engine (GKE). Also, it provides Vulnerability Assessment (VA) for images stored in Azure Container Registries (ACR) and running in Azure Kubernetes Service (AKS).

While these features are considered part of your security hygiene, Defender for Containers also has threat detection for nodes and clusters. The architecture shown in Figure 6-12 represents these capabilities.

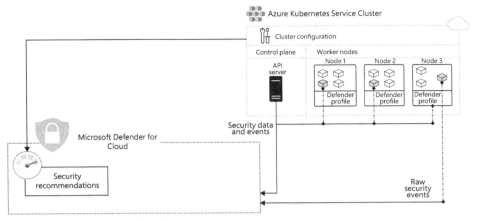

FIGURE 6-12 Defender for Containers

As you can see in Figure 6-12, two major components communicate with Defender for Cloud via the Defender for Containers plan:

- **Defender profile**   This profile is deployed to each node; it provides runtime protections, collects signals, and includes the DaemonSet. For more information on DaemonSet, see *https://kubernetes.io/docs/concepts/workloads/controllers/daemonset.*

- **Azure Policy add-on for Kubernetes**   This component is responsible for collecting cluster and workload configuration for admission control policies. It is deployed in one node of the cluster and also includes Gatekeeper. For more information about Gatekeeper, visit *https://github.com/open-policy-agent/gatekeeper.*

> *TIP*   To enable this plan, you need to enable containers by going to the pricing page. (Use the same steps discussed earlier in this chapter in the "Defender for Servers" section.)

We recommend using the auto-provisioning capability when onboarding containers because auto-provisioning will automatically deploy Azure Arc. For example, when you are configuring a multi-cloud connector, if you configure the default auto-provisioning option to **Off** during the GCP connector onboarding process or afterwards, you will need to manually install Azure Arc-enabled Kubernetes, the Defender extension, and the Azure Policy extensions to each of your GKE clusters to get the full security value out of Defender for Containers.

Vulnerability Assessment

The Vulnerability Assessment (VA) performed by Defender for Containers appears in the Microsoft Defender for Cloud dashboard as a security recommendation, as shown in Figure 6-13.

FIGURE 6-13 Vulnerability Assessment for Containers

When you open this recommendation, you will see the list of checks that ran; when you click each security check, you will see more information about the vulnerability, including remediation steps (if available), relevant Common Vulnerabilities and Exposures (CVEs), Common Vulnerability Scoring System (CVSS) scores, and more. Also, you can view the identified vulnerabilities for one or more subscriptions or a specific registry.

Threat detection

As shown previously in Figure 6-12, Defender for Containers uses threat detection on the cluster level and on the underlying cluster nodes by monitoring the control plane (API server) and the containerized workload itself. Figure 6-14 shows an example of an alert based on Kubernetes audit log analysis.

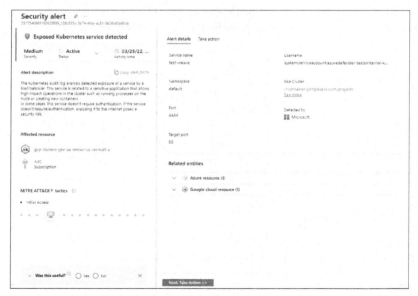

FIGURE 6-14 Threat Detection for Containers

To determine whether the alert is based on the control plane or the runtime workload in the clusters, use the **Copy Alert JSON** button shown in Figure 6-14, paste the content into a Notepad file, and check the suffix, as shown in the alertName field that appears in the raw JSON shown in Listing 6-1.

LISTING 6-1 Alert JSON

```
"type": "Microsoft.Security/Locations/alerts",
 "properties": {
  "vendorName": "Microsoft",
  "alertDisplayName": "Exposed Kubernetes service detected",
  "alertName": "K8S_ExposedService",
  "detectedTimeUtc": "2022-03-25T13:11:21.736406Z",
  "description": "The Kubernetes audit log analysis detected exposure of a service by a
load balancer. This service is related to a sensitive application that allows high impact
operations in the cluster such as running processes on the node or creating new contain-
ers.\nIn some cases, this service doesn't require authentication. If the service doesn't
require authentication, exposing it to the internet poses a security risk.",
  "remediationSteps": "1. Find the external IP address of the service with the command:
kubectl get service [service name] -n [namespace]. The service name and namespace are in
the alert details.\n2. Check whether the service is exposed to the internet by trying to
access to its IP address with the port listed in the alert details.\n3. If the service is
exposed to the internet and is not protected by an authentication mechanism, escalate the
alert to your security information team.",
  "actionTaken": "Undefined",
  "reportedSeverity": "Medium"
```

If it is a control plane security alert, you will see the K8S_ prefix, as shown in the code above, and if it is a runtime workload in the clusters type of alert, you will see the K8S.NODE_ prefix.

> **TIP**   You can see the list of all alerts that can be generated by Defender for Containers at *https://aka.ms/azdforaks*.

Defender for App Service

Azure App Service is a service for hosting web applications, REST APIs, and mobile back ends. It enables you to develop in many languages, such as .NET, .NET Core, Java, Ruby, Node.js, PHP, or Python. Applications run and scale on both Windows and Linux. Defender for Cloud leverages the scale of the cloud to identify attacks on App Service applications; it focuses on emerging attacks while attackers are in the reconnaissance phase and identifies vulnerabilities across multiple websites hosted on Azure.

Defender for App Service detects a multitude of threats by continuously monitoring the VM instance in which the App Service is running and its management interface. It also monitors the requests and responses sent to and from your App Service apps and the underlying sandboxes and VMs. Figure 6-15 shows an example of a Dangling DNS Alert, which is an analytic available in this plan to catch a DNS record that points to a recently deleted App Service resource.

FIGURE 6-15   Dangling DNS Alert triggered by Defender for App Service

Although this is a sample alert generated by the Sample Alert feature, it gives you an idea of the metadata available for this analytic. This type of attack usually takes place when a website is removed, but the custom domain from the DNS registrar is not. In this case, the DNS entry points to a non-existent resource, which means the domain is vulnerable to a takeover. Although Defender for Cloud does not perform a scan DNS registrar for existing dangling DNS entries, it will still trigger an alert when an App Service website is decommissioned and its custom domain (DNS entry) is not deleted.

Defender for Storage

Visibility and control of different workloads are critical when it comes to security hygiene. Exposed storage containers are a typical scenario targeted by threat actors utilizing custom scanners built specifically to identify public containers. Microsoft Defender for Storage is an Azure-native layer of security intelligence that detects unusual and potentially harmful attempts to access or exploit your storage accounts.

Defender for Storage can be enabled for data stored in Azure Blob Storage (Standard/Premium StorageV2, Block Blobs), Azure Files, and Azure Data Lake Storage (ADLS) Gen2. You can enable Defender for Storage on the subscription level just like any other plan, but you can also enable it only on the storage accounts you want to protect. The steps to enable this plan on the subscription level are the same as shown in the "Defender for Servers" section earlier in this chapter. If you only want to enable it on the storage account itself, you can use the `Enable-AzSecurityAdvancedThreatProtection` PowerShell command, as shown in the example below:

```
Enable-AzSecurityAdvancedThreatProtection -ResourceId "/subscriptions/
<subscription-id>/resourceGroups/<resource-group>/providers/Microsoft.Storage/
storageAccounts/<storage-account>/"
```

Defender for Storage works by continually analyzing the telemetry stream generated by the Azure Blob Storage and Azure Files services. If a potential malicious activity is detected, a security alert is generated. Defender for Storage provides alerts based on different types of threats, as shown below:

- **Unusual access to an account** Alerts that fit this category include threats, such as access from a TOR exit node.

- **Unusual behavior in an account** Alerts that are part of this category are the ones where the behavior is a deviation from a learned baseline, such as an unusual deletion of blobs or files.

- **Hash reputation-based malware detection** As files are uploaded to the storage account, they are analyzed by the hash reputation system, which looks to Microsoft Threat Intelligence to determine whether the file is suspicious. It is very important to understand that this is not an antimalware feature because it only looks into the file hash and does not scan the file.

- **Unusual file uploads** Alerts that fit this category are the ones where an upload deviates from the normal pattern, such as uploading cloud service packages and executable files.

- **Public visibility** Alerts in this category are related to break-in attempts using public scanners.

- **Phishing campaigns**   Alerts in this category are related to scenarios in which a piece of content that is hosted on Azure Storage is identified as part of a phishing attack impacting Microsoft 365 users.

Figure 6-16 shows an example of the `Access from an unusual location to a storage file share` alert, where you can see more details about the attack.

FIGURE 6-16   Access From An Unusual Location Alert generated by Defender for Storage

Considerations before enabling Defender for Storage

While our general recommendation is to keep Defender for Storage enabled across every type of storage account at the subscription level, some organizations that need to limit costs might need to prioritize what is most critical to them and enable those things only at the storage account level.

There is also a misunderstanding that storage accounts behind private links don't pose a risk and therefore don't need to have Defender for Storage enabled. The reality is that there are several threats to the storage account behind private links. The most prominent threats are

- Malicious insiders
- Compromised identities
- When lateral movement occurs within the private network when a resource and access keys or access tokens have been compromised
- When identity has been compromised and access privileges have been escalated

For these reasons, exclusively using this rationale is not a recommended approach. Before making this decision, it is important for your organization to perform a risk assessment that considers the following factors:

- The type of information stored in the storage account
- The potential impact if this data is compromised
- Whether an attacker can leverage the storage account as an entry point into your organization

Based on this assessment and the cost estimation that you found using the estimation workbook, you can decide if you want to keep Defender for Storage enabled in the entire subscription or if you want to enable it only on critical storage accounts. Another outcome of this risk assessment is that you always want to have threat detection for all storage accounts but want to exclude storage accounts that don't have critical data that needs to be monitored. If that's the case, use the procedures from *http://aka.ms/D4StorageExclusion* to exclude only the desired storage accounts.

Defender for SQL

Defender for SQL is a protection plan that helps you mitigate potential database vulnerabilities and detect anomalous activities that might indicate threats against your databases. Defender for SQL has evolved over the years and currently has two major plans:

- **Defender for Azure SQL**   This plan includes Azure SQL Database, Azure SQL Managed Instance, and Dedicated SQL pool in Azure Synapse.
- **Defender for SQL servers on machines**   This plan includes the SQL Server running on VMs in Azure, on-premises, or in another cloud provider.

Defender for SQL provides threat detection for anomalous activities indicating unusual and potentially harmful attempts to access or exploit databases. Figure 6-17 shows an example of an alert triggered by this plan.

One important aspect of Figure 6-17 can be seen in the lower-left corner within the **Data Classification** field. This information is populated there because of the native integration with Azure Purview. You will learn more about this integration in Chapter 7, "Better together."

Defender for SQL can be easily enabled on the subscription level of any Azure SQL database you want. No agent is required. However, to use the Defender for SQL servers on machines, you need to enable the plan on the subscription level, and you must onboard the server, which means provisioning the Log Analytics Agent on SQL Server. If your VMs are in Azure, you just need to use the auto-provisioning option in Azure Security Center to automatically onboard the Log Analytics Agent to your Azure VMs.

FIGURE 6-17 Brute-force attack attempt against an SQL database

As part of the onboarding process, you must also enable Azure Arc. We recommend that you use Azure Arc for your SQL servers that are on-premises or in different cloud providers (AWS and GCP), and once they are fully onboarded, you can deploy the Log Analytics Agent. In summary, follow the sequence below to fully onboard:

1. Enable Azure Arc on your machines. (Follow the steps at *http://aka.ms/ ASCbookEnableArc*.)

2. Install the Log Analytics Agent to this machine. You can easily identify which machines are missing the agent by reviewing this Security Center recommendation: `Log Analytics Agent Should Be Installed On Your Windows-Based Azure Arc Machines`.

3. Enable the **SQL Servers On Machines** pricing plan on the **Pricing & Settings** page in Defender for Cloud. The plan will be enabled on all SQL servers and fully active after the first restart of the SQL Server instance.

> **TIP** You can quickly identify Azure Arc-enabled machines using the **Inventory** dashboard. Create a filter based on the **Resource Type** and change the criteria to see only `servers - azure arc`.

Vulnerability Assessment for SQL

Built-in Vulnerability Assessment (VA) is another important capability that comes with Defender for SQL. Defender for SQL will identify that you don't have SQL VA enabled on your workloads and will trigger a recommendation suggesting you enable this feature. Once the feature is on, SQL VA scans your database and gives you a comprehensive list of items that need to be addressed. SQL VA employs a knowledge base of rules that flag security vulnerabilities. It brings awareness of deviations from security best practices, such as misconfigurations, excessive permissions, and unprotected sensitive data.

You can access the assessment from the SQL Databases Should Have Vulnerability Findings Resolved security recommendation, as shown in Figure 6-18.

FIGURE 6-18 VA results in SQL

In this list, you can see all affected resources, and once you click a particular resource, you can visualize the affected databases and the security checks that were performed in more detail, as shown in Figure 6-19.

FIGURE 6-19 List of affected databases

Now that you have this view, you can start remediating each security check. To do that, click the security check you want to remediate, and a new blade with more details about the security check will appear, as shown in Figure 6-20.

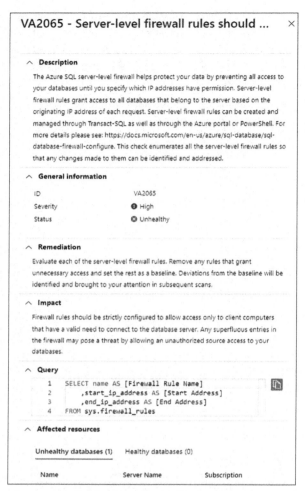

FIGURE 6-20 Details about the security check

After reviewing the details of the security check, you can click the affected database to implement the remediation.

So far, you have accessed SQL VA entirely from the Defender for Cloud dashboard. However, you can also view this information directly from the database. For example, you can go to the SQL Database dashboard, select the database you want to review, and in the left navigation pane, select **Defender For Cloud**. There, you have the consolidated view of all recommendations, alerts, and the Vulnerability Assessment relevant to the selected database, as shown in Figure 6-21.

FIGURE 6-21 Microsoft Defender for Cloud blade integrated with Azure SQL

This is a good visualization for the database owner who needs to know more about the security-related events of the selected database.

Defender for Cosmos DB

Azure Cosmos DB is a fully managed NoSQL database for modern, fast, and flexible app development, capable of having single-digit millisecond response times, automatic and instant scalability, and multiple SDKs and APIs to support a variety of non-relational data models.

In June 2022, Microsoft released the Defender for Cosmos DB plan in general availability. The enabling process is very similar to SQL, where you can enable it on the subscription or resource levels. At the same time, another change was introduced to allow you to enable the database-related plan from a dedicated blade, available on the **Defender Plans** page, as shown in Figure 6-22.

Defender for Azure Cosmos DB monitors your Azure Cosmos DB accounts and detects various attack vectors, such as attacks originating from the application layer, SQL injections, suspicious access patterns, compromised identities, malicious insiders, and direct attacks on the database. Figure 6-23 shows a sample alert generated by Defender for Cosmos DB.

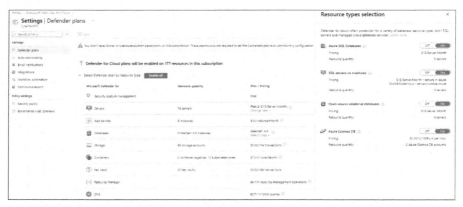

FIGURE 6-22 Database plan blade

FIGURE 6-23 Access From Unusual Location alert

This sample alert is triggered in real scenarios when Defender for Cosmos DB identifies an Azure Cosmos DB account that was accessed from a location considered unfamiliar. This familiarity is based on the usual access pattern.

Defender for Open-Source Relational Databases

Another 2022 addition was the Defender for Open-Source Relational Database, which includes support for Azure Database for PostgreSQL, Azure Database for MySQL, and Azure Database for MariaDB. Just like the other database plans, Defender for Open-Source Relational

Databases includes detection for anomalous activities indicating unusual and potentially harmful attempts to access or exploit databases. Enabling this plan is performed in the same way as shown previously in the "Defender for Cosmos DB section." However, unlike Defender for SQL, this plan doesn't include Vulnerability Assessment for open-source relational databases.

The alerts generated by Defender for Open-Source Relational Databases might have the same alert title across Azure Database for PostgreSQL, Azure Database for MySQL, and Azure Database for MariaDB. However, if you copy the alert in JSON format (as shown previously in this chapter), you will see that the `alertName` field is different. For example, the alert titled `Suspected brute force attack using a valid user` is the same for all three databases, but if you look at the JSON, the `alertName` is `SQL.PostgreSQL_BruteForce`, `SQL.MariaDB_BruteForce`, or `SQL.MySQL_BruteForce`.

Defender for Key Vault

Defender for Key Vault uses machine learning to detect unusual and potentially harmful attempts to access or exploit Key Vault accounts. When this chapter was written, the only option to enable Defender for Key Vault was to enable it on the entire subscription. Figure 6-24 shows an Defender for Key Vault sample alert.

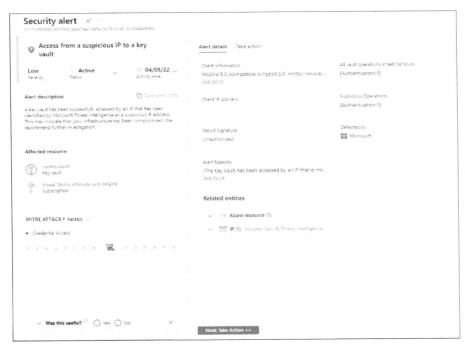

FIGURE 6-24 Access from a suspicious IP to a Key Vault

Defender for Resource Manager

Azure Resource Manager (ARM) is Azure's deployment and management service. ARM provides a management layer that allows you to create, update, and delete resources in your Azure account. These operations can be done via the Azure portal, PowerShell, Azure CLI, REST APIs, and client SDKs.

Threat actors targeting ARM will most likely use toolkits such as Microbust to discover weak configurations and perform post-exploitation actions such as credential dumping. Defender for Resource Manager uses advanced security analytics to detect threats and trigger an alert when suspicious activity occurs. Also, Defender for Resource Manager can detect suspicious resource management operations, including suspicious IP addresses, disabling the antimalware, and executing suspicious scripts in virtual machine extensions. It can also detect lateral movement from the Azure management layer to the Azure resources data plane. Figure 6-25 shows an example of an alert generated by Defender for Resource Manager.

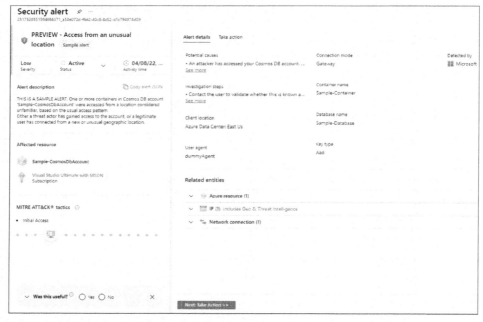

FIGURE 6-25 Defender for Resource Manager alert

Defender for DNS

Defender for DNS is a threat detection that can be enabled if you are using Azure DNS. Azure DNS is a hosting service for DNS domains that leverages Microsoft Azure infrastructure to provide name resolution. According to the 2020 Global DNS Threat Report, in a study performed by the International Data Corporation (IDC), 79 percent of the surveyed organizations experienced a type of DNS attack, and DNS spoofing was the number-one type of attack (39 percent).

MORE INFO You can download the report from *https://www.efficientip.com/ resources/idc-dns-threat-report-2020/.*

Defender for DNS can identify DNS Phishing attacks by analyzing DNS transactions, and it can identify a request for a possible phishing domain. Such activity is frequently performed by threat actors to harvest credentials to remote services. This activity is usually followed by exploiting credentials on the legitimate service. Also, Defender for DNS can identify the following:

- DNS tunneling, which can be used to exfiltrate data from your Azure resources
- Malware communicating with a command-and-control server
- Communication with malicious domains for phishing or cryptomining
- Communication with malicious DNS resolvers

Figure 6-26 shows a sample alert for a suspicious activity detected by Defender for DNS based on an analysis of DNS transactions.

FIGURE 6-26 Defender for DNS alert

The cyberkill chain and fusion alerts

The cyberkill chain is a threat model described in 2011 by analysts from Lockheed Martin. The model was designed to help security teams and researchers organize their thinking about detecting and responding to threats. The model is now generally accepted and is part of the general lexicon of all security professionals.

The original cyberkill chain was divided into these phases:

1. **Reconnaissance** During this phase, the attacker identifies the best targets.

2. **Weaponization** Here, files are altered to make them weapons against a target system and are used to install malicious code.

3. **Delivery**   At this point, weaponized files are placed on the target.

4. **Exploitation**   During this phase, weaponized files are detonated; that is, they're run on the victim system.

5. **Installation**   At this point, a back door is installed on the compromised system, giving the attacker persistent access.

6. **Command-and-control (C&C)**   Here, malware on the compromised system communicates with a C&C system that gives the attacker access to the resources required to carry out their objective.

7. **Actions on objectives**   At this point, the attacker carries out their objectives, which might be predefined or might have evolved based on discovery. The cyberkill chain was defined when on-premises computing was the norm. Now that cloud computing is considered to be a better option, the cyberkill chain must be re-evaluated and updated. A reconfiguration of the cyberkill chain might include the following phases:

   - **Active recon**   In this phase, the attacker uses numerous footprinting methods to identify the operating system or services being used, which will be the focus of the attack.

   - **Delivery**   Because most public cloud assets lack a logged-on user, attackers will need to hack the system—typically by finding unpatched exploits that can be leveraged against the system or service.

   - **Exploitation**   This phase focuses on problems on the server-side instead of the client-side.

   - **Persistence**   Unlike client-side systems, which are rebooted often, server- and service-specific systems are rarely rebooted. The exploit code will need to remain in memory to remain persistent within the system. That is the focus of this stage.

   - **Internal recon**   Attacks against cloud-based systems are server-based. Therefore, rather than installing new tools, the attacker can simply use the server's built-in tools to conduct the attack. This helps the attacker remain undiscovered, as installing new tools could trigger an alert.

Defender has a type of alert called a *security incident*, which is raised in the dashboard whenever the system identifies multiple alerts that, when correlated with each other, indicate that those alerts belong to the same attack. A security incident uses the fusion capability to correlate the alerts that appear to be related to each other.

Figure 6-27 shows an example of what such an attack campaign might look like and what alerts might be raised at the various stages of a cyberkill chain. The figure shows a highly simplified version of the cyberkill chain (outlined in the previous steps) to make it easier to understand how fusion alerts work.

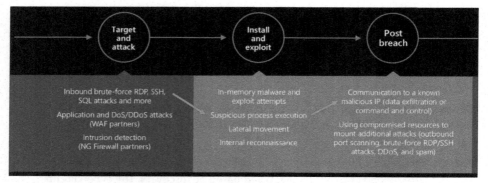

FIGURE 6-27 Microsoft Defender for Servers detections across the cyberkill chain

The sequence in Figure 6-27 goes like this:

1. **Target and attack** In this phase, Defender for Servers detects what appears to be a brute-force attack against the Remote Desktop Protocol (RDP) server on a VM. This determination is made by comparing a baseline of RDP connections to the VM, the current rate of RDP login attempts, and other factors related to RDP logins.

2. **Install and exploit** Here, Defender for Servers detects the execution of a suspicious process on the VM. This suspicious process could be predefined (known-bad malware), or it could be a process that wasn't executed on the machine during previous baselines and is therefore unrecognized. (For example, maybe the process is launched by software recently installed by the admin.) You'll have to correlate this event with other events to find out.

3. **Post-breach** At this point, Defender for Servers has detected what appears to be a communication channel established between the VM and a known-malicious IP address (probably flagged by a threat intelligence feed). There's a very good chance that this is bad, but there is still a chance that it isn't. For example, maybe a security researcher or a red-team member working for the customer connected to the address on purpose. Yes, a connection to a known-bad IP address is serious, but it doesn't guarantee that the VM has been compromised.

Taken individually, each phase of the cyberkill chain indicates something bad might be happening but cannot offer complete certainty. However, when you correlate these findings, you can be almost 100 percent sure that a brute-force RDP attack has compromised the VM, the attacker has installed and run new malware on the machine, and the malware is communicating with a C&C server (likely identified by a threat intelligence feed). As a result, a security incident appears in the alert dashboard in the format shown in Figure 6-28.

FIGURE 6-28 Security incident powered by fusion

On the right side of this dashboard are the individual alerts that are part of this security incident, which help you investigate the alerts (because now you know that there is a correlation between these alerts, and, most likely, they are part of the same attack campaign).

Threat intelligence in Defender for Cloud

As explained throughout this chapter, when a Defender for Cloud plan identifies a threat, it triggers a security alert containing detailed information regarding the event, including suggestions for remediation.

For some alerts, Defender for Cloud will also provide threat intelligence reports to facilitate your investigation. These reports contain information about the detected threats, including the following:

- Attacker's identity or associations (if this information is available)
- Attackers' objectives
- Current and historical attack campaigns (if this information is available)
- Attackers' tactics, tools, and procedures
- Associated indicators of compromise (IoC) such as URLs and file hashes
- Victimology, which is the industry and geographic prevalence to assist you in determining if your Azure resources are at risk
- Mitigation and remediation information

Keep in mind that this information is not always available for all types of alerts. It's only available for the ones that Defender for Cloud can correlate with Microsoft Threat Intelligence and provide more insights to help during the investigation. The alert shown in Figure 6-29 shows an example of an alert that contains a threat intelligence report.

FIGURE 6-29 Alert with enrichment from a threat intelligence report

In the **Alerts Details** tab, there is a link for the report, which, in this case, is called **Report: Shadow Copy Delete**. By clicking this hyperlink, you can download the PDF containing detailed information about this threat, as shown in Figure 6-30.

FIGURE 6-30 Threat intelligence report

Responding to alerts

Throughout this chapter, you saw many examples of how the different Defender for Cloud plans can trigger alerts that are rich in details and information that can assist you in responding to that alert by taking corrective actions to remediate the issue. The approach to investigating each alert can be different according to the alert type and the resource itself. For this example, let's use the Defender for Key Vault alert. Although it has some unique steps, most of the approach applies to most other alerts.

What is unique in a Defender for Key Vault alert is the fact that every alert includes an Object Identifier (ID), the User Principal Name (UPN), or the IP address of the suspicious resource. It is important to highlight that the availability of this information can also vary according to the type of access that occurred. For example, if an application accessed your Key Vault, you will not see the associated UPN, and if the traffic originated from outside of Azure, you wouldn't see an Object ID. With that in mind, we can summarize the response process for an Azure Key Vault alert in the following steps, which are further explained in the coming sections:

- Contact
- Mitigation
- Impact
- Take action

Contact

In this step, you need to verify where the traffic is coming from—in other words, whether the traffic originated from within your Azure tenant. Verify whether you have Key Vault Firewall enabled. If you do, granting access to the user or application likely triggered the alert.

If you can identify the source of the traffic as coming from your own tenant, then contact the user or application owner. If, for some reason, you cannot verify the traffic's source, skip to the next step.

Mitigation

In this step, you assume the access shouldn't have been authorized because you couldn't determine the source of the traffic in the previous step. If the traffic came from an unrecognized IP address, make sure to do the following:

1. Enable the Azure Key Vault firewall (if you don't have it enabled already).
2. Configure the firewall to allow only trusted resources and virtual networks.

However, if the alert source was an unauthorized application or suspicious user, make sure to configure the Key Vault's access policy settings to remove the corresponding security principal or restrict the operations the security principal can perform.

Another scenario is if the alert source has an Azure Active Directory role in your tenant. To respond to this scenario, you should start by contacting your administrator and then determine whether there's a need to reduce or revoke Azure Active Directory permissions.

Impact

Once the attack's impact has been mitigated, you need to investigate the secrets in your Key Vault that were affected. In this step, you will need to do the following:

1. Review the triggered alert.

2. Review the list of the secrets that were accessed and the timestamp.

3. If you have Key Vault diagnostic logs enabled, review the previous operations for the corresponding caller IP, user principal, or Object ID.

Take action

You've already compiled a list of the secrets, keys, and certificates accessed by the suspicious user or application. Your next immediate action is to rotate those objects.

Ensure that affected secrets are disabled or deleted from your Key Vault. If the credentials were used for a specific application, you would need to contact the administrator of the application and ask them to audit their environment for any uses of the compromised credentials since they were compromised. If the compromised credentials were used, the application owner should identify the information that was accessed and mitigate the impact.

Chapter 7

Better together

Microsoft Defender for Cloud can integrate with other Microsoft Security solutions to improve the overall security posture of the workloads and ensure threat detections are streamed to a Security Information and Event Management (SIEM) solution. Also, this integration provides the benefits of an Endpoint Detection and Response (EDR) solution.

In this chapter, you will learn how Defender for Cloud integrates with Microsoft Sentinel, Microsoft Purview, and Microsoft Defender for Endpoint (MDE).

Defender for Cloud and Microsoft Sentinel

Defender for Cloud alerts are published to the Azure Monitor, which enables you to use Event Hub to route Defender for Cloud alerts into an on-premises or cloud-based SIEM solution. The general process occurs in three major phases:

1. Create an Event Hub that will be the destination for your Defender for Cloud data.
2. Stream Azure Monitor logs into the Event Hub.
3. Install and configure the SIEM solution vendor's connector to stream the data from the Event Hub to your SIEM solution.

> **NOTE** Also, you can utilize the Continuous Export feature in Defender for Cloud to export all alerts to a workspace and, from there, send them to your SIEM.

While this is the general process for most of the third-party SIEM solutions, the process is much simpler with Microsoft Sentinel. Microsoft Sentinel is a cloud-native Security Information Event Management (SIEM) and Security Orchestration Automated Response (SOAR) solution. Microsoft Sentinel delivers intelligent security analytics and threat intelligence across the enterprise, providing a single solution for alert detection, threat visibility, proactive hunting, and threat response.

Microsoft Sentinel enables you to collect data across devices, applications, and infrastructure, both on-premises and in multiple clouds. Microsoft Sentinel leverages Log Analytics' workspace for data storage, as shown in Figure 7-1.

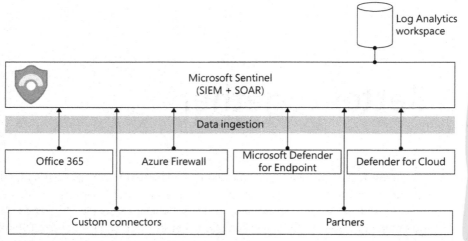

FIGURE 7-1 Microsoft Sentinel data ingestion and storage

To enable Microsoft Sentinel, you need an Azure Subscription, a Log Analytics Workspace, and contributor permissions on the subscription in which the Microsoft Sentinel workspace resides. Also, you need either contributor or reader permissions on the resource group to which the workspace belongs.

If you are using the default workspace created by Defender for Cloud, this workspace will not appear in the list when you try to enable Microsoft Sentinel. The rationale behind this is that default workspaces are managed by the service that created them (in this case, Defender for Cloud), and we want customers to have full control of their workspaces, including managing their retention periods and locations for Microsoft Sentinel. For this reason, you must create your own Log Analytics workspace.

Integration with Microsoft Sentinel

When you configure Defender for Cloud integration with Microsoft Sentinel, all security alerts generated in Defender for Cloud will be streamed to Microsoft Sentinel. Defender for Cloud must be enabled in the target subscription to configure this integration, and you need to be logged in with a user with global administrator or security administrator permissions on each subscription you want to connect. Follow the steps below to configure this integration:

1. Using the Azure portal, click **All Services** in the left navigation pane and type **Sentinel**.
2. Click the **Microsoft Sentinel** option.
3. The **Microsoft Sentinel Workspaces** blade appears for you to either select an existing workspace or create a new one. Because, in this case, you are configuring the integration with Defender for Cloud, the assumption is that Microsoft Sentinel has been already configured. So, select the workspace you are currently using.
4. The Microsoft Sentinel **Overview** page appears; in the left pane, in the **Configuration** section, click **Data Connectors**, as shown in Figure 7-2.

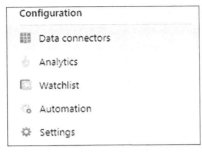

FIGURE 7-2 Configuration section in Microsoft Sentinel

5. The **Microsoft Sentinel—Data Connectors** blade appears. Select **Defender For Cloud**.

6. Click the **Open Connector Page** button, and the **Instructions** tab appears. The instructions are shown on the right side of the page (see Figure 7-3).

FIGURE 7-3 Instructions tab with the options to configure the connector

7. In the **Configuration** section, select the desired **Subscription** and click **Connect**. The status will change rapidly to Connecting; once it finishes, it will show as Connected.

8. If you scroll down on this page, you will see an optional step, **Create Incidents— Recommended!** to enable incident creation, as shown in Figure 7-4.

FIGURE 7-4 Optional step to automatically create incidents in Microsoft Sentinel

9. If you click the **Enable** button, the alerts from Defender for Cloud will automatically generate incidents in Microsoft Sentinel. For this example, you don't need to enable it now.

10. Click the **Close** button to close the blade, and if the Defender for Cloud connector's status doesn't change to Connected, click the **Refresh** button to update; the status should change, as shown in Figure 7-5.

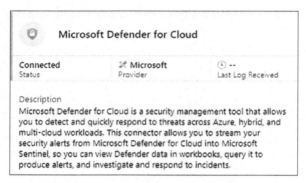

FIGURE 7-5   Defender for Cloud connector status

At this point, the security alerts triggered in Defender for Cloud will appear in Microsoft Sentinel. When you connect Microsoft Defender for Cloud to Microsoft Sentinel, the status of security alerts is synchronized between the two services. If you want to validate this configuration, you can use the Defender for Cloud sample alerts (covered in Chapter 6) feature to simulate some alerts and see the alerts arriving in Microsoft Sentinel.

Accessing alerts in Microsoft Sentinel

As mentioned earlier, during the Defender for Cloud connector configuration, you could automatically enable the alerts generated by Defender for Cloud to generate incidents in Microsoft Sentinel. An incident is an aggregation of all the relevant evidence for a specific investigation, which can include multiple alerts coming from different data sources, as shown in Figure 7-6.

FIGURE 7-6   Microsoft Sentinel performs data aggregation using alerts from multiple data sources

In the **Product Name** field shown in Figure 7-6, the **Network Communication With A Malicious Machine Detected** alert was raised by Defender for Cloud. Because this alert is in the workspace used by Microsoft Sentinel, you can leverage the Microsoft Sentinel ability to search logs to obtain more information about this alert. Go to the Microsoft Sentinel main page, click **Logs** in the left navigation pane, click the **Get Started** button on the right blade, and close the sample queries window that appears. The **Logs** page appears, as shown in Figure 7-7.

FIGURE 7-7 Microsoft Sentinel logs page

This search page uses Kusto Query Language (KQL) for queries. A Kusto query is a read-only request to process data and return results. The request is stated in plain text, using a data-flow model designed to make the syntax easy to read. The query uses schema entities that are organized in a hierarchy similar to SQL's: databases, tables, and columns. Figure 8-6 shows the schema that is available for this workspace, which is located under the **Tables** tab, as shown in Figure 7-7.

You need to start your first query from a specific point of reference. You can use the Defender for Cloud alert about which you are trying to find more information. For this example, you could start a query looking for an alert that contains the "Network communication with a malicious machine detected" string in the description. The query looks similar to this:

```
SecurityAlert
| where Description contains "Network communication with a malicious machine detected 1"
```

The result will appear in table format at the bottom of the page, as shown in Figure 7-8.

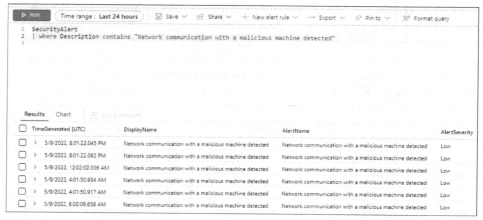

FIGURE 7-8 Query result

NOTE If you want some Kusto Query examples, visit the Microsoft Sentinel GitHub page at *https://github.com/Azure/Azure-Sentinel*.

Defender for Cloud and Microsoft Purview

Microsoft Purview is Microsoft's data governance service that provides rich insights into the sensitivity of your data in Azure. Microsoft Purview has automated data discovery, sensitive data classification, and end-to-end data lineage, which helps organizations manage and govern data in hybrid and multi-cloud environments.

When you have Microsoft Purview enabled on your Azure subscription, Defender for Cloud will automatically get additional metadata that will add information about any potentially sensitive data involved to alerts and recommendations. This information can be very useful to help triage an alert. For example, if you have two high-severity alerts for two storage accounts, which one should you prioritize for a response? You can use the insights from Microsoft Purview to understand which storage account has more critical data, such as personally identifiable information (PII).

Enabling Microsoft Purview is outside the scope of this book, so the steps below assume that you already have Microsoft Purview enabled on your Azure subscription:

1. Using the Azure portal, click **All Services** in the left navigation pane and type **Defender for Cloud**.

2. Click the **Microsoft Defender For Cloud** option.

3. In the main **Overview** dashboard, scroll down on the right side until you see the **Information Protection** tile. If Microsoft Purview is already configured, Defender for Cloud will show some statistics, as shown in Figure 7-9.

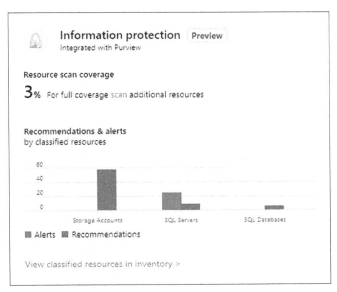

FIGURE 7-9 Information Protection tile

4. Click this tile, and the **Inventory** dashboard appears with a filter set for Data Sensitivity Classification != Unclassified, as shown in Figure 7-10.

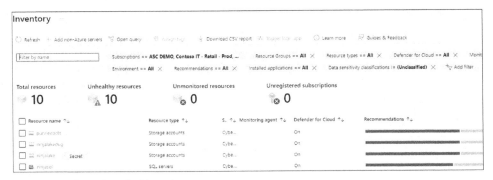

FIGURE 7-10 Inventory dashboard

5. Click the resource for which you want to see the insights. For this example, this resource will be a storage account, showing the insights in the left navigation pane, as shown in Figure 7-11.

Environment
Azure

Location
eastus

Security value

Microsoft Defender for Storage
On

Data classifications

Person's Name (2)
International Banking Account Number (IBAN) (1)
Personal IP Address (1)
U.S. Phone Number (1)
Credit Card Number (1)
Email Address (1)
IP Address (1)

See less

Purview account
purview-EU17NT

FIGURE 7-11 Resource Health page with Purview insights

On the **Resource Health** page, you can see the insights, recommendations, and alerts
related to that resource. Using the insights from Microsoft Purview, you can prioritize which
recommendations should be remediated first, such as deciding which is a proactive action to
avoid a bigger problem. For example, you might choose between a threat actor exploiting a
storage account that is open to the Internet and prioritizing an alert, which is a reactive action
to expedite the proper response for containing the threat.

Defender for Cloud and Microsoft Defender for Endpoint

Microsoft Defender for Cloud integration with Microsoft Defender for Endpoint (MDE) is
enabled by default in the subscription on which Defender for Cloud is enabled, but it requires
Defender for Server (P1 or P2) to be enabled for this integration to work. With this native integration, you get the benefits of a leading Endpoint Detection and Response (EDR); the auto-
deployment to all VMs in Azure, on-premises, or other cloud providers (AWS and GCP); and the
synchronization of alerts from MDE to the Defender for Cloud Security Alerts dashboard. This
integration supports servers running Windows and Linux operating systems. Figure 7-12 shows
an architectural diagram for this integration with Windows Server 2019, Windows Server 2022,
and Linux.

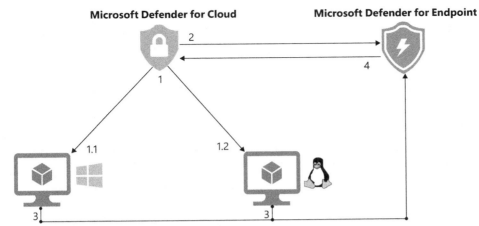

FIGURE 7-12 Architecture diagram for Defender for Cloud and MDE integration

Figure 7-12 shows the following steps:

1. During the onboarding process, Defender for Cloud runs the onboarding script to provision the MDE extension (`MDE.Windows` for Windows and `MDE.Linux` for Linux).

2. Defender for Cloud sends this information to the MDE, which extracts the relevant information to ensure these machines are also visible in the MDE Security Center portal and synchronized.

3. After the onboarding process is finished and MDE is monitoring the machine, MDE will trigger alerts when a suspicious operation occurs and send an alert to the MDE portal first.

4. These alerts will be synchronized with Defender for Cloud and appear in the **Security Alerts** dashboard.

> **NOTE** Defender for Servers P1 deploys the new MDE solution stack for Windows Server 2012 R2 and 2016, which does not use or require installation of the Log Analytics agent.

The alert generated by MDE gets streamed to Defender for Cloud, and it brings together all the insights you need to perform the initial investigation, as shown in Figure 7-13.

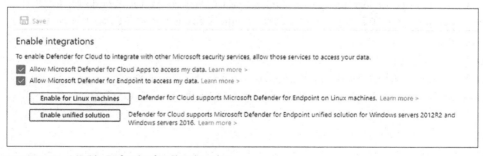

FIGURE 7-13 Security alert triggered by MDE

On the **Alert Details** tab is the **Microsoft Defender For Endpoint** link, which allows you to investigate this alert using the MDE Portal (also known as the *M365 Defender Portal*). This link redirects to *https://securitycenter.microsoft.com/alert/<operationID>*, which opens the details about the machine that triggered the alert.

The computer name and description are shown in the **Affected Resources** section. Notice that the icon represents an Azure Arc icon, which means this computer is located either on-premises or in another cloud provider (AWS or GCP). Azure Arc is a prerequisite for MDE integration to work on non-Azure machines. In other words, you need to onboard Azure Arc first, and then the MDE extension will be deployed.

If you need to disable this integration for some reason—for example, if you already have an EDR solution installed on your servers and don't need MDE—then you should deselect the **Allow Microsoft Defender for Endpoint To Access My Data** checkbox in the **Integrations** section, as shown in Figure 7-14.

FIGURE 7-14 MDE in Defender for Cloud setting

Also on the **Integrations** page is the **Enable For Linux Machines** button. If you've already enabled the MDE integration for Windows (before summer 2021), you just need to click the **Enable For Linux Machines** button to trigger the deployment of MDE for Linux on all existing machines belonging to the subscription and all new machines provisioned in this subscription.

Also, if you've never selected the **Allow Microsoft Defender For Endpoint To Access My Data** option for Windows, when you enable it for the first time and save the changes, Defender for Cloud will automatically deploy MDE for all existing and new Windows and Linux machines.

Before June 2022, the MDE integration automatically included the installation of the new MDE unified solution for machines for Defender for Servers Plan 1 and multicloud connectors with the Defender for Servers Plan 2. Plan 2 for Azure subscriptions enabled the unified solution for Linux machines and Windows 2019 and 2022 servers only. Windows Servers 2012R2 and 2016 used the MDE legacy solution, which was dependent on the Log Analytics agent.

Figure 7-14 shows an example of the **Integrations** page after the June 2022 update, which includes the button **Enable Unified Solution** option. With this addition, Defender for Servers now supports the unified solution for all machines in both Azure subscriptions and multicloud connectors.

Chapter 8

Enhanced security capabilities

Now that you know how to address recommendations to enhance the security posture of your cloud workloads and you understand the importance of threat detection based on the different Defender for Server options, you need to ensure that you also apply security controls to reduce the attack surface. In this chapter, you will learn how to use just-in-time (JIT) virtual machine (VM) access to harden the access to Azure VMs and ensure that your VMs are not always exposed to the Internet.

You will learn how to track changes to your files and registry hives using file integrity monitoring (FIM). Also, you will learn how Microsoft Defender for Cloud uses machine learning to create a list of approved applications on the machines.

Just-in-time virtual machine access

To provide remote access to VMs, the public cloud infrastructure provider must allow all remote management traffic to those VMs. To do this, it uses RDP, SSH, and remote Power-Shell. Using these tools is easy, and as we all know, nothing beats easy. Unfortunately, easy is often the enemy of security, so it's a difficult balancing act.

The reality of remote access changed substantially after COVID-19 because many more people started working remotely. A Gartner CFO Survey in 2020 revealed that 74 percent of the companies surveyed intend to permanently shift some employees to remote work. This means alternative methods for providing remote management traffic access to VMs are primarily utilized. Methods such as point-to-site VPN, site-to-site VPN, and various dedicated WAN link solutions are becoming more prevalent. Despite all that, it is still extremely important to have security policies to dictate how IaaS VMs are exposed to the Internet. If Internet exposure is mandatory, then just-in-time (JIT) VM access should also be mandatory.

RDP or SSH brute-force attacks are the most common types of attacks against VMs in Azure (and other public cloud service providers). VMs are continuously hit by attempts to log in. If you have a strong password policy, it's unlikely your VMs will be compromised, but you shouldn't trust this as your only countermeasure. You can take various steps to reduce the chance of being compromised by a brute-force attack, but you probably don't want to hand over these tasks to your public cloud service provider. However, you might consider letting your public cloud service provider help you with network access to your VMs using management ports (RDP or SSH). Defender for Servers JIT VM access allows you to control who can access predefined management ports on a VM, when that access is granted, and for how long.

You need a set of privileges to work with JIT; these privileges will vary according to the type of operation that you need to perform or that you want to allow a user to perform. You can be very granular about this permission assignment by using these guidelines:

- To configure or edit a JIT policy for a VM, you need to assign these actions to the role:
    - On the subscription or resource group scope associated with the VM: `Microsoft.Security/locations/jitNetworkAccessPolicies/write`
    - On the subscription or resource group scope of the VM: `Microsoft.Compute/virtualMachines/write`
- To request access to a VM, you need to assign these actions to the user:
    - On the subscription or resource group scope associated with the VM: `Microsoft.Security/locations/jitNetworkAccessPolicies/initiate/action`
    - On the subscription or resource group scope associated with the VM: `Microsoft.Security/locations/jitNetworkAccessPolicies/*/read`
    - On the scope of a subscription, resource group, or VM: `Microsoft.Compute/virtualMachines/read`
    - On the scope of a subscription, resource group, or VM: `Microsoft.Network/networkInterfaces/*/read`
- To read JIT policies, you need to assign these actions to the user:
    - `Microsoft.Security/locations/jitNetworkAccessPolicies/read`
    - `Microsoft.Security/locations/jitNetworkAccessPolicies/initiate/action`
    - `Microsoft.Security/policies/read`
    - `Microsoft.Security/pricings/read`
    - `Microsoft.Compute/virtualMachines/read`
    - `Microsoft.Network/*/read`

Also, if you need to see the JIT NSG policy from the VM Networking blade, add the following:

- `Microsoft.Network/networkSecurityGroups/read`
- `Microsoft.Network/networkSecurityGroups/defaultSecurityRules/read`
- `Microsoft.Network/networkSecurityGroups/securityRules/read`

While the permissions above can apply the principle of least privilege, remember that you will need to merge some permissions if you are accessing the Azure portal. For example, to configure or edit a JIT policy for a VM, you will need the given set of privileges and the privileges to read the JIT policies mentioned previously.

Assuming you have the right privileges, you can start by reviewing the Defender for Cloud `Management ports of virtual machines should be protected with just-in-time network access control` recommendation, which recommends that JIT be enabled for Azure VMs. It is very important to understand that Microsoft Defender triggers the recommendation to enable JIT for Cloud, but to enable JIT, you need to have the Defender for Servers plan enabled.

> **NOTE** The recommendation to enable JIT is available for VMs in Azure and EC2 instances in AWS.

Recommendation to enable JIT

This control, which is enabled through Azure network capabilities—rather than through any feature or system on the VM itself—is exerted over incoming connections to the VM. Defender for Cloud will trigger a recommendation when it identifies that a VM needs JIT in Azure or AWS; these recommendations appear in the **Secure Management Ports** security control. The recommendations to enable JIT for Azure and to enable JIT in AWS are shown in Figure 8-1 (the third and fourth recommendations from the top).

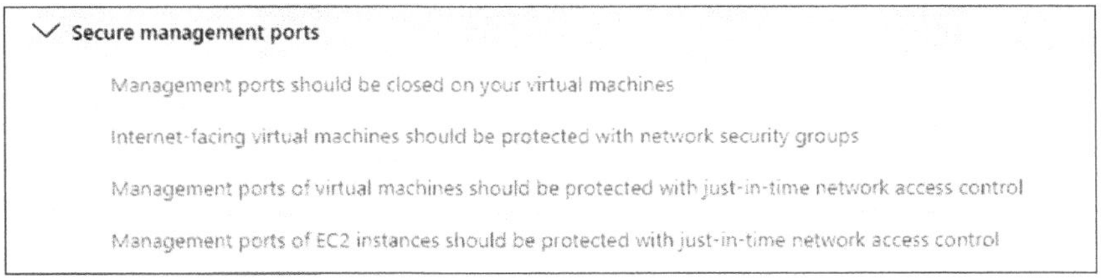

FIGURE 8-1 JIT recommendation

For this example, open the `Management ports of virtual machines should be protected with just-in-time network access control` recommendation. You will see that there are three tabs at the bottom: **Unhealthy Resources** (where JIT is recommended), **Healthy Resources**, and **Not Applicable Resources** (VMs that don't meet the criteria to have JIT enabled). See Figure 8-2 for an example of this page.

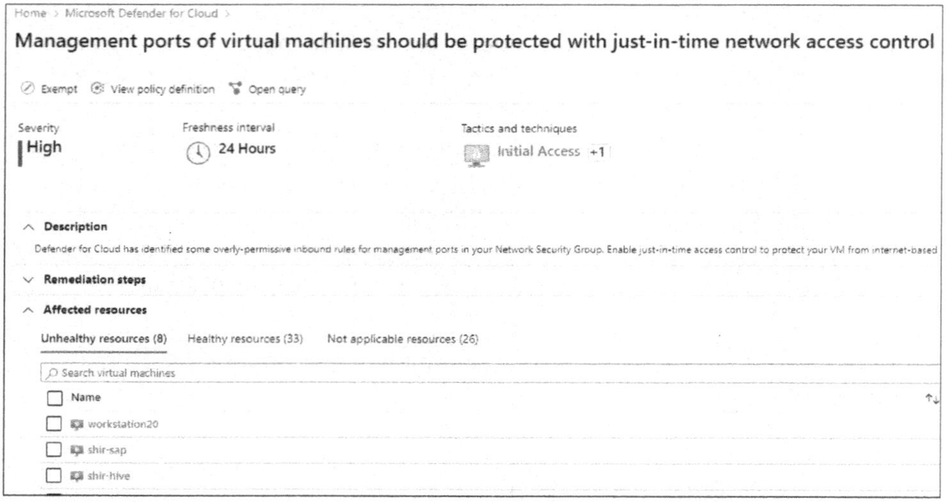

Management ports of virtual machines should be protected with just-in-time network access control

⊘ Exempt   ⊙ View policy definition   ⚲ Open query

Severity	Freshness interval	Tactics and techniques
High	🕐 **24 Hours**	🖥 Initial Access +1

∧ **Description**

Defender for Cloud has identified some overly-permissive inbound rules for management ports in your Network Security Group. Enable just-in-time access control to protect your VM from internet-based

∨ **Remediation steps**

∧ **Affected resources**

Unhealthy resources (8)   Healthy resources (33)   Not applicable resources (26)

🔍 Search virtual machines

☐ Name   ↑↓

☐ 🖥 workstation20

☐ 🖥 shir-sap

☐ 🖥 shir-hive

FIGURE 8-2   JIT recommendation details

> **NOTE**   To understand how Defender for Cloud identifies whether a VM is unhealthy, healthy, or not applicable, see the flowchart at *http://aka.ms/MDCBookJITFlow*.

To enable JIT from this recommendation blade, you just need to choose a VM and click the **Remediate** button. Once you do that, the **JIT VM Access Configuration** page appears, as shown in Figure 8-3.

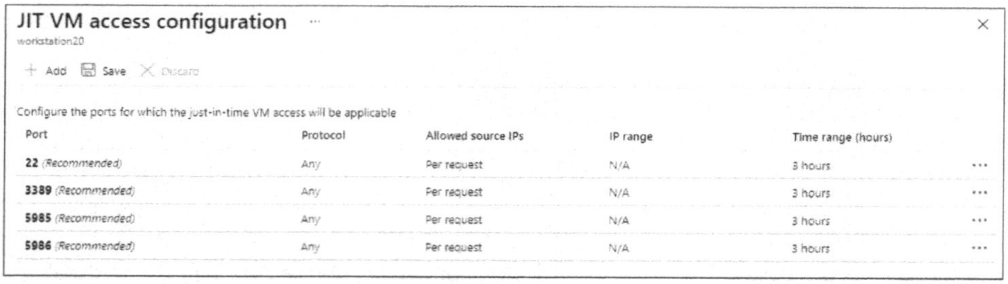

JIT VM access configuration   ···   ✕
workstation20

+ Add   💾 Save   ✕ Discard

Configure the ports for which the just-in-time VM access will be applicable

Port	Protocol	Allowed source IPs	IP range	Time range (hours)	
22 *(Recommended)*	Any	Per request	N/A	3 hours	···
3389 *(Recommended)*	Any	Per request	N/A	3 hours	···
5985 *(Recommended)*	Any	Per request	N/A	3 hours	···
5986 *(Recommended)*	Any	Per request	N/A	3 hours	···

FIGURE 8-3   Selecting the ports that will be allowed

On this page, you can leave the default ports, or you can delete the ones you don't need. By default, the suggested ports are shown here:

- **22: Secure Shell (SSH)**   Commonly used to access Linux machines.
- **3389: Remote Desktop Protocol (RDP)**   Commonly used to access Windows machines.
- **5985: Windows Remote Management (WinRM) 2.0 connection via HTTP**
  Windows Remote Management is a component of the Windows Hardware Management feature that manages server hardware locally and remotely.
- **5986: WinRM 2.0 connection via HTTPs**

To delete a port, you just need to click the ellipsis (**...**) to the right of the desired port and click **Delete**. If you enable JIT on a machine on which you only need access via RDP, then you can delete all the other ports. To configure the properties of the connection, click the port itself. For this example, click **3389**; the **Add Port Configuration** page appears, as shown in Figure 8-4.

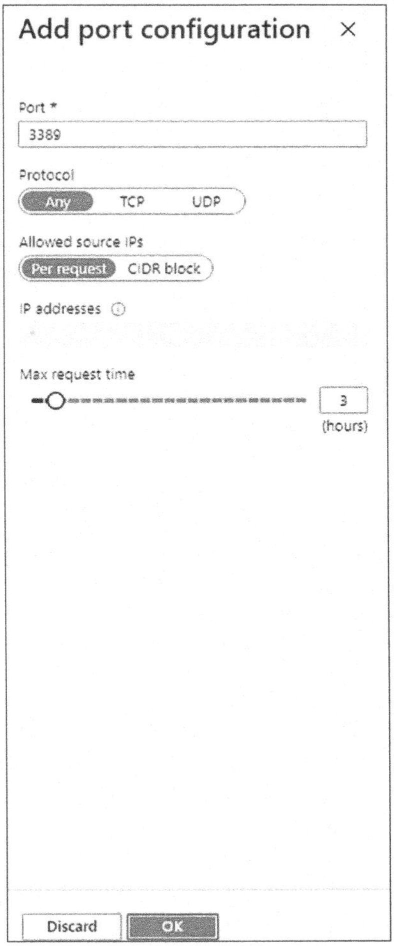

FIGURE 8-4 Port configuration for JIT

Because the goal is to configure RDP, the port and protocol will not change. However, you can customize the allowed source IPs, which can be according to the request, or you can also specify a classless inter-domain routing (CIDR) address block of IPs. Lastly, you can configure the **Max Request Time**, which is the amount of time the port will be open. It is important to mention that the user will not have its connection dropped if the request exceeds this time, though if the user disconnects and tries to connect again, the connection won't work because the port will be closed. Once you finish the configuration, click **OK** to commit the changes and then click **Save**.

JIT dashboard

To access the JIT dashboard, you first need to access the **Workload Protections** dashboard, which is located on the left navigation pane of the Defender for Cloud portal. Once you access this dashboard, you will see **Just In Time VM Access** in the **Advanced Protection** section at the bottom of the page, as shown in Figure 8-5.

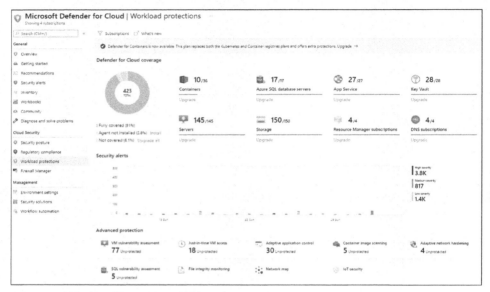

FIGURE 8-5 Workload Protections dashboard

Click the **Just In Time VM Access** option to access the JIT dashboard. There, you will see a comprehensive list of VMs that are **Configured**, **Not Configured**, and **Unsupported**, as shown in Figure 8-6.

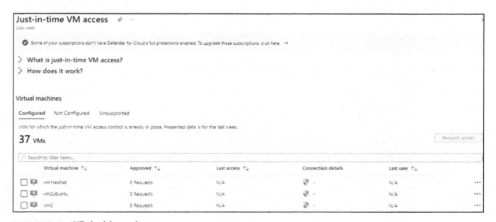

FIGURE 8-6 JIT dashboard

If you are reviewing the VMs that are configured, you can easily identify the number of requests in the **Approved** column, when the VM was last accessed in the **Last Access** column, which port the connection was established in the **Connection Details** column, and the last user who remotely accessed this VM in the **Last User** column. If you need to perform any configuration, you can click the ellipsis (**…**) to the right of the VM to see the following options:

- **Properties**   This option will redirect you to the VM blade, where you can see the VM configuration in Azure.

- **Activity Log**   This option will redirect you to the **Azure Activity Log** page, where you can see previous operations for that VM along with time, date, and subscription.

- **Edit**   This option will redirect you to the page shown previously in Figure 8-3. There, you can change the JIT configuration for that VM.

- **Remove**   This option will remove JIT configuration from this VM.

The **Not Configured** tab, as the name implies, shows a list of machines that support JIT but have not been configured yet. In the example shown in Figure 8-7, some VMs appear with the **Healthy** status because this VM is protected by an NSG that blocks access to management ports; VMs that are shown as **High** severity are protected by an NSG, though access to management ports is allowed.

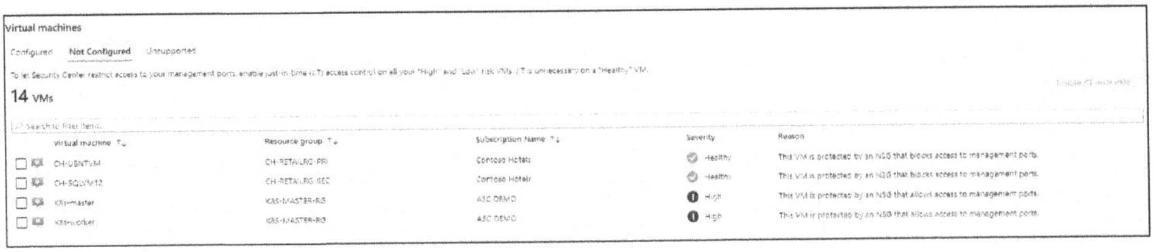

FIGURE 8-7   Machines that are capable of having JIT configured

When evaluating this list, look at the **Severity** column to identify the VMs that need to have JIT enabled. This will help you to prioritize which VMs you should address first.

The **Unsupported** tab shows the VMs that can't have JIT enabled. Reasons JIT cannot be enabled include machines that are missing an NSG and classic VMs. Also, a VM can appear on this tab if the JIT solution is disabled in the subscription's or resource group's security policy.

Requesting access

Once the VM is configured, you can request access to it using the Azure portal or the Defender for Cloud dashboard. If you access the VM properties from the Azure portal and click the **Connect** button to establish an RDP connection, you will see that the **Request Access button** is available, as shown in Figure 8-8.

The same option is available from Defender for Cloud. To access it, open the JIT dashboard and initiate the access request by selecting the VM and clicking the **Request Access** button. The page shown in Figure 8-9 appears, which allows you to configure the request.

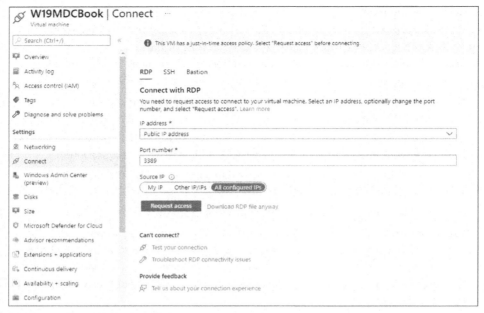

FIGURE 8-8 Request Access option

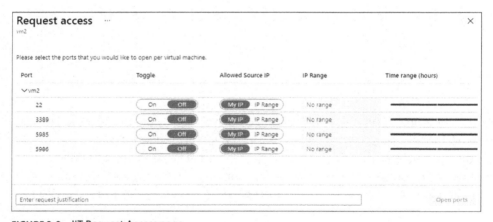

FIGURE 8-9 JIT Request Access page

This page allows the user requesting access to customize the request by providing the port that needs access, the origin IP, the time range for the access, and a justification for this access. Once all this information is configured, the **Open Ports** button will be available to finish the access request.

Using the PowerShell or Defender for Cloud API, you can also configure the JIT VM Access policy. To access a sample PowerShell script, visit *http://aka.ms/ MDCJITVMSample*. To learn more about the API for JIT, visit *http://aka.ms/JITVMAPI*.

File integrity monitoring

File Integrity Monitoring (FIM) helps protect the integrity of your system and applications because Defender for Servers will continuously monitor the behavior of your registry and configuration files. If an abnormal change to the files or malicious behavior is detected, Defender for Servers will track the change, which allows you to stay in control of your files. File Integrity Monitoring is based on Change Tracking and Inventory in Azure Automation. FIM is used to track and identify changes in your VMs and requires Change Tracking and Inventory in Azure Automation to be enabled on the workspace.

VMs connected to the Log Analytics workspace use the Log Analytics agent to collect data about changes to installed software, Microsoft services, Windows registry and files, and Linux daemons on monitored servers. When data is available, the agent sends it to Azure Monitor Logs for processing. FIM is available in the same **Workload Protections** dashboard where you access JIT in the **Advanced Protection** section (see Figure 8-5). If you have multiple workspaces and you access FIM, the last column shows **Enable** or **Upgrade Plan** options. The **Enable** option means you can enable FIM on a workspace; the **Upgrade Plan** option means you can upgrade the plan first and then enable FIM on it, as shown in Figure 8-10.

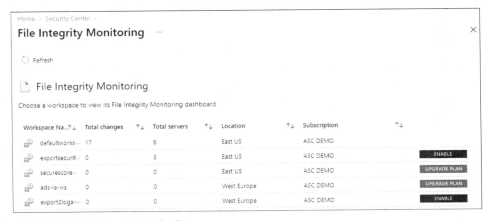

FIGURE 8-10 File Integrity Monitoring

> **IMPORTANT** Workspaces that are shown with the Upgrade Plan button are those that use the free tier and don't have the Defender for Cloud plan enabled on the workspace level.

It might take some time for FIM to identify the total number of computers in the workspace and populate the dashboard. Once it is populated, you will see a dashboard with a summary of statistics that is similar to the screen shown in Figure 8-11.

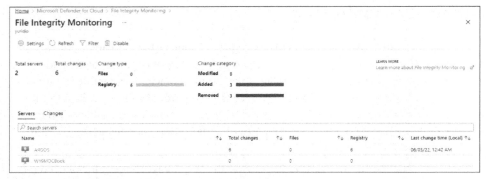

FIGURE 8-11 FIM dashboard

Customizing your settings

Although Defender for Cloud will suggest which files and registry keys you should monitor, you can still customize and add your own preferences. Follow these steps to perform this customization:

1. On the **File Integrity Monitoring** blade, click the **Settings** button, as shown in Figure 8-12.

FIGURE 8-12 Initial screen to customize files and registry settings

2. The **Workspace Configuration** page appears, as shown in Figure 8-13.

FIGURE 8-13 Customizing files and registry values to monitor

3. The **Windows Registry** tab contains all registry keys that can be monitored. Notice that some are set to **False** (in the **Enabled** column), which means that they are not being

monitored, and others are set to **True**, which means that key is currently being monitored. To add a new registry key, click **Add**; the **Add Windows Registry For Change Tracking** page appears, as shown in Figure 8-14.

FIGURE 8-14 Adding a new Windows registry key to monitor

4. In the **Item Name** field, type a friendly name for this registry key.

5. In the **Windows Registry Key** field, type the registry path (for example, HKEY_LOCAL_MACHINE\Software\Microsoft\Windows\CurrentVersion\Run).

6. Click the **Save** button to commit your changes.

While adding a new registry key to monitor is very straightforward, there are more options for configuring Windows files. To see the options available, select the **Windows Files** tab and click the **Add** button. The **Add Windows File For Change Tracking** page appears, as shown in Figure 8-15.

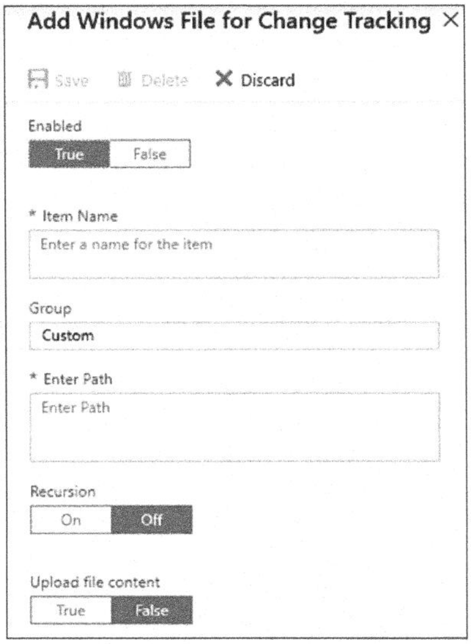

FIGURE 8-15 Adding new files to track changes

In addition to fields for the **Item Name** and path, this page contains the **Recursion** option, which can be set to **On** or **Off**. Recursion allows you to specify wildcards for simplifying tracking across directories. Also, the environment variables allow you to track files across environments with multiple or dynamic drive names.

> **NOTE** If you use wildcards, remember that you can only use the last segment of a path (such as c:\folder*file* or /etc/*.conf).

The **Upload File Content** option can be either **True** (monitor and track when files are uploaded to this folder) or **False** (do not monitor when files are uploaded to this folder).

For Linux files, some unique items are worth mentioning. Choose **Linux Files** > **Add**. The **Add Linux File For Change Tracking** page appears, as shown in Figure 8-16.

FIGURE 8-16 Adding new Linux files to track changes

In the **Path Type** field, you can select whether you want to monitor a file or a directory. The **Use Sudo** option can be set to **On**, which means Sudo will be used when checking for the item, or **Off** (don't use Sudo). The **Links** field determines how symbolic links are dealt with when traversing directories. The available options are:

- **Ignore** This option ignores symbolic links and will not include the referenced files and directories.
- **Follow** This option follows the symbolic links during recursion and includes the referenced files and directories.
- **Manage** This option follows the symbolic links and allows returned content to be altered.

The **File Content** tab (shown in Figure 8-17) contains the relevant settings for enabling this capability, which requires a standard storage account using the Resource Manager deployment model.

FIGURE 8-17 Configuring File Content settings

To connect an existing storage account to this feature, click the **Link** button and select the storage account.

Visualizing changes

Now that you have this feature enabled, you can start tracking the changes from the time FIM was enabled forward. Keep in mind that FIM will not show the changes immediately because the data collection frequency for FIM can vary according to the data type, as shown below:

- For the Windows registry, the frequency is 50 minutes.
- For Windows files, the frequency is 30 minutes.
- For Linux files, the frequency is 15 minutes.

To visualize changes to the registry, follow these steps:

1. On the **File Integrity Monitoring** blade, you will see a snapshot of the changes, as shown in Figure 8-18.

FIGURE 8-18 File Integrity Monitoring after change tracking has started

2. Click the **Changes** tab to see a list of the last 100 changes that have occurred in the monitored system (see Figure 8-19).

FIGURE 8-19 The Changes tab

3. To see more details about what changed, click any of those entities to see the original registry key value and the changes made, as shown in Figure 8-20.

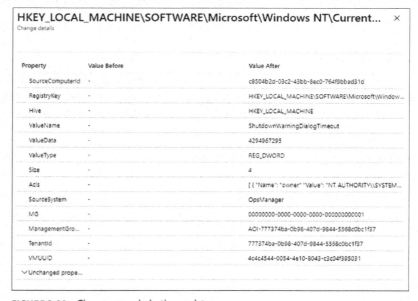

FIGURE 8-20 Changes made in the registry

Adaptive Application Control

Creating restrictions to allow only certain applications to run has always been a goal of on-premises security. The idea behind creating an allowed list of applications is that if you can define and control a predefined list of applications running on a particular operating system, then any other process that runs on the machine represents a possible threat.

This capability existed for many years with Windows Server. While there were some strong advocates for the "application allow list" solution in Windows Server called AppLocker, the basic problem of configuration and maintenance complexity prevented it from being the success it could have been.

One of the implicit goals of the cloud is to make infrastructure transparent to the user. The idea is that the cloud will provide resources desired by the user, and the user can consume these resources without making large investments to understand how and where the resources are run and maintained. Also, users should not need to understand complex constructs that can take many hundreds of hours to gain highly specific professional expertise.

These are still the goals of the cloud, but in most areas, we are still quite a way from that vision because many IT Pros tell us that the cloud is often more complex than on-premises computing. We tell those IT Pros to be patient. Over time, the cloud will fulfill its true vision, and getting things done in the cloud will be much easier than it ever was on-premises.

We can see the implementation of this technology in the Defender for Servers Adaptive Application Control feature. Defender for Servers uses machine learning to learn about the processes running on the virtual machines and the virtual machine's behavior. This learning process usually takes two weeks, and after that period, you will see a recommendation in Defender for Cloud to enable Adaptive Application control, as shown in Figure 8-21.

FIGURE 8-21 Recommendation to enable Adaptive Application Control

When you click the **Adaptive Application Controls For Defining Safe Applications Should Be Enabled On Your Machines** recommendation, you will see one or more groups created by Adaptive Application Control with similar applications that should be allowed, as shown in Figure 8-22.

Group Name	Machines	State	Severity	
ASC DEMO	4			
GROUP5	1	Open - New	High	
GROUP3-EU	1	Open - New	High	
GROUP4-EU	2	Open - New	High	

Enable Adaptive application controls

> What is application control?
> How does it work?

FIGURE 8-22 The alert blade contains the answers to the major investigation's questions.

VMs that have the same set of applications are aggregated into groups. On the **Enable Adaptive Application Controls** page, you can look at the **Machines** column to see how many machines each group contains. To enable Adaptive Application Control for a specific group, click it, and you will see the **Configure Application Control Rules** page, as shown in Figure 8-23.

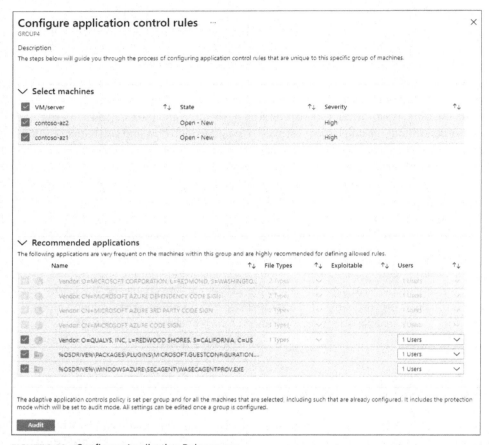

FIGURE 8-23 Configure Application Rules page

On this page, you can select the machines you want to be part of the group or all the VMs suggested by the recommendation. In the **Recommended Application** section, you can disable applications you don't want to be part of the allowed list. Keep in mind that Defender automatically creates this list for servers based on the machine learning analysis of the applications running on the VM. Once you finish, click the **Audit** button to commit the changes.

The button is called **Audit** because you are not blocking other applications from running. Instead, with this feature, you are only auditing the allowed applications and being made aware of applications running outside this scope. When an application outside this group's scope is executed, Defender for Servers will generate an alert.

Configuring Adaptive Application Control

To access the Adaptive Application Control dashboard, go to the Workload protection dashboard, and in the **Advanced Protection** section, click **Adaptive Application Control**. The **Adaptive Application Controls** page appears, as shown in Figure 8-24.

Adaptive application controls   ...   ×

+ Add custom group

> What is application control?
> How does it work?

Configured   Recommended   No recommendation

Groups of machines for which an application allowlist is already applied and can be centrally managed.

Group Name		Machines		Protection Mode		Alerts	
∨ ASC DEMO		7					...
GROUP1		1		Auditing			...
GROUP3		1		Auditing			...
GROUP4		1		Auditing			...
REVIEWGROUP2		1		Auditing			...
GROUP1-EU		1		Auditing			...
GROUP2-EU		1		Auditing			...
GROUP5-EU		1		Auditing			...

FIGURE 8-24 Adaptive application controls dashboard

The first tab contains a list of currently configured groups, and you can quickly see the number of machines in the group in the **Machines** column. The auditing status is shown in the **Protection Mode** column, and any alert triggered for that group is shown in the **Alerts** column. The **Recommended** tab contains a list of recommendations for applying application controls to define a list of known-safe applications (see Figure 8-23 earlier in this section). The **No Recommendation** tab shows a list of machines without a defined allow list of applications, or VMs that don't support this feature. Some scenarios in which a VM might appear in this list include:

- Machines that are missing the Log Analytics agent
- Machines that have the Log Analytics agent installed, but the agent is not sending events to the workspace
- Machines with Windows operating system that have AppLocker policy enabled by either a GPO or a local security policy

Changing policy

To change the configuration of a group, you can click the group to make the **Edit Application Control Policy** page appear, as shown in Figure 8-25.

Edit application control policy
GROUP1

!!! Group settings   + Add rule   🖫 Save   🗑 Delete

> Recent Alerts
> Configured machines
> Publisher allowlist rules
> Path allowlist rules
> Hash allowlist rules

FIGURE 8-25   Edit Application Control Policy page

In the **Recent Alerts** section, you can see the alerts that were triggered by this group. This section is read-only because its intent is to provide easy access to the alerts by group. The same information is available in the **Security Alerts** dashboard. In the **Configured Machines** section, you can either delete a machine from this group or move a machine to another group. When you move a machine from one group to another, the application control policy changes the settings of the destination group. You can also move a machine from a configured group to a non-configured group, though this operation removes any application control rules that were applied to the machine. Essentially, a configured group contains the application control policies, and all machines in it will utilize them.

Under **Publisher Allowlist Rules**, you can select the rule and click the ellipsis (**...**) to the right of the rule, which opens a pop-up menu from which you can select **Edit Rule** or **Delete**, as shown in Figure 8-26.

FIGURE 8-26   Options to edit or delete a publisher allowlist rule

Signed applications have information about their publisher. If you need to edit the publisher information, click **Edit Rule** in the pop-up menu, and you will see the **Edit Rule** page, as shown in Figure 8-27.

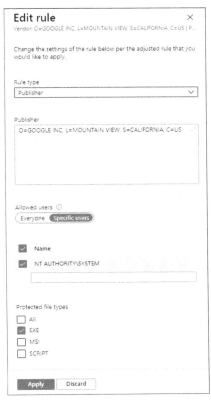

Edit rule　　　　　　　　　　　×

Vendor: O=GOOGLE INC, L=MOUNTAIN VIEW, S=CALIFORNIA, C=US | P...

Change the settings of the rule below per the adjusted rule that you would like to apply.

Rule type

| Publisher | ∨ |

Publisher

| O=GOOGLE INC, L=MOUNTAIN VIEW, S=CALIFORNIA, C=US | ∨ |

Allowed users ⓘ

(Everyone   **Specific users**)

☑ Name

☑ NT AUTHORITY\SYSTEM

[　　　　　　　　　　　　　　]

Protected file types

☐ All
☑ EXE
☐ MSI
☐ SCRIPT

Apply　　Discard

FIGURE 8-27　Options available to customize the publisher rule

It is not very common that you need to change a publisher rule, but in some scenarios, you might have to change which rule can run the applications. Depending on the scenario, you either need to harden the rules to **Specific Users** or open rules for all users by choosing **Everyone**. In the example shown in Figure 8-27, only the system can execute protected `.EXE` files (determined in the **Protected File Types** section). After making the necessary changes, click the **Apply** button.

If you need to create a completely new rule for your specific needs, you can click the **Add Rule** button; the **Add Rule** page appears, as shown in Figure 8-28.

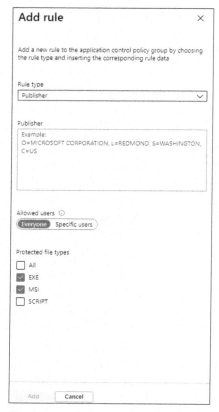

FIGURE 8-28 Options available to create a new rule

On this page, you can select the type of rule that you want to create:

- **Publisher** Identifies an application based on its digital signature and extended attributes. The digital signature contains information about the company that created the application (the publisher).
- **Path** Identifies an application based on the path condition that is provided. This path reflects the application's location in the file system.
- **Hash** Identifies an application based on the file hash.

You will need to configure the appropriate options and set the user's scope based on your selection. In other words, you need to determine whether this rule applies to all users (**Everyone**) or just some users.

The **Path Allowlist Rules** and **Hash Allowlist Rules** on this page will be populated according to the rules you create manually or the rules automatically suggested by Adaptive Application Control.

Application violation

Now that everything is configured, you might start experiencing application violation alerts. Figure 8-29 shows an example of an application violation alert, which is the alert you will receive if an application that is not allowed is executed on the machines that are part of a group configured to use Adaptive Application Control.

FIGURE 8-29 Application violation alert

This alert has all the information you need to evaluate whether this application should be added to the allow list. We created a workflow automation that allows you to trigger a Logic App that will automatically add the file to the allow list. You can download this automation at *http://aka.ms/MDCBookAAA*.

Chapter 9

Accessing Defender for Cloud from APIs

Although Microsoft Defender for Cloud has its own dashboard where you can visualize all security alerts, there are some specific scenarios in which you may want to consume the alert via API. This is a common scenario among organizations that want to build their own dashboards and programmatically manipulate all alerts.

In this chapter, you will learn how to leverage the built-in Defender for Cloud Representational State Transfer (REST) API and the Intelligent Security Graph API to retrieve information using HTTP requests.

Understanding REST API

Representational State Transfer (REST) APIs are service endpoints that support sets of HTTP operations (methods), which provide create, retrieve, update, or delete access capabilities to the service's resources. A REST API request/response pair can be separated into five components: three for the request and two for the response as shown in Figure 9-1.

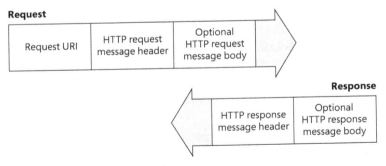

FIGURE 9-1 REST API components

The first part of the request is the *request URI*, which is the main address. This address is made up of the following parts:

1. **Structure**   `{URI-scheme} :// {URI-host} / {resource-path} ? {query-string}`

2. **Example**   `https://management.azure.com/subscriptions/{subscriptionID}/providers/Microsoft.Security/alerts?api-version=2021-11-01`

The second part is the *HTTP request message header*, which is composed of the required HTTP method, such as GET, HEAD, PUT, or POST. Also, you can have other optional headers, such as authentication.

The third part, the optional HTTP request message body, contains supplementary information that may vary according to the method used. For example, a POST method can contain MIME-encoded objects. MIME (Multipurpose Internet Mail Extension) is an Internet standard that initially extended the format of mail messages to support text in character sets other than ASCII. This format is being used in REST APIs, as well. For example, an API call can contain a JSON body. The message body, in this case, would be a JSON representation of a particular setting or resource. When using the request message body, you also need to specify the Content-type request header (in this example: application/JSON).

Below is an example of a POST request against the Microsoft.ResourceGraph/resources API provider:

```
API Method: Post
API URI: https:/management.azure.com/providers/Microsoft.ResourceGraph/
resources?api-version=2021-06-01-preview
Application/JSON body: {"query": "securityresources | where type =~ 'microsoft.security/
assessments'"}
```

In this example, the KQL query securityresources | where type =~ 'microsoft.security/assessments' is submitted to the Azure Resource Graph REST API provider and then executed. The response from this API call will result from the KQL query.

In the response section of Figure 9-1, the first part is the *HTTP status code*, which can also vary according to how the back end is responding to your request. If everything is working properly and this is a successful request, you should receive an HTTP 200 status code. Also, the second response field is optional, and it is there to support the main response. In the Azure Resource Graph example above, the response body will be a MIME-encoded object of the application/JSON type that contains the KQL query result.

Accessing alerts using the Defender for Cloud REST API

Defender for Cloud has its own set of REST API providers, which are divided in to operation groups. Because the list has grown to more than 40 different operation groups, we can only take a look at some of them in this chapter.

- **Alerts**   This operations group represents security alerts that are created in Defender for Cloud.
- **Assessments**   Manage security assessments on your subscriptions that result in Defender for Cloud recommendations.
- **Auto Provisioning Settings**   You can use this operation group to specify provisioning configuration for a subscription.
- **Locations**   This retrieves details of specific locations.
- **Operations**   All available operations.

- **Pricing** Pricing tiers that represent Defender for Cloud plans.
- **Secure Scores** Get the Secure Score information for a specific security control or list the Secure Score for your subscription.
- **Security Contacts** You can use this operation group to retrieve and manage the security contact information for a subscription.
- **Settings** Configuration settings for Defender for Cloud.
- **Workspace Settings** Settings about where your security data and logs are stored (meaning Log Analytics workspace-related settings).

> **MORE INFO** To learn more about the variety of REST API operation groups that Defender for Cloud offers, see *https://aka.ms/MDfC-APIs.*

As you can see, a variety of information and settings can be accessed via API, though this chapter will mainly focus on alerts. The **Alert** operations group has several operations that can be performed, including getting alerts for a resource associated with a resource group or a subscription. For example, to list all the alerts that are associated with a subscription, you can conduct a GET call against the following example URI:

```
https://management.azure.com/subscriptions/{subscriptionID}/providers/Microsoft.Security/
alerts?api-version=2021-11-01
```

The response for this HTTP GET request should be an HTTP 200 header, followed by the body in JSON format, similar to Listing 9-1.

LISTING 9-1 Result of a REST GET request against the Microsoft.Security/alerts API provider

```
{
    "value": [
        {
            "id": "/subscriptions/{subscriptionId}/resourceGroups/ContosoDemo/providers/
Microsoft.Security/locations/westeurope/alerts/2517574460241069999_f6627635-ee1c-46b8-
8899-45bbeedcb396",
            "name": "2517574460241069999_f6627635-ee1c-46b8-8899-45bbeedcb396",
            "type": "Microsoft.Security/Locations/alerts",
            "properties": {
                "status": "Active",
                "timeGeneratedUtc": "2022-02-14T17:11:44.5482146Z",
                "processingEndTimeUtc": "2022-02-14T17:11:42.6273927Z",
                "vendorName": "Microsoft",
                "productName": "Microsoft Defender for Cloud",
                "alertType": "VM_SshBruteForceFailed",
                "startTimeUtc": "2022-02-14T16:06:15.893Z",
                "endTimeUtc": "2022-02-14T16:08:44.243Z",
                "severity": "Medium",
                "isIncident": false,
```

```
            "systemAlertId": "2517574460241069999_f6627635-ee1c-46b8-8899-45bbeedcb396",
            "intent": "Probing",
            "resourceIdentifiers": [
                {
                    "$id": "westeurope_1",
                    "azureResourceId": "/subscriptions/{subscriptionId}/
resourceGroups/ContosoDemo/providers/Microsoft.Compute/virtualMachines/Contoso-Linux-VM",
                    "type": "AzureResource",
                    "azureResourceTenantId": "{tenantId}"
                },
                {
                    "$id": "westeurope_2",
                    "workspaceId": "{workspaceId}",
                    "workspaceSubscriptionId": "{subscriptionId}",
                    "workspaceResourceGroup": "{workspaceResourceGroup} ",
                    "agentId": "{agentId}",
                    "type": "LogAnalytics",
                    "workspaceTenantId": "{tenantId}
                }
            ],
            "compromisedEntity": "Contoso-Linux-VM",
            "alertDisplayName": "Failed SSH brute force attack",
            "description": "Failed SSH brute force attacks were detected on
Contoso-Linux-VM",
            "remediationSteps": [
                "1. In case this is an Azure virtual machine, add the source IP to
NSG block list for 24 hours (see https://azure.microsoft.com/en-us/documentation/articles/
virtual-networks-nsg/) ",
                "2. Enforce the use of strong passwords and do not re-use them
across multiple resources and services (see http://windows.microsoft.com/en-us/Windows7/
Tips-for-creating-strong-passwords-and-passphrases)",
                "3. In case this is an Azure virtual machine, Create an allow list
for SSH access in NSG (see https://azure.microsoft.com/en-us/documentation/articles/
virtual-networks-nsg/) "
            ],
            "extendedProperties": {
                "number of failed authentication attempts to host": "54",
                "accounts used on failed sign in to host attempts": "[\"postgres\",\"an
sible\",\"zabbix\",\"root\",\"public\",\"odoo12\",\"a\",\"csgo\",\"azureuser\",\"mc\",\"20 additional
usernames\"]",
                "was SSH session initiated": "No",
                "resourceType": "Virtual Machine",
                "end Time UTC": "2022-02-14T16:08:44.2430000Z",
                "killChainIntent": "Probing"
            },
            "entities": [
                {
```

```
                    "$id": "westeurope_3",
                    "hostName": "Contoso-Linux-VM",
                    "azureID": "/subscriptions/{subscriptionId}/resourceGroups/
ContosoDemo/providers/Microsoft.Compute/virtualMachines/Contoso-Linux-VM",
                    "omsAgentID": "{agentId}",
                    "type": "host"
                },
                {

                    "$id": "westeurope_4",
                    "address": "209.141.xx.xxx",
                    "location": {
                        "countryCode": "US",
                        "countryName": "United States",
                        "state": "Nevada",
                        "city": "Las Vegas",
                        "longitude": {longitudeInfo},
                        "latitude": {latitudeInfo},
                        "asn": 53667
                    },
                    "type": "ip"
                },
                {
                    "$id": "westeurope_5",
                    "name": " postgres",
                    "ntDomain": " postgres",
                    "host": {
                        "$ref": "westeurope_3"
                    },
                    "isDomainJoined": false,
                    "type": "account"
                },
                [...]
                {
                    "$id": "westeurope_15",
                    "sourceAddress": {
                        "$ref": "westeurope_4"
                    },
                    "type": "network-connection"
                }
            ],
            "alertUri": {alertDeepLink}
        }
    }
  ]
}
```

There is a lot of information that can be consumed when retrieving an alert via REST API. The example above shows an alert that has automatically been fired as a result of a failed SSH brute-force attack on February 14, 2022. The attack was conducted from Las Vegas, Nevada, and the alert contains information about the attacker's IP address, longitude/latitude, accounts that have been used, and much more. While the alert dashboard in Defender for Cloud provides important details about each alert, the REST API brings a different perspective to consuming the same set of data.

In Chapter 5, "Strengthening your security posture," you learned about Logic Apps that can stimulate REST APIs to consume and process data from these APIs. In addition to that, you learned about the Workflow Automation capability within Defender for Cloud. With that knowledge, you can now start building your own automations that are triggered once a new alert is created. In other words, Defender for Cloud comes with its own little SOAR (**S**ecurity **O**rchestration, **A**utomation, and **R**esponse) capability, at least when it comes to automated reaction on alerts.

For example, if Defender for Cloud detects a brute-force attack against one of your virtual machines, you could automatically block the attacking IP address(es) in the machine's Network Security Group (NSG). The information provided by Defender for Cloud will include details that are also published through the Alerts API, as shown in the example above.

> **MORE INFO**   In the Defender for Cloud GitHub repository, the community has published a variety of workflow automations and remediation scripts to react on alerts and recommendations. One of these artifacts is an ARM (Azure Resource Manager) template that will create a Logic App to automatically react on brute-force attacks within the scope of Workflow Automation. You can find this artifact at *https://aka.ms/BlockBruteForce*.

To make yourself familiar with the different APIs that come with Defender for Cloud, Microsoft has added a nice feature to the API reference you already know; see *https://aka.ms/MDfC-APIs*. The API reference is made up of different operation groups and in every operation group, the documentation gives you an overview about the methods that you can use to interact with the respective API provider. In addition to that, you can test all APIs in your own environment directly from the documentation. For that purpose, follow these steps:

1. In the **Alerts-List**, click the **Try It** button shown in Figure 9-2.

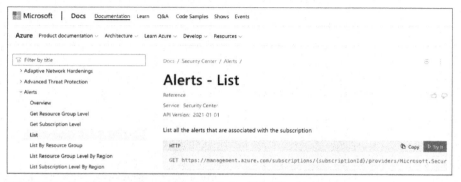

FIGURE 9-2   Explanation of how to list alerts in the DefeAPI reference

2. After clicking the **Try It** button, you are asked to authenticate against Azure Active Directory so you can retrieve information from the API for your environment.

3. Depending on the operation group and method, you might be asked to enter additional information, such as scope (resource group), alert name, or IDs. Figure 9-3 shows how to list alerts for the Contoso subscription in our environment.

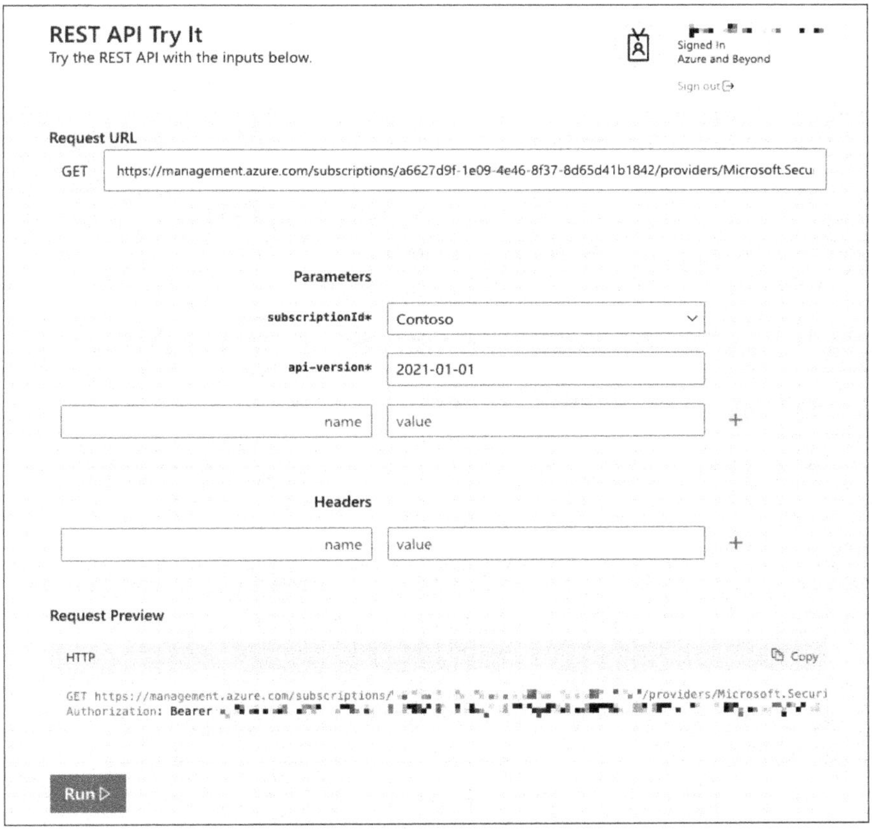

FIGURE 9-3 Defender for Cloud alerts in the Contoso subscription

4. Click the **Run** button.

You should now see the response code 200, which indicates that the API request has been successfully processed, followed by header information and the response body, both in JSON format, as explained earlier in this chapter.

The **Try It** capability is very handy when working with Defender for Cloud API providers because it allows you to learn about the body's schema, which you can then use within your automations, such as Logic Apps. Also, you can easily learn which API versions you can use to retrieve information or manage security settings. API versions reflect different management capabilities over time. If new features are published to an API, or if there are changes in the back end, Microsoft usually does not change existing API versions; instead, Microsoft adds a new one. This allows you to first test and change your automations around existing APIs, instead of being impacted by breaking changes. Unfortunately, if you take a look at the API reference, you will see that there is no dropdown menu to select a valid API version, and there is no information about which API versions exist at all for a particular operation group. But you can use the **Try It** capability to figure that out by simply entering an *invalid* API version, such as 2020-01-02 in the configuration blade. After executing the API request, you will get a response body that contains the following information:

```
{"error":{"code":"InvalidResourceType","message":"The resource type 'alerts' could not be
found in the namespace 'Microsoft.Security' for api version '2020-01-02'. The supported
api-versions are '2015-06-01-preview,2019-01-01,2020-01-01,2021-01-01,2021-11-01'."}}
```

It will tell you that, for the Alerts operation group, only API versions 2015-06-01-preview, 2019-01-01, 2020-01-01, 2021-01-01, and 2021-11-01 are supported. Now, go ahead and play around with the API reference and your environment.

Accessing alerts using the Graph Security API

The Microsoft Graph (*graph.microsoft.com*) is a unified interface to access information from Microsoft online services, such as Azure Active Directory, Microsoft 365, and others. The Graph Security API is based on Microsoft Graph, and can be defined as a unified REST API for integrating security products.

When you make calls to the Graph Security API, they will be federated to all supported Microsoft security products, services, and partners. The results are aggregated in a common schema, which makes correlating alerts from multiple data sources easier. The idea is that when you connect and enrich the alerts, you will be able to easily understand the scope and impact of an attack.

Figure 9-4 shows an easy representation of the different components that can be used with the Graph Security API.

Looking at this diagram from the top, you see that Microsoft 365, Azure, and partner solutions can be Graph Security providers. All Microsoft security products, such as Microsoft 365 Defender, Defender for Cloud, or Microsoft Sentinel, are security providers within this scope. They all integrate with the Graph Security API and will send data to and consume data from it. Graph Security API has many capabilities other than retrieving alerts, including setting actions to alerts or storing information about Microsoft Secure Score (not Secure Score from Defender for Cloud, though). These options are beyond the scope of this chapter, but if you want to learn more about the use of Graph Security API, visit *https://aka.ms/graphsecuritydocs*. Results from the Graph Security API are then exposed so they can be consumed by authenticated applications, such as Microsoft Graph Explorer.

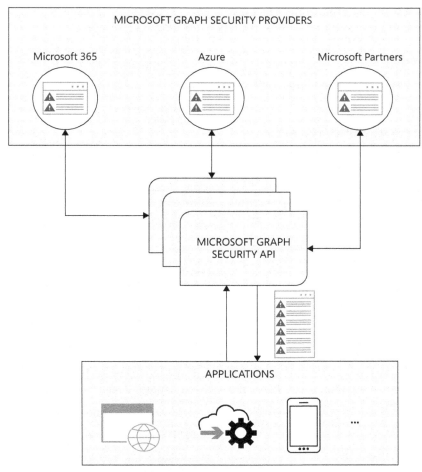

FIGURE 9-4 Graph Security API architectural diagram

After reviewing this diagram, you can also say that the Graph Security API is an intermediary service (or broker) that provides a single programmatic interface to connect multiple security providers (Microsoft and Partners). When planning to build your own application to use the Graph Security API, make sure to cover the following points:

1. **Register your application with Microsoft Graph**   Log in to *portal.azure.com* to add the app to your Azure AD tenant.

2. **Specify permissions and secrets**   You can use **Delegated** if your app accesses the API as a signed-in user, or you can use **Application** if your app has its own Role Base Access Control (RBAC).

3. **Write your code**   You can start by leveraging the sample codes at *http://aka.ms/ graphsecurityapicode.*

4. **Get consent from the organization using your app**   In this step, the Azure AD Admin needs to grant consent for the organization (tenant) to use the app.

> **MORE INFO**   To learn more about registering your application with Azure AD, see the steps at *https://aka.ms/MDfC-AppRegistration*.

Using the Graph Security API

The Graph Security API is accessible through the Microsoft Graph; in other words, it uses the single point of connection (*https://graph.microsoft.com*) with the same REST API syntax and response in JSON format. Security data accessible via the Graph Security API is protected using permissions and Azure AD (AAD) roles. To retrieve alerts from the Graph Security API, including Defender for Cloud alerts, you need to use the HTTP GET request similar to the example below:

```
https://graph.microsoft.com/v1.0/security/alerts
```

One important aspect of this GET request is that it will retrieve all alerts from the service providers that you may have in your tenant, which includes Defender for Cloud, Azure Active Directory Identity Protection, Microsoft Cloud App Security, Microsoft Defender for Endpoints, Microsoft Defender for Identities, Office 365, Cloud App Security, Microsoft Information Protection, Microsoft Sentinel, and other partner providers to which you may have access.

Depending on the number of service providers you have, the amount of data that returns with a simple GET request for all alerts can be substantial. It is a good idea to use filters to target the information that you really want to see. For example, if you want to see only the top 10 high-severity alerts, you can use the GET request below:

```
https://graph.microsoft.com/v1.0/security/alerts?$filter=Severity eq 'High' and $top eq 10
```

The part of the URL in bold represents the filter that was created to retrieve only the information that you needed. If you want to validate your GET request before you start writing your own app, you can use the Microsoft Graph Explorer (*https://developer.microsoft.com/en-us/graph/graph-explorer*) to test the URL. For this example, you would get a result that lists the top 10 high-severity alerts. While this filter helps, it will still show the top 10 high-severity alerts for all security providers to which you have access. If you want to see only alerts generated by Defender for Cloud, you can filter the vendor provider by using the vendorInformation property, as shown in the example below:

```
https://graph.microsoft.com/v1.0/security/alerts?$filter=vendorInformation/provider eq 'ASC'
```

If you use Microsoft Graph Explorer to run this GET request while logged in to a tenant that has Defender for Cloud enabled, this request will retrieve only alerts from Defender for Cloud (see Figure 9-5).

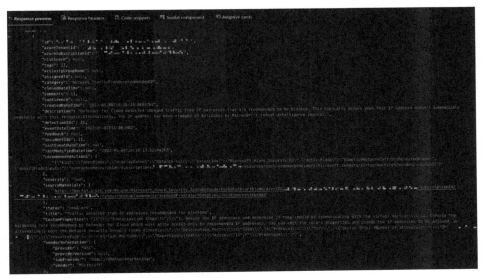

FIGURE 9-5 Graph Explorer

You can also use logical operators to expand your query. For example, if you want to see only high-severity alerts generated by Defender for Cloud, you can use the following GET request.

```
https://graph.microsoft.com/v1.0/security/alerts?$filter=vendorInformation/provider eq 'ASC'
and severity eq 'high'
```

> **MORE INFO** You can find the Graph Security API reference, including information about alert security providers and common use cases, at *https://aka.ms/SecGraphAPI*.

In this chapter, we incorporated the most important resources and API references for both Defender for Cloud's REST APIs and the Graph Security API. If you have read the book until this point, you already have a great overview of Defender for Cloud and all its capabilities. Now, let's move on to the last chapter, where you will learn how to deploy Defender for Cloud at scale.

Chapter 10

Deploying Microsoft Defender for Cloud at scale

I n this fast-evolving cloud world in which threats are constantly changing, security deployment at scale, orchestration, and automated response are mandatory qualities a modern security solution needs to bring so it can help security administrators and SOC analysts react to the challenges they are facing today. In this book, you have already learned how to deploy Microsoft Defender for Cloud to your subscriptions, how to harden your environments, and how to react to alerts. Now, let's bring it all together and see how you can deploy and manage Defender for Cloud at scale. Limitless cloud speed and scale allow you to create as many Azure subscriptions as you like. However, what is a great feature and value proposition of cloud computing also brings manageability and compliance challenges. How can you enforce and achieve compliance across your tenants and potentially, across hundreds of subscriptions in an efficient and automated way? Key concepts to achieve this goal are Azure Resource Manager (ARM) Templates, Azure Policy, and Management Groups.

The three cornerstones of deployment at scale

ARM templates are a declarative way of describing a deployment result in the form of a JSON document, which contains information about the resources (which, in this case, equates to objects) that you want to deploy. It contains the type of resources, names, and their properties. The JSON file can be checked into a source control solution, supports versioning, and enables you to deploy Azure "infrastructure as code."

The two deployment types, incremental and complete, enable you to only deploy what is declared in the template (complete) or to add/update additional resources (incremental). The complete deployment mode deletes all the resources not specified in the template. Therefore, incremental is the default deployment type. This safeguards you from unintentionally deleting resources. An ARM template is idempotent, meaning that either a resource will be created if it does not exist, or an existing resource will be updated. Idempotency allows you to repeatedly deploy the same template without breaking something. Upon deployment of an ARM template, the JSON file is consumed by the Azure Resource Manager API that has a contract with its resource providers. A resource provider is a trusted HTTPS RESTful API Azure endpoint that can provision, delete, and manage services on a user's behalf. Figure 10-1 shows an example of an ARM template for deploying or updating a Log Analytics workspace.

```
1    {
2        "$schema": "http://schema.management.azure.com/schemas/2015-01-01/deploymentTemplate.json",
3        "contentVersion": "1.0.0.0",
4        "parameters": {
5            "omsWorkspaceName": {
6                "type": "string",
7                "metadata": {
8                    "Description": "Assign a name for the Log Analytic Workspace Name"
9                }
10           },
11           "omsWorkspaceLocation": {
12               "type": "string",
13               "metadata": {
14                   "Description": "Location for your workspace"
15               }
16           },
17           "omsSKU": {
18               "type": "string",
19               "defaultValue": "PerGB2018",
20               "allowedValues": [
21                   "Free",
22                   "Standard",
23                   "Premium",
24                   "Unlimited",
25                   "Standalone",
26                   "PerNode",
27                   "PerGB2018"
28               ],
29               "metadata": {
30                   "Description": "Specify the SKU for your OMS Resources"
31               }
32           }
33       },
34       "variables": {},
35       "resources": [
36           {
37               "apiVersion": "2015-11-01-preview",
38               "location": "[parameters('omsWorkspaceLocation')]",
39               "name": "[parameters('omsWorkspaceName')]",
40               "type": "Microsoft.OperationalInsights/workspaces",
41               "properties": {
42                   "sku": {
43                       "name": "[parameters('omsSKU')]"
44                   }
45               }
46           }
47       ],
48       "outputs": {}
49   }
```

FIGURE 10-1 Example of an ARM template with its main sections

The sections highlighted in the template shown in Figure 10-1 are explained below:

- Line 3 (contentVersion) contains the template version to allow source control integration for a CI/CD pipeline.

- The parameters section, starting with line 4, contains parameters that can be used throughout the template. Contrary to variables, parameters in ARM templates are meant to be filled with custom values once the deployment starts. If you deploy an ARM template through Azure portal, the parameters section will be used to fill in custom values during the deployment, such as if you need to provide an email address for an automation artifact to send messages to, or if you define a custom workspace name. As opposed to parameters, variables are only used within the template to define properties; they are not exposed outside the template to be filled with custom values during the deployment.

- The allowedValues array, starting with line 20, is a definition of which values are allowed for a particular parameter. During deployment in Azure portal, you will be able to pick one of these values from a dropdown, instead of manually entering a value.

- The resources section contains the declaration of the Azure resource that is supposed to be created based on an ARM template. Line 37 specifies the API version for a resource provider.

- Lines 38 and 39 show how a parameter is used. Location and name attribute values are references to the corresponding parameter values.

- Line 40 specifies the resource provider type.

Azure Policy is one of the most important governance controls for an Azure environment. It can prevent (deny) you from creating non-compliant resources, it can audit resource compliance (audit and auditIfNotExists), and even remediate non-compliant resources (deployIfNotExists), either upon creation or for existing resources. Make sure to also read Chapter 4, "Policy management," for a deep dive into Azure Policy. The Azure Policy example shown in Figure 10-2 will prevent the creation of websites in Azure for which HTTPS connections are not enforced.

```
 1   {
 2       "mode": "All",
 3       "policyRule": {
 4         "if": {
 5           "allof": [
 6             {
 7               "field": "type",
 8               "equals": "Microsoft.Web/sites"
 9             },
10             {
11               "not": {
12                 "field": "Microsoft.Web/sites/httpsOnly",
13                 "equals": "true"
14               }
15             }
16           ]
17         },
18         "then": {
19           "effect": "deny",
20           "details": {
21             "type": "Microsoft.Web/sites",
22             "existenceCondition": {
23               "field": "Microsoft.Web/sites/httpsOnly",
24               "equals": "true"
25             }
26           }
27         }
28       },
29       "parameters": {}
30   }
```

FIGURE 10-2   Example of a policy definition that will prevent the creation of non-compliant resources

As you already learned in Chapter 4, policy definitions can be grouped with initiative defini-tions, both of which can be assigned to a scope within a policy assignment. The highest scope within this context are management groups which build the third cornerstone for supporting management at scale. They provide a level of scope above subscriptions and, therefore, are great for configuring the same settings on numerous subscriptions at the same time. When you organize subscriptions into a management group, you can apply governance conditions in a single place. All the subscriptions in a management group inherit the conditions applied to that management group. You can also build a hierarchy of management groups, with a root management group at the top of each directory. Conditions applied to the root management group or to a management group flow down to lower management groups and subscriptions. An example of a management group hierarchy is shown in Figure 10-3.

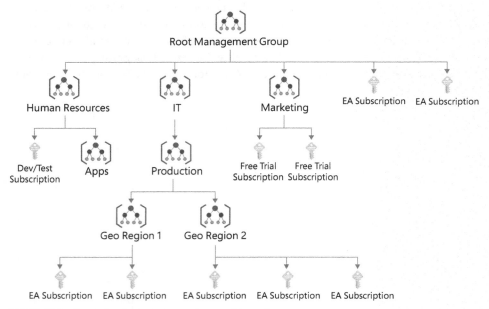

FIGURE 10-3 Example of a management group hierarchy

Defender for Cloud, Azure Policy, and Management Groups-better together

When a new subscription is created and the subscription is registered with the Microsoft Secu-rity Resource Provider (RP), the default behavior is that the Azure Security Benchmark policy initiative is provisioned and assigned at the subscription level. The exception is if the subscrip-tion resides in a Management Group that already has the Azure Security Benchmark initiative assigned. In this case, the initiative will not be re-assigned to any of the subscriptions within that management group. This approach has several advantages:

- You define your governance conditions in a single place, either at the Root Management Group or at the lower management groups.
- You can assign deny policies at a high-level that cannot be overridden at a lower level.
- There is a clear view of your compliance state across your management groups and subscriptions.

> **MORE INFO** In case you have the Azure Security Benchmark policy initiative assigned to a management group other than the tenant root management group, and if someone creates a new subscription without moving it to the correct subordinate management group, Defender for Cloud might not be enabled on this subscription. For identifying subscriptions that are not managed by Defender for Cloud within this context, you can find an automation artifact at *https://aka.ms/MDfCSubMgmt*.

As you have learned throughout this book, Defender for Cloud has grown into a very mature security management platform with many tuning capabilities to change its behavior according to your needs. Now, let's take a look at how to bring them all together so you can make it the best tool for managing your environment's security posture at scale.

Best practices for managing Defender for Cloud at scale

The best approach for managing Defender for Cloud at scale is to define compliance conditions that apply to your organization, group them in an Azure Policy initiative, and assign them at the highest level in your management group hierarchy. For most organizations, it is the best approach to use the built-in Azure Security Benchmark policy initiative definition and assign it to the organization's root management group. It is best to use the built-in definition, because Microsoft will maintain the initiative and all its policy definitions, so you can make sure to always get the latest changes and recommendations for your environment. In addition to that, make sure to follow these best practices:

- Tailor the Azure Security Benchmark according to your needs. Make sure to leverage resource exemptions on resources, resource groups, or subscriptions to exempt them from being assessed toward a particular recommendation, or completely disable a particular assessment in case it does not apply to your environment at all.
- Create *additional* custom initiative definitions to add custom recommendations if needed. Also, make sure to create custom policy definitions according to your compliance needs, such as `deny` or `deployIfNotExists` rules.

- Do not remove the Azure Security Benchmark assignment and only work with custom initiatives as you will lose access to secure score calculation and will have to manually watch out for future additions and changes toward recommendations.

- Deploy and maintain policy and initiative definitions using ARM templates as Infrastructure as Code (IaC). That way, you can make sure to have a documented process, tests, and documentation for any change that is made.

- Don't be tempted to manually configure Defender for Cloud. Instead, make sure to leverage Azure Policy and ARM templates whenever possible.

- Ask yourself if you can provision a new tenant or subscription with automation only. That way, you can be sure that every resource, scope, or subscription will exactly adhere to your organization's governance rules.

- First, test with `audit` or `auditIfNotExists` policies before using the `deny` effect to prevent breaking changes to your environment and to see if the policy definition will have the expected result.

How to get started with ARM templates

Using ARM templates as a declarative language for describing IaC deployments has a lot of advantages compared to imperative languages, such as PowerShell. With ARM templates, you just have to define (declare) the deployment result—what your environment is supposed to look like, once it is deployed—whereas, with PowerShell, you would have to define settings, sub-resources, and resources themselves in the correct order so the deployment will succeed. ARM templates can be used in a CI/CD pipeline to deploy resources, which makes it a great tool for modern DevOps deployments. But, compared to PowerShell, the learning curve might be slightly higher as ARM templates are using JSON syntax. With this last section, we want to provide you with some guidance on how to learn using ARM templates.

Export templates from the Azure portal

The easiest way to create your first ARM template is using the Azure portal for creating and deploying Azure resources. When you move through the portal, no matter if you are looking at a resource group or at a particular resource, the toolbar on the left side will provide you with a section called **Automation** in which you find the **Export Template** option. Once you select that option, an ARM template is generated that will contain all resources with its dependencies, as shown in Figure 10-4.

FIGURE 10-4 Export an ARM template from Azure portal

Depending on the scope you have been navigating, the ARM template will contain a single resource or the complete content of a resource group. Using the **Export Template** option is a great way to familiarize yourself with ARM templates because it is based on the resources you have already created and so you can cross reference the template to the existing resource and its settings and configurations. You can also use the **Export Template** feature to export and generalize resources which you then can make available for further deployments. For example, you can use this option to export an existing resource, make sure to change every static value, such as "location":"westus2" to dynamic values, such as "location":"[resourceGroup().location]" and then publish the object as an ARM template on GitHub.

Use Visual Studio Code to create ARM templates

Visual Studio Code (VSCode) is a free code editor that runs on Windows, Linux, and macOS operating systems. With the Azure Resource Manager Tools extension, it provides language support, resource snippets, and resource autocompletion, making your life as an IaC developer easy. To start with VSCode and ARM templates, follow these instructions. (Make sure to have the Azure Resource Manager Tools extension [*https://aka.ms/MDfC-VSCodeArmTools*] installed in VSCode.)

1. Open Visual Studio Code, create a new file, and store it as myTemplate.json.

2. Enter **arm** in the code editor, as shown in Figure 10-5.

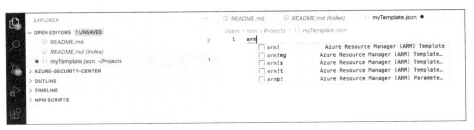

FIGURE 10-5 Start a new ARM template in Visual Studio Code

3. Autocompletion will immediately display valid commands. Select **arm!**, so a new template structure is created in the code section, as shown in Figure 10-6.

```
ⓘ README.md        ⓘ README.md (index)        ≡ myTemplate.json ●

Users > tom > Projects >  ≡ myTemplate.json
  1   {
  2       "$schema": "https://schema.management.azure.com/schemas/2019-04-01/deploymentTemplate.json#",
  3       "contentVersion": "1.0.0.0",
          Select or create a parameter file to enable full validation...
  4       "parameters": {},
  5       "functions": [],
  6       "variables": {},
  7       "resources": [],
  8       "outputs": {}
  9   }
```

FIGURE 10-6   An empty ARM template is created

4. You can now continue with creating parameters and resources. Functions, variables, and outputs are optional and can be removed if they are not used within the template.

5. Make sure to leverage the ARM Tools extension's autocompletion capabilities. For example, when you navigate to the **resources** section and enter "**work**", it will propose `arm-log-analytics-workspace` as a resource template. Once you select the item, it will add necessary information to the **resources** section, as shown in Figure 10-7.

```
ⓘ README.md        ⓘ README.md (index)        ≡ myTemplate.json ●

Users > tom > Projects >  ≡ myTemplate.json
  1   {
  2       "$schema": "https://schema.management.azure.com/schemas/2019-04-01/deploymentTemplate.json#",
  3       "contentVersion": "1.0.0.0",
          Select or create a parameter file to enable full validation...
  4       "parameters": {},
  5       "functions": [],
  6       "variables": {},
  7       "resources": [
  8           {
  9               "name": "logAnalyticsWorkspace1",
 10               "type": "Microsoft.OperationalInsights/workspaces",
 11               "apiVersion": "2015-11-01-preview",
 12               "location": "[resourceGroup().location]",
 13               "properties": {
 14                   "sku": {
 15                       "name": "Free"
 16                   },
 17                   "features": {
 18                       "searchVersion": 1
 19                   }
 20               }
 21           }
 22       ],
 23       "outputs": {}
 24   }
```

FIGURE 10-7   Add a Log Analytics workspace to your ARM template

6. You can now change the workspace's static **name** value to a **parameter** value, which will allow you to define the workspace name during deployment, not when creating the template. To do so, declare a new parameter in the parameters section and then add it as a reference to the workspace's name value, as shown in Figure 10-8.

```
 ⓘ README.md        ⓘ README.md (Index)        myTemplate.json ●

Users > tom > Projects > ≡ myTemplate.json
  1   {
  2       "$schema": "https://schema.management.azure.com/schemas/2019-04-01/deploymentTemplate.json#",
  3       "contentVersion": "1.0.0.0",
          Select or create a parameter file to enable full validation...
  4       "parameters": {
  5           "workspacename": {
  6               "type": "string"
  7           }
  8       },
  9       "functions": [],
 10       "variables": {},
 11       "resources": [
 12           {
 13               "name": "[parameters('workspacename')]",
 14               "type": "Microsoft.OperationalInsights/workspaces",
 15               "apiVersion": "2015-11-01-preview",
 16               "location": "[resourceGroup().location]",
 17               "properties": {
 18                   "sku": {
 19                       "name": "Free"
 20                   },
 21                   "features": {
 22                       "searchVersion": 1
 23                   }
 24               }
 25           }
```

FIGURE 10-8   Change a static name value to a dynamic parameter

7. Once you have created your ARM template, you have several options of deploying it. You can either use Azure CLI or PowerShell or create a custom deployment in the Azure portal. You also can attach the template to your deployment pipeline.

> **MORE INFO**   For more information about using Visual Studio Code to create ARM templates, see *https://aka.ms/MDfC-VSCode.*

ARM templates provide adaptability, and they are a great way to deploy resources to Azure. You can leverage ARM templates to basically deploy any type of resources that can be created using the Azure Resource Manager, which includes Log Analytics workspaces, policy and policy set (initiative) definitions, policy assignments, Defender plans, and much more. So, with ARM templates, you have a great tool to deploy governance—and security-related resources at scale.

Now that you know how to integrate Microsoft Defender for Cloud into your environment, tune the tool according to your needs, and deploy relevant guardrails and security configurations at scale, we look forward to seeing your security posture increase.

Microsoft Defender for DevOps

By George Wilburn,
Principal PM
Defender for DevOps

Attackers know there is a treasure trove of information in source code. This has turned source code management systems into an increasingly high-value attack target. Regardless of whether attackers leverage the source code for initial access or as an exfiltration point, or use it to harvest valuable data such as credentials, the source code and systems that house it must now be on the frontline of the defense. Adversaries can find ways to attack running systems by exfiltrating and examining source code. While the source code itself is valuable—think *ransomware scenarios and corporate infiltration points*—if adversaries can command and control the source code lifecycle, they can achieve a ripple effect, allowing them to infiltrate customers who install compromised software.

Preventing and detecting these attacks is high on the priority list of most CISOs and Security organizations today, and Microsoft is positioned to help its customers protect these source code assets against this modern threat.

In this appendix, you will learn more about the latest addition to Microsoft Defender for Cloud services, Defender for DevOps.

Shift left

Source code management systems, such as GitHub and Azure DevOps, are complicated systems with a lot of moving parts that are difficult to monitor. Developers are constantly pushing and pulling updates to source code. With the distributed nature of Git, source code repositories are forked and cloned continuously to other repositories and local machines. With every software push into source code management systems, builds are initiated. These builds require build definitions, credentials, dependencies, and more to get the software ready to push to production. Once built, the solution runs a company's SaaS offering, is deployed as a cloud workload, or is prepared to be pulled down as updates or patches to existing systems. All this is to say that the software supply chain comprises a lot of activity that requires monitoring and provides numerous opportunities for attacks in the software lifecycle. Monitoring all this activity can generate false-positives, and distinguishing innocuous behavior from malicious behavior is difficult.

The cybersecurity industry recognizes that source code management systems, source code, and the build and deployment pipelines must be protected. Security operators have frequently been caught off-guard by the latest attacks on source code management systems and have lacked comprehensive knowledge of these assets and systems and the ability to trace them back to a development team or owner. Security organizations need visibility into these systems and the security of the source code throughout the development lifecycle. Microsoft's latest Defender for Cloud product—Defender for DevOps—helps Security Operations gain visibility into the security of source code management systems and source code. This helps customers understand—at enterprise scale—whether their code repositories are staying secure and their software is being developed securely. With this visibility, security teams can take action to harden the security of pre-deployment systems and assets by shifting security activities left to uncover security issues before they make it to production.

Microsoft's CEO, Satya Nadella, has asserted that every company is now a software company. As companies in every industry—from financial services to manufacturing to healthcare—have become more reliant on software to run their business, they must increasingly rely on their developers to create robust and secure code. However, most developers are not security experts and need help solving security issues while they code and when code is checked into source code management systems. Defender for DevOps offers dual-layered protection by looking for security issues as code moves through the development lifecycle—first, on the developer's local machine, and then as code is checked into a repository and moves through the build process. Providing developers with security tools is not new, but it is now a critical part of the defense-in-depth story that enables companies to protect critical software assets and ensure security across the development ecosystem.

As security and development teams work together to address the great DevSecOps divide and connect security, operations, and development, securing the pipeline is where their efforts converge in shifting security to the left (see Figure A-1 later in this chapter). The pipeline is where the security team implements processes and tools to address security posture and compliance requirements, and the development team passes code through their checks to ensure software meets operational deployment requirements as code makes its way to production. Defender for DevOps bridges the gap in this journey toward secure code by helping companies start from a secure position and helping teams operate securely and efficiently throughout the code build and deployment lifecycle.

In this appendix, you will learn how to use Microsoft Defender for Cloud (MDC) to monitor the security posture of your source code management systems, understand new DevOps recommendations in MDC, configure the Microsoft Security DevOps tools, and find vulnerabilities in code.

Understanding Defender for DevOps

Defender for DevOps is a new addition to the Microsoft Defender for Cloud family that helps you discover, monitor, and detect threats to your source code management systems and source code. The service requires a connection to the source code management systems to allow it to discover resources such as repositories, organizations, projects, and code and to initiate assessments of the security posture of these assets.

Defender for DevOps also provides a dedicated dashboard to visualize the discovered assets and configure additional features such as pull request annotations and analytics about the source code management system activities. As illustrated in Figure A-1, Defender for DevOps connects your source code management systems to Defender for Cloud to utilize MDC's rich security capabilities to shift security left and protect your pre-deployment assets.

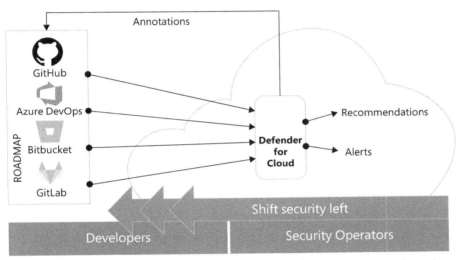

FIGURE A-1 Defender for DevOps connects source code management systems to Microsoft Defender for Cloud

Defender for DevOps brings the security and development teams together and enables collaboration between security operators (SecOps) and developers as code is developed and security issues are discovered and remediated. Let's examine one scenario where Defender for DevOps can help your organization bridge the division between your security and development teams. In MDC, security operators receive security recommendations about issues discovered in repositories and source code. This new information helps SecOps understand, locate, and provide guidance to act on DevOps-related issues, though developers must address these security issues in the code. Now, SecOps can communicate directly with developers by enabling pull request annotations with information about the issue, location, and actionable steps to remediate. Developers, in turn, use the same information provided in the pull request annotations to fix security issues before the code is merged.

Preventing security issues from getting to production is a crucial step in securing the software development lifecycle. Now, when a security incident arises and SecOps and developers come together to review and take action, both teams have the same information from Defender for DevOps, unlocking more meaningful and richer conversations to address identified security risks.

To maintain the security posture of source code management systems, Defender for DevOps provides always-on checks, such as ensuring authorization and authentication settings are configured and ensuring good code hygiene is followed in repositories by assessing whether code, secret, and dependency scanning is enabled. Additionally, assessments are performed on the security configuration of pipelines, service connections, webhooks, and many other configurations to ensure the system is operating securely. These posture assessments ensure that developers work in a secure, hardened environment and that their code is protected from adversaries.

For developers, Defender for DevOps provides the Microsoft Security DevOps (MSDO) tools that can be configured on every repository. These tools help ensure that, as developers check in code, the code is secure and free from common security defects, such as secrets left in code, code security vulnerabilities, Infrastructure as Code (IaC) security risks, and container vulnerabilities. The MSDO tools can also be leveraged from the command-line interface in developers' local environments to help them find and fix security vulnerabilities before pushing code to a repository. If desired, the same tools can even be configured to break a build and not allow code to be deployed to production until developers resolve all identified security issues.

In summary, Defender for DevOps offers new capabilities in three critical areas:

1. Discovery and visibility of source code management systems provide an inventory of DevOps assets—a known blind spot for security organizations—and enables statistics about security vulnerabilities and improvements

2. Continuous posture assessment ensures the SCMS is configured securely and provides recommendations with remediation guidance to address security posture misconfigurations.

3. Code vulnerability management finds and prevents vulnerable source code, IaC templates, containers, and secrets and helps developers find and address security vulnerabilities while code is written.

Defender for DevOps unites security operators and developers like never before. It enables each team to work in the same familiar environments, tools, and experiences that they're used to—SecOps in Microsoft Defender for Cloud and developers in their chosen development environments. It allows each team flexibility in when and where they address discovered security issues—during development, at the pipeline, and in security operations. Teams can communicate seamlessly and collaborate across multiple layers of protection, enabling security organizations to shift left and address security early in the development lifecycle.

Connect your source code management system to Defender for Cloud

To start using Defender for DevOps, you must connect your source code management system (SCMS) to Microsoft Defender for Cloud. By onboarding your SCMS to MDC, you authenticate to your source code management system(s), such as Azure DevOps and GitHub, and then grant authorization to Defender for DevOps to access your repositories.

Start setting up an SCMS connection to Defender for DevOps by logging into the Azure portal, opening Microsoft Defender for Cloud, and clicking **Environment Settings**, where you'll find the **Add Environment** menu. Next, click a source code management system in the menu to begin adding your connector. Connecting to GitHub is shown in Figure A-2.

FIGURE A-2   Using the Add environment menu to connect to GitHub

The next onboarding steps require you to give your connector a **Name** and select a **Region**, **Subscription**, and **Resource Group** where the connector will be stored, as shown in Figure A-3.

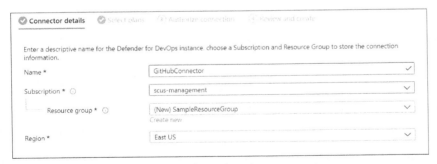

FIGURE A-3   Basic information required to onboard your connector

The steps shown in Figure A-4 authorize your GitHub account. After granting authorization, the installation adds the Defender for DevOps GitHub App to your organization and allows the Defender for DevOps service to access your repositories.

FIGURE A-4   Defender for DevOps authorization and app installation

After onboarding is complete, your source code management system's connector is displayed as one of the connectors in MDC's **Environment Settings** blade, as shown in Figure A-5. You can change the repositories you selected during onboarding by clicking the connector.

FIGURE A-5   SCMS connector in Environment settings

The Defender for DevOps service now starts discovering your repositories and analyzing them for any security issues. Once discovered, the **Inventory** dashboard shows the repositories, and the **Recommendations** dashboard shows any security issues related to a repository.

Once you have enabled Defender for DevOps, Defender for Cloud continuously scans your source code management system's resources and provides security recommendations. If any security issues are found in repositories, a recommendation is created for each type of finding. Remediating these issues reduces your attack surface and increases your Secure Score.

Defender for DevOps analyzes your repositories and creates recommendations that help you harden the security posture of

- Source code management systems, repositories, projects, and organizations
- Source code files, credentials in code, and dependencies in your solutions
- Infrastructure as Code templates
- Container images and Docker files

Defender for DevOps' recommendations seamlessly enhance Defender for Cloud's recommendations by utilizing the same MDC dashboard and the same familiar recommendations experience. Recommendations can be numerous in large and complex environments, so the filtering and exemption capabilities in the **Recommendations** dashboard can help you manage your investigations and remediate findings. For example, to see recommendations specific to GitHub, you can filter by **Resource Type** to show only **GitHub Repositories**, as shown in Figure A-6.

FIGURE A-6 Recommendations filtered by Resource Type: GitHub Repositories

To see additional details about a specific recommendation, simply click it to see more information in the recommendation's context blade. In the example shown in Figure A-7, you can see the result of the **Code Repositories Should Have Secret Scanning Findings Resolved** recommendation.

FIGURE A-7 Defender for DevOps Recommendation to resolve secrets found in repositories

When reviewing the findings in this recommendation, you can see that Defender for DevOps found multiple secrets in the code repositories. Secrets found in repositories can be leaked or discovered by adversaries, compromising an application or service. All these credentials should be assumed to be compromised. Clicking each credential displays the context blade where additional information can be found to assist in your investigation, such as a deep link to the location of the file containing the credential. To remediate this recommendation, the credential should be removed from the source code and rotated out of its source system. The code containing this credential should be refactored to use a secure secret store such as Azure Key Vault.

Configure pull request annotations

As you learned earlier, Defender for DevOps has new capabilities like pull-request annotations that help security operators assist developers when adopting security best practices early in the development cycle. Also, these new capabilities help security operators address high-risk vulnerabilities quickly and easily before those vulnerabilities make it into production. Defender for DevOps provides the centralized configuration for pull-request annotations and a way to keep track of the current status of all annotations across the DevOps estate.

Security operators can enable pull-request annotations so that developers receive security findings directly on their pull requests to remediate security issues before merging into the main branch. Developers can then interact with the pull-request annotations to determine when the issue can be prioritized and fixed or explain why an issue cannot be remediated, meaning it needs to be dismissed or suppressed until a later release.

This capability facilitates bidirectional communication between security operators and developers about discovered security issues, recommended guidance to remediate, and which security issues developers have accepted and fixed, have not fixed, or will fix in a later release.

Discover security issues when developers commit code

Defender for DevOps has a set of static analysis tools called Microsoft Security DevOps (MSDO). MSDO contains a combination of Microsoft and open-source tools that scan for security vulnerabilities. These tools scan for credentials left in code files, security vulnerabilities in Infrastructure as Code templates, vulnerable containers and Docker files, and more. You can configure the MSDO tools to break a build—that is, not allow the code to continue moving to the next development step—if any security issues are discovered during the automated scan. This helps prevent developers from merging un-remediated vulnerabilities into a main branch and deploying them to production.

As security teams mature their DevSecOps practices, they can set up the MSDO tools to run automatically when a developer commits code to a repository. This layer of protection helps find and block code vulnerabilities and prevents them from making it to a production resource. To add this layer of protection, you need to configure the MSDO tools in your GitHub work-flows or Azure DevOps pipelines.

For example, you can configure the MSDO tools to run in Azure DevOps on a pipeline. Start the configuration by selecting a project and clicking **Pipelines**, as shown in Figure A-8, to cre-ate a new pipeline.

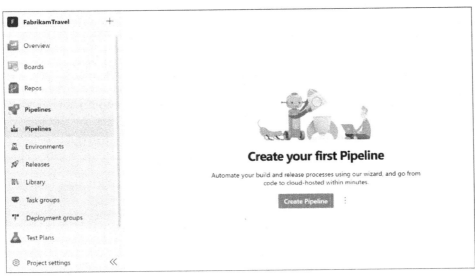

FIGURE A-8 Create a new pipeline in Azure DevOps

The YAML code shown in Figure A-9 is an example of how to create a new pipeline. As shown in the following sample, by including the input parameter break = true, if any security issues are found, the build will break until all security issues are resolved, and the scan completes successfully.

After successfully creating the pipeline, you are ready to scan your code for security vulnerabilities.

```
# Starter pipeline
# Start with a minimal pipeline that you can customize to b
uild and deploy your code.
# Add steps that build, run tests, deploy, and more:
# https://aka.ms/yaml

trigger:
- main

pool:
  vmImage: windows-latest

steps:
- task: UseDotNet@2
  displayName: 'Use dotnet'
  inputs:
    version: 3.1.x
- task: UseDotNet@2
  displayName: 'Use dotnet'
  inputs:
    version: 5.0.x
- task: UseDotNet@2
  displayName: 'Use dotnet'
  inputs:
    version: 6.0.x
- task: MicrosoftSecurityDevOps@1
  displayName: 'Microsoft Security DevOps'
  #Optional to break build
  inputs:
    break: true
```

FIGURE A-9 Create a new pipeline in Azure DevOps

One of the MSDO tools that security operators have most highly anticipated is the Microsoft
Credential Scanner tool. During the MSDO scan of Azure DevOps, the Credential Scanner finds
secrets that developers have checked in. The increase in attacks on source code management
systems helps your organization find and remediate credential leaks and keep them out of
source code files. Scan results from the MSDO Credential Scanner are shown in Figure A-10.

FIGURE A-10 MSDO results filtered for Credential Scanner showing a Storage Account Key found in code

Discover security issues in Infrastructure as Code (IaC)

One of the most requested capabilities is the ability to scan Infrastructure as Code templates for security issues and security best practices in your CI/CD pipelines. If you would like to run only IaC scanning and not the other MSDO tools, this can be done by enabling the MSDO tools and configuring them to scan only Infrastructure as Code templates.

The example shown in Figure A-11 has the lines that you should add to your workflow so that it will only perform IaC scanning.

```
26        # Run analyzers
27      - name: Run Microsoft Security DevOps Analysis
28        uses: microsoft/security-devops-action@preview
29        id: msdo
30        with:
31          categories: 'IaC'
```

FIGURE A-11   Sample code to scan only IaC files

To see the IaC scan results in GitHub, after your workflow is configured and runs on your code, click the **Security** tab in your repository and then click **Code Scanning Alerts**, as shown in Figure A-12.

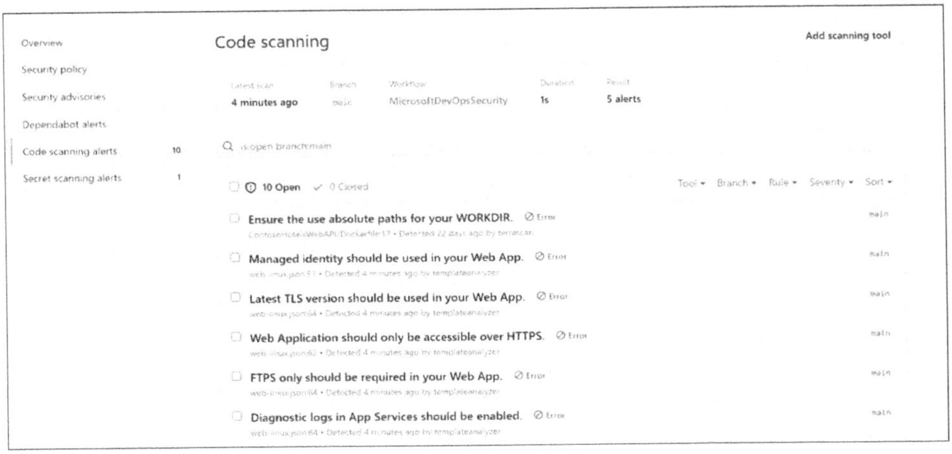

FIGURE A-12   IaC scan results in the GitHub Code scanning dashboard

To see the IaC scan results in Azure DevOps, click your pipeline's **Summary** tab, as shown in Figure A-13.

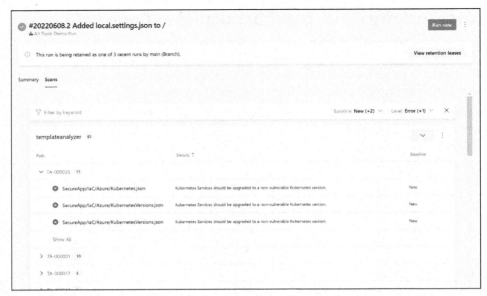

FIGURE A-13   IaC scan results in the Azure DevOps SARIF SAST Scans Tab viewer

Discover security issues during development

The MSDO tools can be configured to run on a pipeline, as explored in a previous section, but also have a command-line option that can be downloaded to a developer's local machine to help find security issues during development.

Let's look at one of these MSDO CLI tools—the ARM Template Best Practice Analyzer (BPA)—in more detail. ARM templates are Infrastructure as Code JSON files used to create Azure resources through automation. This tool analyzes ARM templates for best practices and security issues. It also helps developers address these issues by providing recommended steps to easily fix security issues. The Template Analyzer results example in the figure below shows security issues related to the `azuredeploy.json` ARM template. The terminal in the lower half of Figure A-14 shows the Template Analyzer output with these discovered issues from the `azuredeploy.json` ARM template being developed in the screen's top half.

FIGURE A-14 MSDO Template Analyzer

Exploiting leaked credentials is a primary mechanism used to breach cloud resources. Leaked credentials should be remediated before code is pushed into a repository. Another MSDO CLI tool that helps developers find and address this security issue is the Credential Scanner tool. This tool scans all files in your code project and notifies developers when it finds a credential. Figure A-15 shows a code file named `GenerateLicenseFile.cs` that contains a general password.

FIGURE A-15 MSDO Credential Scanner

Index

A

access management, 12
Adaptive Application Control, 215-216
   application violation, 221
   changing policy, 217-220
   configuring, 217
adaptive network hardening, 134-135
ADE (Azure Disk Encryption), 19-20
AKS (Azure Kubernetes Service), 23-25
alerts, 31, 155-157. *See also* Security Alerts dashboard
   accessing
      in Microsoft Sentinel, 192-194
      using Defender for Cloud REST API, 224-230
      using Graph Security API, 230-232
   application violation, 221
   ARG (Azure Resource Graph), 163
   Defender for Storage, 171-172
   DNS, 170-171
   filtering, 158-159
   fusion, 182-185
   PowerShell activity, 165-166
   responding to, 187
      contact, 187
      impact, 188
      mitigation, 187-188

      take action, 188
   simulating, 157-158
   suppressing, 161-163
allowing recommendations, 84
API(s)
   Graph Security
      accessing alerts, 232-233
      using, 232-233
   REST (Representational State Transfer)
      accessing alerts using, 224-230
      GET request, 225-228
      providers, 224-225
      request/response pair, 223-224
      testing, 228-230
application violation alert, 221
architecture, Microsoft Defender for Cloud
   Log Analytics Agent, 31-32
   recommendations and alerts, 31
   vulnerability assessment integration with Qualys, 32
   workspaces, 32
ARG (Azure Resource Graph), alerts, 163
ARM templates, 89, 235-237, 240
   Best Practice Analyzer, 256-257
   creating, 241-243
   exporting from Azure Portal, 240-241
assessment(s)
   creating for AWS and GCP, 99-103

   security, 105
assigning, Azure security benchmark, 65
assignments, Azure Policy, 68
assume-breach philosophy, 8
attack(s). *See also* threat(s)
   detection, 7-8
   file-less, 2
   local privilege escalation, 5
   paths, 149-152
   phishing, 2-3, 6
   spearphishing, 3
   vectors, 4
AuditD, 166
auditing, SQL, 136-138
authentication, multi-factor, 118-119
auto-deployment, guest configuration agent, 57
automation
   remediation of security recommendations, 138-140
   resource exemptions and, 141-143
auto-provisioning, 51-52
   Log Analytics agent for Azure Arc servers, 55-56
   Log Analytics agent for VMs, 52-54
   Microsoft Defender for Containers, 58-59
   at-scale, 66
   vulnerability assessment solutions, 56-57

AWS (Amazon Web Service)
connecting to, 59-62
creating custom assessments,
99-103
VMs, onboarding, 62-63
Azure
AD Identity Protection, 21
built-in role definitions, 47-48
container security, 22-23
defense-in-depth, 17
logging, 21-22
RBAC (role-based access
control), 14
security, 13-14
DDoS protection, 17-19
network protection, 15-17
VM protection, 14-15
storage protection, 19-20
subscriptions, 14
Azure Active Directory
Identity Protection, 21
Security Defaults, 119
Azure Activity Log, 22
Azure Blueprints, 85-86
Blueprint assignment, 86
Blueprint definition, 86
creating, 87-88
Azure Key Vault, 20
Azure Policy, 67-68, 70, 237-238
assignments, 68
definitions, 68, 69-70
initiative, 68
policy, 69
exemptions, 70-72
regulatory compliance policy
initiatives, 91
Azure Security Benchmark,
73-75, 93, 238-239
assigning, 65
Secure Score, 82-83
recommendations, 74-75
Azure SQL, auditing, 136-138
Azure Storage API, scan
phases, 9
Azure Storage Firewall, 20

B

behavioral analysis, 155-156
best practices
Defender for Cloud
management at scale,
239-240
policy, 88-90
Blob storage, 9
Blueprint
assignment, 86
definition, 86, 87-88
botnets, 3
building your own compliance
initiative, 96-99
built-in policy definitions, 64
bulletproof hosting services, 1-2
BYOL (bring your own license), 40

C

C2 (command-and-control)
server, 4
CIS (Center of Internet
Security), 74
cloud
security
Azure, 13-14
compliance, 11
data protection, 13
endpoint protection,
12-13
identity and access
management, 12
operational, 12
risk management, 11-12
threats, 9-11
weaponization, 9-10
Cloud Security Map, building
your own views, 152-153
cloud solution provider (CSP), 11
code injection, 2, 3
Colonial Pipeline incident, 1
complete deployment, 235-236

compliance. See also regulatory
standards and compliance
cloud security, 11
initiative, building, 96-99
regulatory, 90-96
compute, recommendations, 121
connectors, AWS and GCP,
99-103
containers, 120-121
recommendations, 128
security, 22-23
Vulnerability Assessment,
167-168
contextual security, 143-144
Continuous Export, 112
pulling Secure Score data,
112-114
Secure Score over time report,
114-115
controls
for compute, 121
Enable Endpoint Protection,
129-131
Enable MFA, 118-119
Manage Access and
Permissions, 118-121
Remediate Vulnerabilities,
125-128
Secure Management Ports,
121-124
counter-antivirus (CAV)
services, 1-2
creating
ARM templates, 241-243
Blueprint definition, 87-88
custom assessments for AWS
and GCP, 99-103
custom policies, 78-83
exemptions, 110-111
external access prevention
rule, 123-124
policy exemptions, 71-72
rules, 220
Credential Scanner tool, 257

CSPM (Cloud Security Posture Management), 27, 28
  recommendations, 35, 36-38
  workflow, 35-36
CVE-2021-44228, 3
CWPP (Cloud Workload Protection Platform), 28, 38-39
cybercrime
  code injection, 2
  Colonial Pipeline incident, 1
  counter-antivirus (CAV) services, 1-2
  email phishing, 2-3
  Ransomware as a Service (RaaS), 1-2
cyberkill chain, 3-5, 182-185
Cybersecurity and Infrastructure Security Agency (CISA)
  Alert Report (AA22-040A), 1
  Analysis Report (AR21-013A), 6

D

dashboards, 33-34
  FIM, 210
  JIT, 206-207
  NSG Hardening, 134
  Regulatory Compliance, 92-94
  Security Alerts, 157-161
  Security Posture, 106-107
  Workload Protections, 38, 131
data plane logs, 21
data protection, 13
DDoS (distributed denial-of-service), Azure security, 17-19
default workspaces, 46-47
Defender for App Service, 169-171
Defender for Azure Storage, 20
Defender for Containers, 166-167. See also containers
  auto-provisioning, 58-59
  threat detection, 168-169

Vulnerability Assessment, 167-168
Defender for Cosmos DB, 177-178
Defender for DNS, 181-182
Defender for Key Vault, 179
Defender for Open-Source Relational Databases, 178-179
Defender for Resource Manager, 180-181
Defender for Servers, 28-29, 48-49
  Adaptive Application Control, 215-216
    application violation, 221
    changing policy, 217-220
    configuring, 217
  alerts, 157
  behavioral analysis, 155-156
  for Linux, 166-167
  plans, 164-165
  for Windows, 165-166
Defender for SQL, 173-174
  onboarding, 174
  plans, 173
  VA (vulnerability assessment), 174-177
Defender for Storage. See also storage
  alerts, 171-172
  considerations before enabling, 172-173
defense-in-depth, 13, 17, 68
definitions
  Azure Policy, 68, 69-70
  Blueprint, 86
denying recommendations, 84
deployment and deployment scenarios
  CSPM (Cloud Security Posture Management), 35-38
  CWPP (Cloud Workload Protection Platform), 38-39
  Microsoft Defender for Containers, 58-59
  multi-cloud, 39-40

detection, 7-8
DevOps, pipeline, 246
disabling, recommendations, 76
DNS alerts, 170-171
domain dominance, 5
downgrade notification, Secure Score, 115
due date, recommendation, 145

E

EDR (endpoint protection and response), 12-13, 42
email
  phishing, 2-3, 6
  spearphishing, 3
Enable Endpoint Protection control, 129-131
Enable MFA control, 118-119
endpoints, Enable Endpoint Protection control, 129-131
exemptions
  Azure Policy, 70-72
  creating, 110-111
  policy, 109-110
  resource, 141-143
exporting ARM templates from Azure Portal, 240-241

F

file-less attacks, 2, 3
filtering
  recommendations, 116-117
  Security Alerts, 158-159
FIM (File Integrity Monitoring), 209-210
  customizing your settings, 210-213
  visualizing changes, 213-214
fine-tuning
  policies, 75-78
  Secure Score, 109-111

firewall(s), Azure Storage, 20
frameworks, MITRE ATT&CK, 5
free tier, Microsoft Defender for
Cloud, 28

G

GCP, creating custom
assessments, 99-103
GitHub, 9, 38, 228
governance, 81, 90, 237
rules, 145-148
security, 143-145
grace period, recommendation,
145
Graph Security API
accessing alerts, 230-232
using, 232-233
group policy, 19-20
guest configuration agent,
auto-deployment, 57

H-I

HTTPS (Hypertext Transfer
Protocol Secure), 136
IaC (infrastructure as code)
scanning, 255-256
identity, 12
implementation, policy, 81
improving security posture, 6-8
incremental deployment, 235-236
InfoSec Institute, 7-8
initiative definition, Azure
Policy, 68
intel, 4
isolation, AKS clusters, 24

J

JIT (just-in-time) VM access,
201-203
dashboard, 206-207

FIM (File Integrity
Monitoring), 209-210
permission assignment,
202-203
recommendations, 203-205
requesting, 207-208
JSON (JavaScript Object
Notation), policy definitions, 89

K-L

KQL (Kusto Query Language),
99, 102
Kubernetes, 6
leaked credentials, 257
Linux systems
Defender for Servers, 166-167
Log Analytics Agent, 31
local privilege escalation
attack, 5
Lockheed Martin cyberkill chain,
4-5, 182-185
Log Analytics agent/workspace,
45
Defender for Servers, 48-49
deploying to Azure Arc
machines, 55-56
enabling Defender for Cloud,
49-50
Linux systems, 31
VMs, auto-provisioning,
52-54
Windows systems, 31-32
Log4J vulnerability, 3, 143
logging, Azure, 21-22
Logic App, 141-143
logical isolation, AKS clusters, 24

M

Manage Access and Permissions
control, 118-121
management groups, 238-239

MFA (multi-factor
authentication), 118-119
Microsoft
assume-breach philosophy, 8
red-teaming, 8
Microsoft Defender for Cloud, 3, 18
alerts, 31, 156-157. See also
alerts; Security Alerts
dashboard
accessing using REST API,
224-230
filtering, 158-159
fusion, 182-185
simulating, 157-158
suppressing, 161-163
Azure Security Benchmark,
73-75
connecting to source code
management system,
249-251
Continuous Export, 112
pulling Secure Score data,
112-114
Secure Score over time
report, 114-115
CSPM (Cloud Security Posture
Management), 27, 28
recommendations, 35,
36-38
workflow, 35-36
CWPP (Cloud Workload
Protection Platform), 28,
38-39
dashboards, 33-34
NSG Hardening, 134
Regulatory Compliance,
92-94
Security Alerts, 157-161
Security Posture, 106-107
Workload Protections,
38, 131
Defender for Servers, 28-29
deploying at scale
ARM templates, 235-237,
240-243

best practices, 239-240

management groups, 238-239

deployment scenarios, 27-28

EDR (endpoint protection and response), 42

free tier, 28

GitHub repository, 38, 228

integration with other solutions

  Microsoft Defender for Endpoint, 196-199

  Microsoft Purview, 194-196

  Microsoft Sentinel, C07.008-192

Log Analytics agent, 31-32, 45

MITRE ATT&CK tactics, 5

multi-cloud deployment, 39-40

multi-tenant, 42-43

networking

  adaptive hardening, 134-135

  network map, 132-134

onboarding. *See also* auto-provisioning; onboarding

  assigning Azure security benchmark, 65

  auto-provisioning, 51-63

  AWS VMs, 62-63

  connecting to AWS, 59-62

  designing your environment, 46-49

  planning your Azure environment, 45-46

  plans, 48-49

  RBAC (role-based access control), 47-48

  registering the Microsoft. Security resource provider, 63-65

  subscriptions at scale, 63

  VMs, 49-51

planning adoption, 34-35

plans, 29

policy(ies). *See also* policy(ies)

  custom, 78-83

  fine-tuning, 75-78

pricing tier names, 64-65

recommendations, 31. *See also* recommendations

  compute, 121

  container security, 128

  controls, 117

  data and storage, 135-136

  disabling, 76

  Enable Endpoint Protection control, 129-131

  Enable MFA control, 118-119

  filtering, 116-117

  finding only your own, 148-149

  JIT, 203-205

  Manage Access and Permissions control, 119-121

  Remediate Vulnerabilities control, 125-128

  remediating, 115-116, 138-140

  Secure Management Ports control, 121-124

regulatory standards and compliance, 92-94

security. *See also* security

  governance, 143-148

  misconfigurations, 83-85

stakeholders, 34

threat intelligence, 185-186

threat protection, 155-156

use cases, 34

vulnerability(ies)

  assessment integration with Qualys, 32

  remediating, 125-128

workspaces, 32, 46-47

Microsoft Defender for DevOps, 245

developer tools, 248

IaC scanning, 255-256

MSDO (Microsoft Security DevOps) tools, 253-254

  ARM Template Best Practice Analyzer, 256-257

  Credential Scanner, 257

onboarding your SCMS, 249-251

pull request annotations, 252

recommendations, 251-252

SecOps and, 247-248

security assessments, 248

Microsoft Defender for Endpoint, integration with Microsoft Defender for Cloud, 196-199

Microsoft Defender for Storage, 9

Microsoft Digital Defense Report 2021, 1, 2

Microsoft Purview, integration with Microsoft Defender for Cloud, 194-196

Microsoft Security Intelligence Report Volume 22, 9

Microsoft Sentinel

  accessing alerts, 192-194

  integration with Microsoft Defender for Cloud, C07.008-192

Microsoft.Security resource provider

  registering, 63-65

  retrieving Secure Score data, 111-112

misconfiguration, 9, 83-85

MITRE ATT&CK framework, 5

monitoring

  file integrity. *See* FIM (File Integrity Monitoring)

  policies, 81

MSDO (Microsoft Security DevOps) tools

ARM Template Best Practice
Analyzer, 256-257
Credential Scanner, 257
multi-tenant, 42-43

N

Nadella, S., 246
networking, 131-132
adaptive hardening, 134-135
network map, 132-134
NIST (National Institute of
Standards and Technology), 74
Nitol botnet, 3
notifications. See also alerts,
Secure Score downgrade, 115
NSGs (network security groups),
16
adaptive network hardening,
134-135
security rules, 17

O

onboarding
assign the Azure security
benchmark, 65
auto-provisioning, 51-52,
56-57
Log Analytics agent for
Azure Arc servers,
55-56
Log Analytics agent for
VMs, 52-54
AWS VMs, 62-63
connecting to AWS, 59-62
Defender for SQL, 174
designing your environment,
46-49
guest configuration agent,
auto-deployment, 57
Microsoft Defender for
Containers, 58-59

planning your Azure
environment for Defender
for Cloud, 45-46
plans, 48-49
RBAC (role-based access
control), 47-48
registering the Microsoft.
Security resource provider,
63-65
source code management
system, 249-251
subscriptions at scale, 63
VMs from an Azure
subscription, 49-51
operational security, 12
ownership
recommendation, 144-145
subscription, 120

P

permissions, JIT (just-in-time)
VM access, 202-203
phishing, 2-3, 6
planning adoption, Microsoft
Defender for Cloud, 34-35
plans
Defender for Containers,
166-167
Defender for Servers, 164-165
Defender for SQL, 173
Microsoft Defender for
Cloud, 29
policy(ies). See also Azure Policy;
Azure Security Benchmark;
group policy; regulatory
standards and compliance
Adaptive Application Control,
217-220
Azure Policy, 67-68, 70
assignments, 68
definitions, 68, 69-70
exemptions, 70-72
initiative definition, 68

policy definition, 69
best practices, 88-90
built-in, 64
custom, 78-83
Enable Azure Security
Center, 63
exemptions, 109-111
fine-tuning, 75-78
governance, 81
implementation, 81
monitoring, 81
network, 24
recommendations, 80
subscription, 77-78
PowerShell activity alerts,
165-166
pricing tier names, 64-65
privileged access, 13
proactive security, 83
publisher rules, 219
pull request annotations, 252

Q

Qualys
auto-provisioning, 56-57
vulnerability assessment
integration, 32
query(ies)
ARG (Azure Resource Graph),
163
assessment, 103
building your own, 152-153
KQL (Kusto Query Language),
102

R

Ransomware as a Service (RaaS),
1, 2
RBAC (role-based access control)
Azure, 14
onboarding, 47-48

recommendations, 31, 35.
See also Secure Score
allowing/denying, 84
Azure Security Benchmark,
74-75
compute, 121
container security, 128
controls, 117
Enable Endpoint
Protection, 129-131
Enable MFA, 118-119
Manage Access and
Permissions, 118-121
Remediate Vulnerabilities,
125-128
Secure Management Ports,
121-124
CSPM (Cloud Security Posture
Management), 36-38
data and storage, 135-136
Defender for DevOps,
251-252
disabling, 76
due date, 145
filtering, 116-117
finding only your own, 148-149
grace period, 145
JIT, 203-205
ownership, 144-145
policy, 80
remediating, 115-116, 138-140
VA (vulnerability assessment),
167-168
red-teaming, 8
registration, Microsoft.Security
resource provider, 63-65
regulatory standards and
compliance
Azure Policy, 90-91
building your own
compliance initiative, 96-99
customizing your experience,
94-96
Microsoft Defender for Cloud,
92-94

remediating
recommendations, 115-116,
138-140
vulnerabilities, 125-128
reports
Cybersecurity and
Infrastructure Security
Agency (CISA)
Alert Report (AA22-040A), 1
Analysis Report (AR21-
013A), 6
Secure Score, 111-112, 114-115
requesting JIT access, 207-208
resource(s)
attack path, 149-152
exemptions, 141-143
responding to alerts, 187
contact, 187
impact, 188
mitigation, 187-188
take action, 188
REST (Representational State
Transfer) API
accessing alerts using,
224-230
GET request, 225-228
providers, 224-225
request/response pair, 223-224
REvil, 2
risk management, 11-12
rules
Alert Suppression, 161-163
creating, 220
external access preventions,
creating, 123-124
governance, 145-148
publisher, 219

S

search box, Security Alerts
dashboard, 159
Secure Management Ports
control, 121-124

Secure Score, 34, 37, 82-83.
See also recommendations
calculating influence per
resource, 109
Continuous Export, 112-114
downgrade notification, 115
fine-tuning, 109-111
improving security posture,
105-109
preview recommendations,
108
recommendations
for compute, 121
container security, 128
controls, 117
data and storage, 135-136
Enable Endpoint
Protection control,
129-131
Enable MFA control,
118-119
filtering, 116-117
finding only your own,
148-149
Manage Access and
Permissions control,
118-121
ownership, 144-145
Remediate Vulnerabilities
control, 125-128
remediating, 115-116,
138-140
Secure Management Ports
control, 121-124
reports, 111-112, 114-115
security controls, 107-108
Take Action tab, 160
vulnerabilities, remediating,
125-128
security
alerts, 156-157. *See also* alerts
accessing using Graph
Security API, 230-232
accessing using REST API,
224-230

application violation, 221
ARG (Azure Resource Graph), 163
DNS, 170-171
filtering, 158-159
fusion, 182-185
PowerShell activity, 165-166
simulating, 157-158
suppressing, 161-163
assessment, 105
Azure
    cloud, 13-14
    containers, 22-23
    DDoS protection, 17-19
    logging, 21-22
    network protection, 15-17
    storage protection, 19-20
    VMs, 14-15
cloud
    compliance, 11
    data protection, 13
    endpoint protection, 12-13
    identity and access
        management, 12
    operational, 12
    risk management, 11-12
contextual, 143-144
FIM (File Integrity
    Monitoring), 209-210
    customizing your settings,
        210-213
    visualizing changes,
        213-214
governance, 81, 143-148
incident, 183-184
misconfiguration, 83-85
posture, improving, 6-8
    Secure Score, 105-109
    VA (vulnerability
        assessment), 40-41
proactive, 83
threat protection, 155-156
Security Alerts dashboard, 157-161
Alert Details page, 159

filtering alerts, 158-159
Full alert page, 160
search box, 159
simulating alerts, 157-158
Security Posture dashboard,
    106-107
segmentation, VNet, 17
SIEM (Security Information Event
    Management), 189
simulating, alerts, 157-158
SOAR (Security Orchestration
    Automated Response),
    189, 228
SolarWinds, 4
source code management
    system, 1, 245-246. See also
    Microsoft Defender for
    DevOps
    connecting to Defender for
        Cloud, 249-251
    GitHub, 9, 38, 228
spearphishing, 3
SQL, auditing, 136-138
stakeholders, 34
storage
    ADE (Azure Disk Encryption),
        19-20
    Blob, 9
    recommendations,
        135-136
Storage Firewall, 20
"Strengthening Security
    Configurations to Defend
    Against Attackers Targeting
    Cloud Services", 6
subscription(s)
    Azure, 14
    onboarding, 46
        at scale, 63
        VMs, 49-51
    ownership, 120
    policy assignments, 77-78
supply chain attacks, 4
suppressing, alerts, 161-163

T

templates, ARM, 89, 235-237, 240
    Best Practice Analyzer, 256-257
    creating, 241-243
    exporting ARM templates
        from Azure Portal, 240-241
testing APIs, 228-230
threat(s)
    actors, 6, 7-8
    cloud, 9-11
        misconfiguration, 9
        weaponization, 9-10
    detection, 168-169
        Defender for App Service,
            169-171
        Defender for Cloud,
            185-186
        Defender for Cosmos DB,
            177-178
        Defender for DNS, 181-182
        Defender for Key Vault, 179
        Defender for Open-Source
            Relational Databases,
            178-179
        Defender for Resource
            Manager, 180-181
        Defender for SQL, 173-177
        Defender for Storage,
            171-173
    phishing attacks, 6
    protection, 155-157
    ransomware, 6
tiles, Microsoft Defender for
    Cloud dashboard, 33-34
tools, MSDO (Microsoft Security
    DevOps), 253-254, 256-257
    ARM Template Best Practice
        Analyzer, 256-257
    Credential Scanner, 257
TVM (Microsoft Defender
    for Endpoint's Threat and
    Vulnerability Management),
    auto-provisioning, 56-57

U-V

VA (vulnerability assessment), 40-41, 167-168
  auto-provisioning, 56-57
  Defender for SQL, 174-177
Verizon Data Breach Report 2020, 6
VMBA (Virtual Machine Behavioral Analysis), 155-156
VMs (virtual machines)
  AWS (Amazon Web Service), onboarding, 62-63
  FIM (File Integrity Monitoring), 209-210

customizing your settings, 210-213
  visualizing changes, 213-214
JIT (just-in-time) access, 201-203
  permissions, 202-203
  recommendations, 203-205
  requesting, 207-208
Log Analytics agent, auto-provisioning, 52-54
onboarding, 49-51
security, 14-15
VNets (virtual networks)
  Azure, 15-17
  segmentation, 17

VSCode (Visual Studio Code), creating ARM templates, 241-243
vulnerabilities
  CVE-2021-44228, 3
  remediating, 125-128

W-X-Y-Z

Windows systems, Defender for Servers, 165-166
workflow, CSPM (Cloud Security Posture Management), 35-36
Workload Protections dashboard, 38, 131
workspaces, 32, 46-47